"You think you know what it's like?" Gaius sco ed, leaning against the sturdy wooden barricade that separated the raucous crowd from the dusty chariot track. His eyes gleamed with the same fiery passion that burned in the chests of the horsesguard. Sextius would soon thunder past. "You sit in your cushioned seat, sipping wine and watching the world's most dangerous sport, but you have no idea!"

"I've seen plenty of races, Gaius," his friend, Titus, replied with a smug grin, adjusting his toga. "It's just a bunch of horses and men fighting for a piece of metal, isn't it?"

Gaius threw his head back and laughed, the sound lost in the sound of the crowd. "Just a bunch of horses? This is the heart of Rome, the very essence of our spirit! The roar of the chariots, the clash of the teams, the smell of victory!" He pointed to the towering Circus Maximus, its grandeur casting a shadow over the bustling city. "This is where we come to live, to breathe, to feel alive!"

The air was thick with the anticipation of the games to come. The Circus Maximus, a colossal stadium that could swallow a small town whole, was a marvel of ancient engineering. Its spina, a long central barrier adorned with statues and obelisks, split the arena in two, while the carceres at the far end held the chariots in their starting positions, poised like sprinters in a marble cage. The scent of sweat and animal musk mingled with the sweet incense that wafted from the nearby temples, a heady mix that set the pulse racing.

As the sun climbed higher, the shadows grew shorter and the tension grew thicker. The four great factions of the circus, the Blues, the Gold, the Reds, and the Whites, had painted the city with their colors. Their

rivalries were legendary, their fan clubs as devoted as any religious sect. The factions were more than just teams; they were the lifeblood of the city, a reflection of the social fabric that stretched from the emperor's own box to the lowest seats, where the poor and the desperate came to find escape from their struggles.

The Senate, once the bastion of Roman virtue, now danced to the tune of the imperial family's whims, their allegiances as fickle as the wind. Meanwhile, the people of Rome seethed with unrest, their bellies empty from scarcity and their spirits bruised by heavy taxes. The games were their solace, a temporary balm to the wounds of life, and the charioteers their champions, fighting not just for glory, but for the very soul of the empire.

The day's race was about to begin, and the air was charged with excitement and the promise of bloodshed. The crowd surged forward eager for the spectacle. Amidst the sea of faces, a young charioteer named Thidius for the red faction stood tall, his eyes fixed on the distant carceres. He was a man of few words, but his grip on the reins spoke volumes of his determination. This was more than just a race for him; it was a battle for honor, for his family, and for the future of Rome itself. The roar of the crowd grew deafening as the starting mechanism creaked and groaned, the gates poised to swing open and unleash the fury of the chariots. Unseen by the masses, a shadowy figure lurked in the background, his intentions as murky as the whispers of rebellion that slithered through the city's alleyways.

The chariots shot forward, a blur of color and motion. The clatter of hooves and the grind of wheels filled the air, drowning out the cries of the spectators. Thidius steered his chariot with a precision honed from years of practice and countless battles. The factions' rivalries played out before them, each team vying for dominance in a dance of speed and strategy. The spina loomed ahead, a jagged backbone slicing through the arena, where the chariots would race, their wheels almost grazing the stone.

As the chariots approached the first turn, the tension was palpable. The teams jockeyed for position, their drivers leaning out, whips cracking in the air. Suddenly, a rogue chariot from the Red faction veered sharply, colliding with one of the Golds. The sound of shattering wood and screaming horses pierced the din as the Gilds chariot flipped, sending its driver sprawling into the dust. The crowd gasped, a collective intake of breath that was swiftly followed by a frenzied chant for their fallen hero.

Gaius and Titus watched, their faces a mix of horror and fascination. The race was chaos, a microcosm of the political games played out in the Senate. The emperor's box remained silent, the ruler's expression unreadable as he observed the unfolding disaster. It was clear to all that the balance of power in Rome was as precarious as the chariots on the track, and a single misstep could send everything tumbling into oblivion.

Thidius knew he had to act. The race was a minefield, with danger lurking around every turn. He urged his horses on, his heart pounding in his chest. This was his chance to not only win the race but to strike a blow for the people, to show that not all heroes wore togas and wielded swords. His eyes narrowed, and he focused on the finish line, the prize within his grasp. But little did he know that his actions today would set in motion a series of events that would shake the very foundations of the eternal city. The charioteers' gambit was about to begin.

The chariots circled the spina, their wheels kicking up clouds of dust that billowed into the stands. The air was a cacophony of noise—the crack of whips, the roar of the crowd, and the grinding of metal on stone. Thidius felt the heat of the sun on his back and the cold sweat on his palms. His mind raced, calculating the best path, the swiftest move that would secure his victory. The chariots grew closer, their shadows merging into a single, terrifying specter.

The shadowy figure in the background watched with keen interest, his hand resting on the pommel of his sword. This race was more than just a sporting event; it was a chessboard where the fate of Rome would be decided. His plan was complex, a tapestry of alliances and betrayals that would either crown a new emperor or plunge the city into civil war. His gaze never left Thidius, the unknowing pawn in a game of power that had been centuries in the making.

The race grew more brutal with every lap. Chariots crashed, sending their riders flying into the air like rag dolls. The crowd reveled in the carnage, their cries of joy and horror echoing o the ancient walls. Thidius deftly avoided the wreckage, his skills and instincts honed by years of struggle and hardship. The finish line was in sight, and he could almost taste victory. But as he rounded the final turn, the shadowy figure's hand tightened on his sword, and a cold smile spread across his lips.

The Reds and Blues were neck and neck, their drivers' eyes locked in a silent challenge. Suddenly, a flash of movement in the stands caught Thidius's eye—a glint of steel, a hint of malice. Without hesitation, he steered his chariot towards the danger, risking everything for a shot at the lead. The shadowy figure tensed, his plan threatening to unravel before it had even begun. As the chariots thundered past, he saw his opportunity slipping away.

With a roar that could have been heard in the furthest reaches of the empire, Thidius surged ahead, his horses responding to his desperate call. The finish line loomed closer, a thin ribbon of hope against the backdrop of chaos. The shadowy figure's smile vanished, replaced by a snarl of frustration. He would not be denied so easily.

The race was a blur of color and fury as the chariots streaked towards the end. The crowd erupted into a frenzy, their shouts a battle cry that seemed to lift the very air. Thidius felt the wind in his hair, the sting of dust in his eyes, and the raw power of the beasts beneath him. In that moment, he knew he was not just racing for himself but for Rome. And as the chariots crossed the line, it was his that emerged victorious, the crowd's roar a thunderous salute to the underdog who had dared to defy the odds.

The shadowy figure melted into the shadows, his eyes never leaving Thidius. This was not the end, merely the beginning of a dance of power and destiny. As the victor's laurels were placed upon the charioteer's head, the whispers of the city grew louder, the rumblings of discontent shaking the very ground beneath the Circus Maximus. Rome was a powder keg, and the charioteer had just lit the fuse. The Gambit had been set in motion, and the fate of the empire rested on the shoulders of one man, a hero born from the dust and the roar of the chariots.

In the aftermath of the race, Aurelius found himself the center of attention. The Reds showered him with praise and gold, eager to claim him as their own. His victory had not gone unnoticed by the powerful figures who pulled the strings from the shadows. Livia watched from afar, her heart swelling with pride, her father's glare a silent rebuke. Their love was a flame that burned brightly, but it threatened to consume them both if it was ever exposed to the harsh light of day.

Quintus, his mentor, o ered a solemn nod from the sidelines. He had seen this game before, had played it himself in his youth. The allure of wealth and power was intoxicating, but it was a path that led to ruin for those who didn't know when to step aside. He approached Aurelius, his eyes filled with a warning that the young man was too intoxicated with victory to heed.

"You've made powerful enemies today," he said, his voice gru with concern. "And more powerful friends. Choose your alliances wisely, for the games are never just about winning. They are the theater of life, where the gods play out their own dramas through the lives of men."

Thidius, now basking in the adoration of the people, felt a twinge of doubt. The victory had come at a cost, one he hadn't anticipated. The shadowy figure had been watching, waiting for his moment. And now, the charioteer of the Red faction had unwittingly become a player in a game that was as old as Rome itself.

The days that followed saw Rome alive with whispers and intrigue. The Senate buzzed with speculation, the emperor's spies scrambling to understand the implications of the race. Thidius, now the toast of the city, was invited to grand parties, showered with gifts, and o ered deals that would make a senator blush. Yet, amidst the revelry, he remained haunted by the shadowy figure and the steely glint in his eye.

As he strolled through the bustling streets, the cobblestones stained with the blood of fallen champions, Thidius couldn't shake the feeling that he was being watched. The city was a labyrinth of alliances and betrayals, and he had unwittingly stepped into the heart of the maze. His rivalry with Aurelius had taken on a new dimension, one that went beyond the race track and into the very fabric of the empire.

The rivalry between the two charioteers grew more intense with each passing day. Every race was a battle, every victory a declaration of war. Yet, amidst the clamor of the arena, the whispers grew louder, the stakes higher. The shadowy figure had not forgotten Thidius's defiance and bided his time, waiting for the perfect moment to strike.

The pivotal moment came when Thidius was approached by a patrician, his toga a stark contrast to the dusty street. "You have something I need," the man said, his voice smooth as oiled leather. "And I have something you want. Information, power, the love of a certain lady. All can be yours, for a price."

Thidius knew he was being tested, that his next move could alter the course of his life. The smell of the arena, the taste of victory, and the touch of Livia's hand were all at stake. He looked into the man's eyes, searching for an answer, but all he found was the cold, hard truth of the world he had entered.

In that moment, Thidius understood that he was no longer just a charioteer but a player in the grand scheme of Rome. And as he took the patrician's hand, sealing a pact that would bind him to a destiny he could not foresee, the shadowy figure watched from the shadows, his smile as sharp as the blade he kept hidden beneath his cloak. The charioteer of fortune had made his choice, and now he would have to live with the consequences.

The following days were a whirlwind of secret meetings and whispered promises. Thidius found himself navigating a world of deceit and manipulation, a world where a single misstep could mean his downfall He trained harder than ever before, pushing his body and his horses to their limits, driven by the knowledge that each victory brought him closer to the heart of the conspiracy that threatened to consume him.

The rivalry between the Golds and the Reds grew more bitter with each race, and Aurelius watched his rival with a newfound respect and a hint of fear. He knew that Thidius had been approached by the same shadowy figures that had once o ered him a path to power. Yet, the young charioteer remained steadfast, his eyes never straying from the prize that awaited him beyond the arena walls.

Livia, caught between her love for Thidius and her duty to her family, found herself torn. Her father, a prominent member of the Senate, had made it clear that any union between them was impossible. Yet, as she watched Thidius from the safety of the patrician's box, her heart ached for the man who had captured her soul with his courage and his unyielding spirit.

The day of the next great race dawned, the air thick with the scent of jasmine and the promise of rain. The factions were on edge, their supporters ready to spill into the streets if their champions were denied victory. The emperor himself would be in attendance, his mood as unpredictable as the weather.

As the chariots lined up in the carceres, Sextius took a deep breath, his hand trembling slightly on the reins. The shadowy figure was nowhere to be seen, but his presence was felt in the tension that coiled around the track like a serpent waiting to strike. The starting mechanism creaked, the gates swung open, and the chariots surged forward, a living tapestry of speed and fury.

The race was a blur of color and sound, the chariots weaving in and out of each other like a deadly ballet. Thidius and Sextius were inseparable, their chariots locked in a dance that seemed to transcend the mere mortal struggle for supremacy. Each knew that this race was about more than just the laurels; it was about the future of Rome, and their places in it.

The shadowy figure's plan was unfolding before his eyes, the pieces of his grand gambit moving into place. The charioteers were pawns in a game that could end in only one way—with the rise of a new power that would shake the very foundations of the empire. And as the chariots approached the final turn, the fate of Rome rested on the outcome of this race, a race that would be remembered for generations to come.

Thidius felt the weight of his decision as the chariots drew closer to the finish line. The patrician's o er had been tempting, but he had chosen honor over power. His eyes searched the crowd for Livia, her beauty a beacon in the sea of faces. He knew that if he could just hold on, if he could just win, he might be able to claim not only victory but also the love that had been denied to him.

Sextius, driven by his own ambition and the whispers of the shadows, pushed his horses to their limits. The prize was within his grasp, and he would not let it slip away. His heart pounded in his chest, the roar of the crowd a deafening crescendo that threatened to drown out the voice of his conscience. Yet, as he looked across at Thidius, he saw a reflection of what he once was—a man who raced for glory, not for the machinations of the powerful.

The chariots hurtled towards the finish, the gap between them narrowing with every heartbeat. The crowd was on its feet, the air electric with anticipation. Thidius leaned into the turn, his muscles screaming in protest, while Sextius searched for an opening, his eyes as cold as the steel of his chariot's axle. It was a battle not just of speed and skill but of wills, a contest that would determine the course of their lives and the fate of Rome.

The chariots thundered across the line, so close that it was impossible to tell who had won. The crowd erupted into a frenzy, the factions' fans tearing at each other's clothes, their passions a mirror of the chaos that threatened to engulf the city. The shadowy figure watched with a mix of satisfaction and unease. The gamble had paid o , but the stakes had grown higher than he had ever imagined.

As the dust settled and the judges conferred, the tension grew unbearable. The emperor leaned forward in his seat, his eyes narrowed in concentration, his hand tightening around the hilt of his dagger. The fate of his reign could hinge on the outcome of this race, the whispers of rebellion growing louder with every passing moment.

Finally, the decision was made. The Gold faction's chariot had won by a nose, and the crowd exploded in a cacophony of cheers and jeers. Sextius felt a surge of relief and pride, but as he looked into the shadowy figure's eyes, he knew that the battle was far from over. The charioteer of fortune had claimed his victory, but at what cost?

The shadowy figure stepped forward, a knowing smile playing on his lips. "Well done, my friend," he said, his voice low and dangerous. "But remember, the games are never truly over. The real race is just beginning." With that, he vanished into the crowd, leaving Sextius to ponder the true price of his triumph.

The days that followed were a whirlwind of celebration and treachery. Sextius victory had not brought him the peace he sought but had instead cast him into the heart of a storm he could not control. The shadowy figure's words echoed in his mind, a constant reminder of the precarious path he now trod. The emperor's box remained cold and silent, a stark contrast to the jubilation that filled the rest of the Circus Maximus.

Thidius heart was torn between his love for Livia and the whispers of power that called to him from the shadows. The patrician who had o ered him the pact was ever present, his smile as false as the peace that hung over Rome. His eyes promised a future of wealth and influence, but Thidius knew that such promises came with a steep cost .

The day of the final race dawned, the sun a fiery sphere in the heavens. The air was thick with the scent of fear and anticipation. The shadowy figure had arranged for a grand finale that would either secure his power or see it crumble to dust. As the chariots took their positions, the factions' supporters held their breath, their eyes on the prize that was more than just a race.

The starting mechanism released with a thunderous boom, and the chariots leaped forward, a living tapestry of power and betrayal. Sextius focused on the race ahead, his every move a silent declaration of his intent to change the course of history. The African, his eyes reflecting the shadows that had claimed him, pursued with a ferocity that belied his own inner turmoil. The chariots clashed, wheels sparking against the stone as the two men became the embodiment of Rome's tumultuous spirit.

As they rounded the spina, the shadowy figure watched with a tension that belied his usual calm. This race was not merely for bragging rights or wealth; it was the culmination of a plan that had been centuries in the making. His eyes darted between Sextius and the African, the two pawns he had so carefully maneuvered into position. But even as the chariots raced towards destiny, he knew that the true battle was not on the track but in the hearts of those who watched from the stands. Marcus's chariot pulled ahead, the very essence of Rome's hope and defiance. The African, driven by the whispers of the shadows, gave chase, his eyes narrowed to slits of determination.

In the emperor's box, Augustus gaze was as sharp as a falcon's. He sensed the shifting tides of power, the undercurrents of revolt that the charioteers had unwittingly become the figureheads of. His thumb hovered over the button that would release the trapdoors beneath the stands, his mind racing with the consequences of his decision.

Sextius felt the eyes of the city upon him, the weight of their hopes and dreams, his duty to the people, and his desire to free Rome from the clutches of corruption fueled his every move. As he took the final turn, the shadowy figure's plan coalesced in his mind. He had to win, not just for the sake of the race but for the soul of the empire.

As the chariots thundered towards the finish line, he made a decision that would resonate through the annals of history.

With a sudden surge of speed, the African's chariot shot forward, the gap between them closing with every heartbeat. Sextius felt the cold touch of the shadowy figure's hand on his shoulder, a silent reminder of the pact he had made. Yet, as he looked into the eyes of his rival, he saw not malice but a spark of redemption. The two chariots remained locked in their deadly embrace, the fate of Rome hanging in the balance.

The crowd held its collective breath as the chariots raced towards the finish, the air pregnant with the promise of change. The shadowy figure watched, his smile fading as the reality of his failure dawned. The emperor's thumb hovered, his eyes never leaving the track, the power of his decision a silent thunder in the air.

Sextius felt the ground shake beneath him as the African's chariot drew alongside. Their eyes met, a silent conversation passing between them —a plea for understanding, a question of loyalty. In that moment, the rivalry between them transcended the games and became a struggle for the very soul of Rome.

As the chariots crossed the line, it was impossible to discern the victor. The shadowy figure's plan had been thwarted, the delicate balance of power now teetering on the edge of a knife. The tension in the air was palpable, the fate of the empire hanging on the decision of two men who had been raised to be nothing more than entertainment for the masses.

The shadowy figure stepped forward, his hand reaching for his sword. But before he could act, the unthinkable happened. Sextius, his eyes filled with a newfound clarity, pulled his chariot aside, conceding the race to the African. The crowd erupted in a roar of disbelief and anger, the factions' supporters clashing in a frenzy of confusion.

The African, stunned by his rival's gesture, reined in his horses, his heart racing. The shadowy figure's grip on his sword tightened, the fury in his eyes a stark contrast to the sudden stillness that had descended upon the Circus Maximus. The charioteers' destinies had become inextricably linked, their futures as intertwined as the reins that bound them to their horses.

expose the shadowy figure's corrupt influence, turning the upcoming race into a declaration of war against the city's entrenched corruption and setting the stage for a pivotal confrontation.

Aurelius, once the favored son of the shadows, knew the faction's secrets better than anyone. His rise to stardom had been swift, propelled by the very hand that now sought to control him. His early life, spent in the stables of a minor racing team, had taught him the value of loyalty and the cost of ambition. His father, a stoic and hardworking man, had instilled in him a love for the horses and the art of the race. But it was his mother's death, her gentle spirit lost to the harsh world of the arena, that had left him vulnerable to the whispers of power.

Now, with the weight of the city's hope upon his shoulders, Aurelius felt the tug of his past, the echoes of his father's lessons. He knew that he had to make amends, to use his newfound fame to bring the corruption into the light. His rivalry with Marcus had once been fueled by the desire to be the best, but now it was a battle for the very essence of Rome.

Marcus, born into a world of hardship, had always been driven by the need to provide for his family. His father's work as a stable hand had provided him with the skills and the passion for the sport, but it was his mother's unwavering belief in his destiny that had set him on this path. Her death had left him with a fierce determination to succeed, to become a beacon of hope for those who had none.

Under the tutelage of the wise and battle-hardened Quintus, Marcus had learned not only the tactics of the race but the tactics of survival. The aging ex-charioteer had recognized the fire within the young man, the potential to be more than just a champion. He had taught Marcus that victory came not just from speed and strength but from honor and integrity, lessons that would serve him well in the treacherous world of politics.

The first opportunity to drive for a prominent faction had come as a stroke of luck. An injured charioteer had left a seat open in a minor race, and Marcus, hungry for the chance to prove himself, had filled the void. His surprising victory, a David and Goliath moment that had the crowd on their feet, had caught the eye of the talent scouts. They saw in him a spark that could be fanned into a flame that would illuminate the entire city.

The Green faction had come calling, their o ers of wealth and fame too tempting to refuse. The Green's were the darlings of the Circus Maximus, a bastion of power and prestige that could elevate a man from obscurity to legend in the blink of an eye. Marcus had accepted their o er, eager to provide for his family and to honor the memory of his mother. The training was intense, pushing him to the limits of his endurance, but he embraced it, knowing that it was the price of greatness.

The internal politics of the Green faction were as treacherous as the race itself. Rivalries simmered just beneath the surface, a cauldron of ambition and envy that threatened to boil over at any moment. Marcus had to navigate these waters with the grace of a dolphin, making allies and enemies with every step. Yet, he remained true to himself, never compromising his values for the sake of expedience.

His first major victory had come with a cost. The jealousy of established charioteers had been a bitter pill to swallow, their snide comments and underhanded tactics a stark reminder of the serpents that lurked in the shadows of success. Yet, Marcus had persevered, his focus unwavering. He had learned to ignore the whispers of doubt and the sting o betrayal, channeling his anger into every race.

The string of impressive victories that followed had made him a star, the people's champion. His fan base grew with every race, their love for him a testament to the hope he represented. The Senate took notice, the whispers of his name a siren's song that echoed through the marble halls of power. The shadowy figure watched from the shadows, his smile widening as he saw the pawn he had long ago placed on the board begin to ascend to the heights he had foreseen.

The pressure and expectations grew with every victory, a burden that weighed on Marcus's shoulders like the armor of a legionary. Yet, he knew that this was his destiny, a path laid before him by the gods themselves. He raced not just for the roar of the crowd but for the whispers of history that would one day tell his tale.

Behind the scenes, the shadowy figure worked tirelessly. His network of power brokers, wealthy patrons, and corrupt o cials had been carefully cultivated over decades. The factions were his playthings, their every move a piece in his grand design. The Circus Maximus was not just a stage for entertainment but a battleground for the future of Rome.

The whispers grew louder, the stakes higher. The underground betting syndicates placed their bets on the outcome of the races, their vested interest in the games as potent as the incense that filled the air. Bribes changed hands with the ease of a merchant's coins, and the promise of power was as intoxicating as the finest wine. Marcus felt the tug of these unseen forces, the allure of the dark pact that had been o ered to him.

But he was not alone in his struggle. Aurelius, the enigmatic charioteer of the Red faction, had his own demons to face. The shadowy figure had once whispered sweet nothings of power and riches in his ear, promising him the world in exchange for his soul. Yet, as the games grew more perilous, Aurelius began to question the path he had chosen.

The wealthy patrons who had once showered him with gifts and adoration now held his fate in their hands, their whispers of influence as potent as the finest incense that clouded the air of the Circus Maximus. The corrupt o cials who had promised him victory now demanded more than he was willing to give, their greedy fingers reaching into every corner of his life.

The underground betting syndicates, the invisible hand that manipulated the outcome of the races, had grown bold in their demands. They knew that the charioteers were merely pawns in their grand scheme, their lives as expendable as the wooden tokens that represented them in the games of the rich.

The charioteers' rivalry grew, not just on the track but in the shadowy corridors of power. Each victory, each loss, was a move in a chess game played by those who pulled the strings from afar. Marcus felt the sting of betrayal as he learned of the depths to which the shadowy figure had sunk, his heart heavy with the knowledge that his friend had been coerced into playing a role in this twisted Gambit.

Yet, amidst the chaos, a spark of rebellion began to flicker. The factions, once loyal to their shadowy benefactors, began to question the price of their success. The whispers grew into murmurs, the murmurs into shouts, and soon the very fabric of the games began to unravel.

The charioteers, once blinded by the glitz and glamour of their world, had seen the darkness that lurked beneath.

Their hearts now heavy with the knowledge of the shadowy figure's manipulations, Marcus and Aurelius found themselves at a crossroads. The whispers of revolution grew louder, the people's desperation a constant drumbeat in the streets of Rome. The price of bread had skyrocketed, the granaries empty, and the Senate's indi erence to their plight had kindled a fire of anger in the bellies of the once-proud citizens.

The factions, once the playthings of the elite, had become the breeding grounds for rebellion. The people looked to their heroes, the charioteers, as a symbol of hope amidst the chaos. The shadowy figure watched from the shadows, his smile fading as he realized that the games had become something he could no longer control.

Marcus and Aurelius knew that their next race would be their most dangerous yet. It was no longer about the roar of the crowd or the spoils of victory but about the very future of Rome. They had to win not just for themselves but for the people, to show that the spirit of the Republic still burned brightly despite the shadow that had fallen over the city.

The night before the tournament races, a group of desperate citizens gathered in the shadow of the Colosseum. Their faces were etched with hunger and anger, their eyes gleaming with the desperation of those who had nothing left to lose. Marcus and Aurelius, their hearts swelling with a newfound purpose, stood before them, their voices strong and clear.

"We fight not just for the prize of the circus," Marcus declared, his eyes alight with the fire of rebellion, "but for the very soul of Rome. The Senate has forgotten its duty, the emperor is a tyrant, and we, the people, are left to starve in the shadow of their excess."

The crowd erupted into a frenzy, their hunger for change as palpable as the scent of the burning torches that lit the night. They had come from every corner of the city, driven by the whispers of hope that had spread through the streets like wildfire. The charioteers, once mere entertainers, had become the face of their struggle.

Aurelius stepped forward, his voice as commanding as the roar of his chariot's wheels. "We stand together, as one. We fight for bread, for justice, for the Rome that once was, and the Rome that can be again. Let the games be our battleground, and our victory, the spark that ignites the flame of revolution!"

The citizens of Rome looked to their new leaders, their spirits buoyed by the charioteers' fiery words. They had tasted the bitter fruit of the elite's neglect, and now they thirsted for change.

In the shadow of the Colosseum, whispers grew into a roar. The factions, once united by the love of the games, now found common ground in their anger. They were the heart of the city, the very lifeblood that pumped through its veins, and they had been betrayed. The time had come to take back what was rightfully theirs.

The shadowy figure watched from afar, his plan unraveling before his eyes. He had not anticipated the depth of the people's anger, the fervor of their desperation. His grip on the city had always been tight, but now it slipped like sand through his fingers. The games had become a catalyst for something far more dangerous than mere political maneuvering—a full-blown revolution.

Marcus and Aurelius, now the unwitting leaders of this uprising, knew that they had to act swiftly. The people's desperation was a volatile force that could either be harnessed for change or lead to chaos. They turned to the factions, their former rivals now united by a common cause.

The Whispering War had begun. The Green and Red factions, once fierce adversaries in the circus, now stood side by side, their charioteers the generals of a rebellion that would shake the very foundations of the empire. The shadowy figure's influence had turned the games into a battleground for power, but the people had transformed it into a war for survival.

The factions' supporters took up arms, their loyalties to their teams now symbolizing their commitment to the overthrow of the corrupt regime. The streets of Rome became a tapestry of color, the air thick with the scent of rebellion. The Senate trembled, their feasts of opulence interrupted by the cacophony of the mob's approach.

The Senate chamber, once a bastion of power, now reeked of fear. The shadowy figure, his identity still concealed, urged the Senators to stand firm, to crush the insurgents before they could take root. But the whispers of dissent had spread too far, too fast. The Senate was a house divided, and the cracks in its foundation grew with every pounding step of the enraged citizens.

Marcus and Aurelius watched from the sidelines, the gravity of their situation weighing heavily upon them. They had not anticipated the ferocity of the people's response, the depth of their anger. Yet, as the shadows grew longer and the screams grew louder, they knew that there was no turning back. The genie of revolution had been released from its bottle, and it would not be easily contained.

The Senate was overrun, the once-mighty lions of Rome now the hunted. The citizens, their fury unbridled, tore through the marble halls, seeking out the men who had feasted on their su ering. The Senate was no more, their blood a crimson river that flowed through the streets, a grim testament to the price of power.

The emperor, his own fear now a living, breathing entity, called for his Praetorian Guard. Yet, even the mightiest of legions could not stem the tide of the people's wrath. Nero, the Golden Child, watched as his city burned, his dreams of grandeur turning to ash before his very eyes. The Great Fire of Rome had been but a spark compared to the conflagration that now engulfed the Senate.

The once-mighty Senate lay in ruins, a monument to their own greed and decadence. The blood of the elite painted the streets, a crimson path that led directly to the steps of the Palatine Hill. The citizens, their faces twisted by hunger and anger, had become the instruments of their own vengeance. They had been pawns in the shadowy figure's game, but now they had become the players, and the board was set for a revolution that would echo through the annals of history.

The air grew thick with the acrid smell of burning buildings, the cries of the dying a cacophony that seemed to fuel the flames of rebellion. Marcus and Aurelius looked upon the carnage, their hearts torn between the hope of change and the horror of what it had cost. They had become the heroes of a cause that had spiralled out of control, their chariots now the vanguard of a revolution that threatened to consume the very fabric of Rome.

The shadowy figure watched from the shadows, his smile now a grimace of defeat. He had underestimated the people's spirit, the bond that could be forged in the crucible of despair. His plan, so meticulously crafted over the millennia, had been undone by the very pawns he had sought to manipulate. Yet, even in his failure, he knew that the seeds of discord had been sown, and the harvest would be ripe for his kind to feast upon.

The citizens of Rome had become a ravenous beast, their hunger for justice an insatiable maw that consumed everything in its path. The Senate, once the bastion of power and corruption, now lay in ruins, its members slaughtered without mercy. The crimson tide of their blood painted the marble floors, a macabre dance of death that mirrored the crimson sands of the Colosseum. The air was thick with the scent of iron and fear, the once-proud lions of the Republic now reduced to cowering prey. It was time to turn to the king and do the same.

Marcus and Aurelius, at the forefront of the rebellion, led their makeshift army to the Palatine Hill. The roar of the mob grew louder with every step they took, the echoes of their anger bouncing o the ancient stones of the palace walls. The king's guard, once an unstoppable force, now looked upon them with fear in their eyes.

They knew that the tide had turned, that the power had shifted, and that their lives were now measured in moments.

The battle for the king's chamber was swift and brutal. The charioteers, now seasoned warriors in the fight for Rome's soul, tore through the ranks of the guard with the same ferocity they had once shown in the circus. Swords clashed, shields shattered, and lives were extinguished in the blink of an eye. The guard, once the embodiment of imperial might, now lay broken and defeated before the people they had sworn to protect.

The doors to the chamber stood open, the path to the king clear Marcus and Aurelius stepped over the fallen bodies, their hearts racing with anticipation and dread. They had come so far, sacrificed so much and now the moment of truth was upon them. Yet, as they entered the opulent chamber, their eyes fell upon a scene that none had anticipated. The king's throne sat empty, the room abandoned save fo the flickering candles and the distant echoes of the battle outside.

The king's guard, a once-mighty phalanx of loyal soldiers, lay scattered, their armor dented and bloodied. Yet, there was no sign of the king himself. The whispers grew to a crescendo, the very air thick with the scent of betrayal. The shadowy figure had played his final card, retreating into the shadows like the coward he was.

Panic and confusion reigned supreme as the rebels searched the chamber. The king's chamber was a labyrinth of opulence, each corner hiding a potential escape route for the man they sought. Yet, it was in the heart of the chaos that they found their first clue—a secret passage, hidden behind a tapestry depicting the grandeur of Rome's past .

The passage was narrow, the air stale with the scent of dust and the faint whi of something... darker. Marcus and Aurelius, flanked by the most trusted of their faction members, descended into the bowels of the palace. The shadows danced around them, cast by the flickering torches that lined the walls. Their steps echoed through the passage, a stark reminder that they were no longer in the grand halls of power but in the belly of the beast.

The battle with the king's guard had been fiercer than any race they had ever run. The guards had fought with the desperation of men who knew their lives were forfeit if they failed. Yet, the charioteers had prevailed, their newfound unity a force that could not be stopped. The corridor grew narrower, the walls closing in around them like the jaws of a giant serpent, but they pressed on, driven by the cries of their people outside.

Finally, they reached a chamber, the air heavy with the scent of fear and betrayal. The throne, a monstrosity of gold and jewels, sat empty, a silent sentinel to the king's absence. The room was in shambles, the opulent furnishings smashed and overturned. Upon the wall, a hastily scrawled message in crimson ink read, "The Senate will be reborn, chosen by the people."

The charioteers stared at the words, their hearts racing. The shadowy figure had outwitted them once again. Nero had vanished, leaving behind a promise of change that seemed too good to be true. Marcus and Aurelius knew that this was but a ploy to calm the storm that had engulfed Rome. Yet, hope flickered within them—perhaps this was the opening they needed to restore balance to the city they loved.

Marcus took the lead, his voice steady and strong. "We must be vigilant. The king's words may soothe the mob's anger, but we cannot let our guard down. We will help the people organize fair elections, and together we will ensure that the Senate is rebuilt from the ashes of corruption."

The rebels nodded, their eyes alight with the same determination. The revolution had begun in the circus, but it would not end there. They had become the architects of a new Rome, one that would rise from the embers of the old, a phoenix born of the flames of rebellion.

The shadowy figure watched from the shadows, his smile a cold calculating grin. His plan had taken a detour, but it had not been entirely derailed. Nero, the puppet king, had retreated to the safety o his hidden chamber, his fear palpable. Yet, from the ashes of chaos, a new strategy began to form in the figure's mind. He whispered into the king's ear, the words a seductive serenade that promised power and control.

The king, his voice trembling, called out to the people of Rome. He promised a new Senate, chosen by the very citizens who now sought his head. It was a desperate gambit, a last-ditch attempt to maintain his grip on the city. The whispers grew, spreading like wildfire through the streets. The people, their anger momentarily abated, whispered of hope amidst the ash.

Marcus and Aurelius, now the reluctant leaders of the revolution, knew that this was a ploy, a false dawn meant to lull them into complacency. Yet, they saw the glimmer of possibility in the chaos. If they could guide the people through this transition, perhaps they could shape the new Senate in the image of the Republic they so desperately longed for.

The elections were a tumultuous a air, the air of the city thick with the scent of hope and suspicion. Marcus and Aurelius had managed to organize the people into a semblance of order, but the shadowy figure's influence remained, casting a pall over the proceedings. Three candidates had emerged, each a symbol of the forces that had brought Rome to this precipice.

The first was a man named Gaius, a warrior whose valor on the battlefield was legendary. His eyes were cold and hard, his voice like the clang of iron on iron as he spoke of strength and order, the virtues that had once made Rome great. He was a product of the old guard, a son of the Senate, and his words resonated with those who longed for the stability of the past.

The second was a nobleman named Lucius, his fingers stained with the ink of a thousand treaties and his pockets heavy with the gold of the elite. He spoke of compromise and diplomacy, of the need to balance the scales of power lest the city tip into anarchy. His words were like honey, sweet and sticky, coating the ears of those who feared the loss of their own privileges.

And then there was Titus, a simple farmer whose eloquence and knowledge surpassed that of any scholar. His hands were calloused from the plow, his eyes clear with the wisdom of one who had seen the land su er under the yoke of the Senate's neglect. He spoke of new ideas, of innovation and reform, of a Rome that served all its citizens, not just the few. His voice was the gentle rain that could nurture the seeds of change.

The debate raged in the Forum, the heart of Rome, where once the greatest orators had swayed the masses with their words. The three candidates stood upon the rostra, the stone podium where countless leaders had addressed their people. The whispers of the crowd grew into a roar as each man presented his vision for the future.

Gaius spoke of the need for a strong hand to guide the Republic, his words stirring the embers of national pride. "We must stand firm against the barbarians at our gates," he declared, "and restore the might of our legions." The crowd, weary of the endless wars that had bled the city dry, roared in approval.

Lucius, the nobleman, countered with a vision of harmony and balance. "Our city is a tapestry," he argued, "and each thread must be carefully woven to ensure its strength. We must work together, regardless of our stations in life." The Senate loyalists nodded in agreement, whispering among themselves about the stability he o ered.

Titus, the farmer-scholar, took his turn, his voice a calming force amidst the tumult. "Rome is more than just swords and gold," he said, his eyes scanning the sea of faces before him. "It is the collective wisdom of its people, the sweat of their brows, and the dreams they hold for their children." His words resonated with the common folk, who had long been trampled under the boots of the elite.

The debate grew heated, the three men's ideologies clashing like the chariots of the Circus Maximus. Each spoke of his vision for Rome, their words a battle cry to their supporters. The air was thick with the scent of sweat and ambition, the very essence of power.

Marcus and Aurelius watched from the sidelines, their hearts racing as the fate of Rome hung in the balance. They had never imagined that their rivalry on the racetrack would lead to this moment, the shaping of their city's destiny. The whispers grew to a crescendo as the citizens of Rome leaned in, hungry for the words that could lead them out of the shadow of tyranny.

The third candidate, Titus, spoke with a passion that seemed to ignite the very air around him. He spoke of a Rome where the soil was not just a battleground but a cradle for new life, where the power of the Senate was not absolute but tempered by the will of the people. He was already the people's choice but after the debate, he clearly was the frontrunner.

The shadowy figure watched with growing unease as Titus's words resonated with the crowd. He knew that this man, with his talk of unity and change, posed a grave threat to his own plans. He had hoped to use the chaos to install a puppet, but Titus had the potential to become so much more.

Marcus and Aurelius looked at each other, their hearts swelling with hope. Titus was not just a symbol of change but a beacon of it. They had started this journey as rivals, unknowingly pawns in a game of power and manipulation. Now, standing on the precipice of a new Rome, they were bound by a shared vision of a better future.

The shadowy figure, however, saw Titus as a threat to his millennia-long scheme. He could not allow this farmer to dismantle the corrupt system that had served him so well. As the elections approached, whispers grew louder in the dark corners of the city, of plots and poisons, of hidden blades and bribes. The shadowy figure had not survived the ebb and flow of empires by playing fair.

On the eve of the vote, a plot was uncovered. An assassin, paid by the shadowy figure, had infiltrated Titus's camp. The charioteers and their allies had grown suspicious of the increasing tension and had fortified their position around the farmer-scholar. The air was thick with tension as the sun set, the whispers of treachery and deceit louder than ever.

Aurelius and Marcus, their friendship forged in the crucible of rebellion, stood side by side with Titus. They knew that the shadowy figure would not relinquish his grip easily. The stakes had never been higher, and the shadowy figure had proven himself a formidable opponent. Yet, as they faced the coming storm, they felt a unity that surpassed their former rivalry.

The day of the election dawned, the air still heavy with the scent of uncertainty and fear. The shadowy figure had retreated into the shadows once more, his hand visible only through the whispers that rippled through the city like a malignant wind. Marcus, Aurelius, and Titus gathered in the Forum, the heart of Rome, where the fate of the Republic would be decided.

The voting process was fraught with tension. Guards patrolled the perimeter, their eyes sharp for any sign of trouble. Marcus and Aurelius had rallied their factions to stand as a united front, protecting the integrity of the vote. Yet, the whispers of the shadowy figure's influence remained, casting doubt on every action, every decision.

As the sun reached its zenith, the votes were counted. The tension in the Forum was palpable, the whispers of the crowd a symphony of anticipation and fear. The shadowy figure's agents had infiltrated every corner of the city, their whispers of doubt and chaos threatening to drown out the cries for change. Yet, when the results were announced, a collective gasp filled the air—Titus had won by a landslide.

The farmer-scholar, once a mere pawn in the shadowy figure's grand scheme, now stood before the people of Rome as their chosen leader. His eyes shone with a mix of disbelief and determination as he took the podium. The crowd erupted into a deafening roar, their cheers echoing through the ancient streets like the thunder of a new era.

Marcus and Aurelius, their hearts racing with hope and anxiety, shared a brief nod of understanding. They had become more than just charioteers; they were the guardians of a revolution. Their eyes scanned the crowd, searching for any sign of the shadowy figure's next move. But for now, the shadowy figure remained hidden, biding his time, licking his wounds.

The days that followed were a whirlwind of activity. Titus, with the unyielding support of Marcus and Aurelius, began the monumental task of rebuilding the Senate. The corrupt o cials were weeded out, one by one, and replaced with men and women with good core beliefs. Men and women who won't just give into the desire of wealth giving up their power.

The power brokers who had once controlled the chariot factions from the shadows found themselves in the limelight, their illicit dealings now the subject of public scrutiny. The wealthy patrons who had financed the factions for their own gain found their pockets lighter, their influence waning as the new Senate began to assert its authority. The underground betting syndicates, once the lifeblood of the games, were dismantled brick by brick as the games themselves were reformed to be a spectacle of honor and skill rather than a playground for the corrupt.

The shadowy figure watched from his hiding place, his rage simmering like a pot left unattended. He had not anticipated the swiftness of the charioteers' rise to power, nor the loyalty they had inspired in the people. Yet, he was not one to accept defeat easily. His hand reached for the amulet that hung around his neck, a talisman of ancient power that had seen the fall of empires.

The king, Nero, had realized that his survival depended on the will of the people. In a desperate bid to regain their trust, he had ordered the shadowy figure's capture. The man who had once whispered sweet nothings of power and control into his ear was now a liability, a symbol of the very corruption that had brought Rome to its knees. The figure was brought before the public, his once-shadowy visage now illuminated by the harsh sun of the Colosseum.

The execution was swift and brutal. The shadowy figure was dragged into the arena, his once-proud frame now bruised and broken. He was thrown to the ground, the amulet ripped from his neck and held aloft by a grinning gladiator. Nero, seated on his throne, his eyes wild with a mix of fear and desperation, announced to the crowd, "Cheat the games, and you cheat life itself. Let this be a lesson to all who would seek to manipulate Rome's fate for their own gain!"

The gladiator plunged his sword into the shadowy figure's chest, and with a final gasp, the puppet master's life drained away into the sands. The crowd roared in approval, the spectacle of his death a cathartic release for their anger and frustration. Yet, amidst the cheers and the echoes of the king's decree, a single whisper of doubt remained—the shadowy figure was one man, but the corruption he had fostered was a hydra with many heads.

Marcus and Aurelius knew that the battle was far from over. The shadowy figure's death was a victory, but the monster of corruption he had created still lurked in the shadows of Rome. They worked tirelessly alongside Titus, implementing reforms that would ensure the Senate's integrity and transparency. The games were no longer a stage for political manipulation but a place where heroes were truly born, where the spirit of Rome could shine.

But the whispers grew. The shadowy figure had had his hands in many pies, and his loyalists remained, biding their time. They whispered of a new leader, a new hope for those who craved power. They whispered of a conspiracy to bring down the new Senate and restore the old ways. The charioteers turned senators knew that the seeds of corruption had not been fully eradicated.

Marcus and Aurelius patrolled the streets, their eyes sharp for any sign of trouble. They had become the faces of the revolution, and with that came a responsibility to protect the very people they had once entertained. The chariot races had been a catalyst for change, but now they were a symbol of a new Rome, a Rome that valued honor and justice over greed and deceit.

Their days were filled with the mundane tasks of governance, but their nights were haunted by whispers of the shadowy figure's lingering influence. They knew that the real battle was not in the arena but in the hearts and minds of the people. To truly win, they had to convince Rome that change was not just a fleeting dream but a tangible reality.

The new racing season approached, and with it, the unveiling of the Gold Faction, a faction owned by the king himself. The Gold Faction's stables were filled with the finest Spanish stallions, beasts that could outrun the wind. The chariots were adorned with gold and precious gems, and the drivers, handpicked by Nero, were promised wealth and power beyond their wildest dreams. The whispers grew louder, the temptation of easy victory beckoning to those who had once known only struggle.

Marcus and Aurelius watched the first race of the season from the Senate's private box, their stomachs knotted with tension. The Gold Faction's chariots sped around the Circus Maximus, the thunder of hooves a stark reminder of the power struggle playing out before their eyes. The crowd roared in awe at the speed and skill of the new faction, and for a moment, it seemed as if the shadowy figure's legacy had found new life.

Yet, as the race unfolded, the charioteers of the Gold Faction began to show signs of strain. The pressure of performing for the king had made them sloppy, their once-perfect form now marred by desperation. Marcus and Aurelius, their eyes never leaving the track, noticed the subtle mistakes, the missed opportunities for strategy that only those who had felt the thrill of victory and the sting of defeat could spot.

The whispers grew quieter as the race progressed. The Gold Faction's dominance was not as absolute as had been promised. The charioteers of the old factions, the Greens and the Reds, who had once been pawns in the shadowy figure's game, began to push back. Their determination, fueled by the hope of a new Rome, made them fiercer competitors than they had ever been before.

The final lap approached, and the Gold Faction's lead began to falter. A chariot from the Reds, driven by a young and fiery newcomer named Caius, made a daring move, slipping through the tightly packed field. The crowd's allegiance shifted, their cheers now a cacophony of hope for the underdogs. Marcus and Aurelius leaned forward in their seats, their eyes glued to the race.

Caius's chariot, propelled by a combination of skill and sheer will, drew closer to the Gold Faction's leader. The tension in the air was palpable, the roar of the crowd a physical force that seemed to push the chariots forward. The Gold Faction's driver, a seasoned but corrupt veteran, sensed the shift in momentum. He glanced back, his eyes narrowing in a mix of anger and fear.

In that moment, the crowd saw what Marcus and Aurelius had known all along—the Gold Faction was not untouchable. The whispers grew louder, a collective murmur of rebellion against the king's attempt to hijack their beloved games. The charioteers of the old factions, the Greens and the Reds, seemed to draw strength from the people's energy, pushing their horses to their limits.

The final turn of the race was upon them, and Caius of the Reds took the inside track, his stallions' eyes ablaze with determination. The Gold Faction leader, desperate to maintain his lead, made a reckless move, cutting Caius o . The crowd gasped as the two chariots collided, sending splinters of wood flying into the air. Marcus and Aurelius leaped to their feet, their hearts in their throats.

But Caius was not to be deterred. He steered his damaged chariot around the wreckage, the crowd's roar lifting him like the very breath of the gods. The Gold Faction's leader, his chariot wobbling, tried to regain control, but it was too late. Caius surged ahead, the crimson dust of the track billowing in his wake. The finish line was a blur of color and sound, the once-silent whispers now a deafening cry for a new hero.

The race concluded with Caius standing victorious, the Gold Faction's dominance shattered. The crowd erupted into a frenzy, their chants of "Caius! Caius!" shaking the very foundations of the Circus Maximus. Marcus and Aurelius, their hearts pounding in their chests, knew that this moment was more than just a victory on the track; it was a victory for the soul of Rome.

They approached the young charioteer, his face a mask of exhilaration and shock. Caius looked up at them, his eyes wide with the weight of what he had just achieved. "You've shown us that hope is not lost," Marcus said, his voice hoarse from the roar of the crowd. "But you must also understand the darkness that still lingers in the shadows of this city."

Aurelius took Caius aside, his eyes filled with the wisdom of one who had seen the worst of human nature. "The shadowy figure is gone, but his influence remains," he whispered. "The games are a powerful tool, and there are always those who seek to wield it for their own ends." He spoke of the bribes, the sabotage, the whispers that had once controlled the fate of charioteers and races. Caius listened intently, his expression sobering as he realized the gravity of his newfound role.

Marcus stepped in, placing a firm hand on Caius's shoulder. "We will train you, not just in the art of racing but in the art of navigating the political maelstrom that is Rome. You have a gift, a gift that can inspire and unite. But you must be vigilant."

Together, the three men set to work. Marcus and Aurelius shared their knowledge of the track, their strategies, and their tactics. They taught

Caius to read the subtle cues of his horses, to anticipate the moves of his opponents, and to stay one step ahead of the game. But more than that, they taught him about the shadowy alliances that lurked beneath the surface of Roman society.

As Caius's skills grew, so too did his understanding of the shadowy underbelly of the chariot games. Marcus and Aurelius were candid with him, sharing tales of their own encounters with the shadowy figure and his ilk. They revealed the complex web of bribery, blackmail, and deceit that had once governed the races, and how the stakes had stretched far beyond the arena's sands, reaching into the very fabric of Rome's power structure.

Under their tutelage, Caius's racing acumen grew as did his sense of responsibility. Training sessions were no longer just about speed and strategy; they were lessons in integrity and vigilance. Marcus and Aurelius taught him that every race was a battle not just for victory but for the very soul of Rome. They shared with him the unsavory tactics they had encountered in their own careers—how bribes were whispered in dark alleyways, how chariots were sabotaged under the guise of 'accidental' mishaps, and how the fate of races could be bought and sold like commodities in the marketplace.

Caius's eyes were opened to the labyrinthine world of political machinations and the stakes that went far beyond the prize money. He began to see the chariot races as a microcosm of Rome itself, a place where the powerful few sought to manipulate the many for their own ends. Marcus and Aurelius warned him of the whispers that still echoed through the city, the whispers that sought to corrupt the pure spirit of competition.

The day of the fateful race dawned, the sun casting a foreboding light over the Circus Maximus. Caius, his heart racing with both excitement and fear, took his place at the starting line. The Gold Faction's chariots gleamed menacingly beside him, their drivers filled with arrogance and greed. The king, Nero, watched from his box, a cruel smile playing on his lips as he knew the fate he had sealed for the young upstart.

The signal was given, and the chariots shot forward like bolts of lightning. Caius's stallions, responding to his firm but gentle touch, surged ahead, their muscles rippling with power. The crowd, hungry for a hero, roared their support. But unbeknownst to Caius, a silent enemy had been introduced into the race.

Midway through the race, as the chariots thundered around the final turn, the axle on Caius's chariot snapped with a sound that was drowned out by the deafening cheers of the spectators. The crimson chariot, once a symbol of hope, became a twisted mess of wood and metal, spinning out of control. Caius was thrown into the air, his body a ragdoll to the whims of fate.

The world around him blurred into a chaotic tableau of color and sound. He could see the shadowy figure's grinning face in the dust, feel the malicious whispers that had once held Rome in their thrall. As Caius hurtled through the air, time seemed to slow, allowing him a moment of clarity amidst the chaos. The king's treachery had struck again, aiming to crush the last ember of hope that had been lit by the charioteers' revolution.

Marcus and Aurelius watched in horror as Caius's chariot disintegrated into a shower of splinters. The crowd's cheer turned to a collective gasp of disbelief and fear. The shadowy figure's legacy had once again reached out from the grave to claim a piece of the city they had sworn to protect.

Marcus's mind raced, piecing together the puzzle of this new betrayal. His eyes searched the crowd for any sign of the king's hand, for any hint of the saboteur. Meanwhile, Aurelius, his own heart heavy with the burden of their shared past, knew that they could not let this stand. The people needed a hero, a beacon of light in the gathering storm of corruption.

The race continued, the Gold Faction's chariots now free to claim victory without challenge. But the victory was hollow, a facade painted over the cracks of a city on the brink. Marcus and Aurelius knew that they had to act swiftly, to cut o the head of the hydra before it could regrow. They descended from the Senate's box, their steps determined, their eyes scanning the frantic scene for any clue to the saboteur's identity.

Days later, they received a letter from their hometowns, a response to their desperate call for help. Two men, the best horse handlers and racers their cities had to o er, had arrived in Rome. They were brothers, Castor and Pollux, their reputation preceding them like the gleaming aura of heroes. The siblings were known for their unrivaled bond with horses, a bond that had brought them fame and victory across the empire.

The brothers were assigned to the Red and Green factions respectively, their arrival greeted with a mix of skepticism and hope. The charioteers eyed each other warily, aware that they had been pawns in a much larger game. But with the arrival of Castor and Pollux, they felt a shift in the air, a newfound strength in their unity against the corruption that had plagued their sport.

Under the tutelage of Marcus and Aurelius, the brothers quickly became the new faces of the factions. Castor, with his fiery temperament, embodied the spirit of the Reds, while Pollux, cool and calculating, was the embodiment of the Greens' cunning. They trained tirelessly, not just in the art of horse racing but in the subtleties of Rome's political landscape. They were taught to recognize the whispers of corruption and to stand firm in the face of temptation.

The charioteers watched their new leaders with a mix of admiration and trepidation. The stakes had never been higher, and the shadow of the shadowy figure still loomed large. Yet, with every practice lap, every strategy session, the whispers grew quieter. The people of Rome began to believe again, their spirits lifting like the dust of the Circus Maximus in the wake of a chariot's charge.

Word of the king's new allies spread through the underground, a murmur that grew into a roar. Fixers from across the city sought their favor, o ering bribes and promises of victory in exchange for their complicity. Marcus and Aurelius, however, remained steadfast in their resolve. They knew that to allow corruption to infiltrate the new order would be to invite the shadowy figure's return.

The brothers Castor and Pollux quickly mastered the art of subtle sabotage, their skill at managing their horses' performance becoming almost supernatural. They coordinated with other racers who had seen the light, orchestrating complex fixes that ba led the corrupt o cials and wealthy patrons who had once held sway over the games. Their network grew, a web of loyalty and honor that stretched across the factions, leaving the shadowy figure's minions isolated and impotent .

Marcus and Aurelius worked tirelessly to ensure that the chariot games remained a bastion of hope and fairness in the new Rome. They watched over Castor and Pollux like hawks, guiding them through the treacherous waters of politics and corruption that surrounded the sport. Yet, the whispers grew more insistent, and the shadowy figure's influence began to spread once again.

The king's name became synonymous with manipulation, his network of contacts extending its tendrils into every corner of the chariot world. Through bribery and blackmail, he ensured that the odds remained in his favor, his reputation as a skilled fixer spreading like wildfire in the underground. O ers for his "services" grew more frequent, each one more tempting than the last.

In the public eye, he remained a dedicated owner, his talents for finding good racers for the track seemingly unmatched. Yet, behind closed doors, he mastered the art of subtle sabotage. He coordinated with corrupt drivers from across the factions, using coded messages and secret meetings to orchestrate complex fixes that no one could trace back to him. His success grew, and so too did the whispers of his involvement in the very corruption he had once railed against.

As he climbed the ranks, the king's hunger for power grew insatiable. He used his newfound influence to win key races, leveraging his corrupt connections for better opportunities. Wealthy patrons, desperate to be seen backing a winner, flocked to his side, filling his co ers with gold and promises of support. His name was on everyone's lips, and his chariot was the one to bet on.

But with great power came great risk. One day, he found himself embroiled in a race-fixing scandal of unprecedented proportions. The stakes were high: the outcome of this race would determine the fate of a powerful o cial, and the king had been promised a fortune for his help. The whispers grew to a crescendo, reaching the ears of those who had once been his allies, and even some of his closest friends began to question his motives.

The king knew he had to tread carefully. He had built a network of corrupt o cials and wealthy patrons who could bring him down with a single word. Yet, the thrill of manipulation had become his lifeblood, and he couldn't resist the siren call of power.

In the weeks leading up to the race, the king met with the o cial in question in a series of secret meetings. They plotted and schemed, their greedy whispers echoing in the shadows of the city's darkest alleyways. The king's mind raced with the intricacies of the plan: which drivers to bribe, which chariots to sabotage, which horses to drug. The weight of his actions bore down on him, a heavy burden that only the sweet taste of victory could ease.

The day of the race arrived, and the Circus Maximus was alive with the electric energy of anticipation. The crowd, blissfully unaware of the shadowy dealings behind the scenes, roared for their favorites.

The king, now a notorious figure in the underground, felt the weight of his deception heavy on his shoulders. Yet, as he took his place in the royal box, the allure of power was too strong to resist. His eyes scanned the track, his mind racing with the intricate dance of sabotage he had orchestrated. His heart pounded in his chest, not with excitement for the race, but with the fear of discovery.

As the chariots thundered out of the starting gates, the crowd erupted into a frenzy. The king watched with bated breath as the race unfolded exactly as he had planned. His chosen chariot, driven by a bribed and coerced driver, took an early lead. The whispers grew to a crescendo, the crowd's roar masking the sound of his own racing heart .

But amidst the chaos, something unexpected occurred. One of the underdogs, a young and unassuming racer named Calidus, began to gain ground. His driving was not flashy or aggressive, but rather precise and intelligent, his horse responding to his every command as if they were one. Marcus and Aurelius watched with bated breath as Calidus steadily closed the gap between him and the Gold Faction's leader.

The king's eyes narrowed, his pulse quickening. This was not part of the plan. He had not accounted for such a skilled and determined competitor. The whispers grew frantic, the network of corruption buzzing with tension. In the final stretch, Calidus pulled alongside the Gold Faction's chariot, their wheels almost touching. The crowd's roar grew deafening as they sensed the possibility of an upset.

Marcus and Aurelius watched with a mix of awe and dread. They knew that if Calidus won, it could be the spark that ignited a full-blown rebellion against the corruption that had long plagued the games. But if the king's chariot prevailed, it would only serve to strengthen his grip on the sport, and by extension, the city itself.

The final turn approached, and the king made his move. He whispered a command to his personal guard, and a saboteur, disguised as a track worker, rushed out with a pouch of poisoned sand. The saboteur tossed the sand into the path of Calidus's horse, aiming to blind it and cause a catastrophic wreck. The air grew thick with the scent of treachery, the very essence of the shadowy figure's legacy.

But Calidus, sensing the danger, reacted with a swiftness that belied his youth. He steered his horse clear of the deadly cloud, his eyes never leaving the prize ahead. The crowd held its collective breath as the two chariots thundered towards the finish line, the king's plot hanging in the balance.

In the royal box, the king's heart raced as he watched Calidus's horse leap over the final hurdle, its hooves barely touching the ground. The whisper of fate grew to a deafening roar, and the world around him seemed to slow to a crawl. The finish was a blur of motion, the crimson of Calidus's chariot a stark contrast against the dusty track.

As the dust settled and the crowd erupted in a cacophony of cheers, it was clear: Calidus had won. The king's face paled, the color draining from his cheeks like the last light of a dying sun. The whispers grew to a deafening crescendo, the tide of public opinion turning against him.

His network of corruption had been outmaneuvered by a pure-hearted outsider, and the taste of defeat was bitter on his tongue.

Marcus and Aurelius, their hearts pounding with a mix of excitement and dread, descended into the arena. They approached Calidus, who sat in his chariot, panting heavily but grinning from ear to ear. "You have shown us all what it truly means to race for Rome," Marcus said, his voice hoarse from shouting over the din of the crowd. "But beware, for the shadowy figure's legacy is not easily vanquished."

The whispers grew louder, and the king's network of corruption began to fray at the edges. As the truth of his manipulations spread through the city, his allies grew wary, and the once-solid ground beneath his feet began to shift. The king knew he had to act fast. He called for a private audience with Calidus, a meeting that was shrouded in mystery and intrigue.

The young charioteer arrived at the palace, surrounded by whispers of treachery and suspicion. He had been summoned by the king himself, and the weight of the moment was not lost on him. As he stepped into the opulent chamber, the king's cold gaze bore into him like a dagger. "You've proven yourself quite the contender, Calidus," the king said, his voice dripping with insincerity. "I see a bright future for you in the games. A future that could be made even brighter with a... strategic partnership."

Calidus knew what the king was hinting at, and his stomach churned with revulsion. The whispers of corruption had grown louder since he had first stepped into the world of chariot racing, and he had vowed to stay true to the sport's original spirit. Yet, as he looked into the king's eyes, he saw the desperation behind the façade of power. The king was o ering him a chance to join the very thing he had sworn to fight against.

Calidus took a deep breath, steeling himself against the temptation. "Your majesty," he began, his voice firm despite the tremor in his chest, "I race for honor and for Rome, not for personal gain or to be a pawn in the games of the powerful." The king's smile never wavered, but his eyes narrowed, the glint of steel in their depths.

The king leaned back in his throne, considering Calidus for a long moment. "Very well," he said finally, his tone deceptively mild. "But know this: the chariot games are a reflection of our city's soul. If you wish to remain pure, you may find yourself an outcast in your own sport."

The meeting ended with an unspoken threat hanging in the air, and Calidus left the palace feeling the weight of his decision. The whispers grew more insistent as he walked the streets of Rome, his thoughts racing with the implications of his refusal. He knew he had made a powerful enemy, but he also knew that he had chosen the right path.

Marcus and Aurelius, upon hearing of Calidus's encounter, were torn between pride in their pupil's resolve and fear for his safety. They knew the king's network was vast and unforgiving, and to deny a partnership with the king was like singing your life away.

During a night of feasting and revelry, the king sat at his usual table, surrounded by his shady partners in crime. His smile was forced, his eyes darting around the room as he searched for signs of betrayal. Little did he know that the very men he had once counted as allies had grown tired of his failures and his insatiable hunger for power. They had seen the writing on the wall and knew that their survival was now contingent on cutting ties with the failing regime.

One of the men, a pockmarked individual with a twisted smile, slipped a vial of clear liquid into the king's cup. The potent poison was known to cause a swift and painless death, leaving no trace of foul play. The room buzzed with the tension of unspoken words and unseen gestures, the whispers of treachery thick in the air.

The king, lost in his own thoughts of failure and vengeance, did not notice as the cup was passed to him. He took a deep drink, the sweet wine doing little to ease the bitterness of his defeat. His eyes widened slightly as the room around him began to spin, the laughter and chatter of his guests fading into a distant hum.

As the king's body slumped to the floor, the room erupted into chaos. The men who had once been his confidants now turned on him, their knives flashing in the torchlight. The whispers grew to shouts, accusations flying as the king's network of corruption crumbled before their very eyes.

Calidus, who had been invited to the festivities as a gesture of goodwill, watched in horror as the men he had once admired descended into a frenzy of betrayal. He knew that he had played a part in this, that his victory had been the catalyst for the king's downfall .

In the aftermath of the chaos, the king's younger brother, a man of unassuming nature and a reputation for fairness, claimed the throne. Unlike his brother, he was a man of the people, and his first act as ruler was to double the grain output, ensuring that no Roman would go hungry. The whispers of his benevolence spread like wildfire through the streets, and the people's hope was rekindled.

The new king, known now as Augustus, set his sights on rebuilding Rome's soul. He founded libraries and universities, filling them with the works of great thinkers and philosophers. The city became a beacon of knowledge and wisdom, drawing scholars from across the empire like a lodestone. The chariot games, once a tool of political manipulation, were transformed into a celebration of unity and skill.

In the Senate, his reforms were met with a mix of skepticism and hope. Many feared that his public promises of change and prosperity were just empty words to win their favor. Yet, as the months passed, the whispers of skepticism gave way to murmurs of admiration. Augustus walked the fine line between the Senate's old guard and the burgeoning revolutionaries, seeking to please both without compromising his vision for a just society.

The Senate chambers buzzed with the sound of quills scratching parchment as new laws were drafted. Restrictions on speech and assembly were loosened, allowing the people to voice their opinions without fear of retribution. Public forums grew crowded with eager listeners, eager to hear the latest debates on philosophy, science, and governance. The air was charged with the scent of ink and parchment, a testament to the flourishing of scholarly pursuits.

Marcus and Aurelius watched the transformation with a mix of pride and trepidation. They knew that the shadow of corruption still lurked in the corners of the city, waiting for the right moment to strike. Yet, they also saw the potential for a new Rome, one where the chariot games were a symbol of unity rather than division.

The new king, Augustus, took to the podium in the heart of the city, his voice strong and clear as he addressed the gathered masses. He spoke of a Rome where the Senate served the people, not the other way around. His words were met with a tentative silence, the crowd unsure if they could trust the promises of another ruler. Yet, as he outlined his plans for reform, the whispers of skepticism began to give way to hope.

He spoke of redistributing wealth and land, of ensuring that every Roman had the opportunity to rise above their station. He promised to establish public schools and libraries, to give the children of the poor the same education as the sons of the wealthy. The Senate murmured among themselves, some nodding in agreement, others raising skeptical eyebrows. The whispers grew louder as Augustus spoke of opening the doors to freedom of speech and assembly, a radical notion in a city where dissent had once been met with swift and brutal punishment.

The populace, accustomed to the empty promises of a thousand leaders before him, listened with guarded hope. Augustus promised that no one shall go dirty anymore, the plans to build an aqueduct to fill every area in the city quality baths has been implemented. Humans had seen empires rise and fall on the backs of grandiose claims and had learned to trust their gut rather than their hearts. Yet, there was something in Augustus's eyes, a spark of genuine conviction that had been absent in the eyes of his predecessors. The air was thick with the scent of change.

In the days that followed, Augustus's words became actions. The Senate, though begrudgingly, passed laws that redistributed wealth and land to the plebeians. The first public schools were founded, their walls adorned with frescoes of philosophers and poets, their halls echoing with the laughter of children eager to learn. The air of the city grew lighter, the whispers of fear and corruption replaced by the chatter of scholarly debates and the promise of a better tomorrow.

The chariot games, once a stage for political posturing and shady deals, were reborn as a spectacle of unity and skill. Marcus and Aurelius worked alongside the new king, ensuring that the races remained fair and honorable. The factions, though they retained their colors and fierce rivalries, became less about political allegiance and more about the camaraderie of the racetrack.

The city's forums, once the domain of conspiracy and treachery, were now filled with the sound of public lectures and spirited debates. Philosophers and scientists from across the empire flocked to Rome, drawn by the promise of academic freedom and patronage from the enlightened new regime. The smell of ink and parchment grew stronger, as ideas once spoken in hushed tones were now shared openly, inspiring a new generation of thinkers and leaders.

Artists painted frescoes of Marcus and Aurelius standing alongside Augustus, the trio symbolizing the new era of enlightenment. In the forums, once the breeding ground for whispers and plots, philosophers and scientists now held public lectures, their voices carrying over the heads of the curious crowd. The air was no longer thick with conspiracy but with the scent of parchment and ink, as ideas were shared openly, and the pursuit of knowledge became a public a air.

New academies and research institutions began to sprout like flowers in the springtime, their hallowed halls echoing with the footsteps of eager scholars. The once-forbidden texts were now openly debated, and the city buzzed with the excitement of discovery. Philosophers from Greece, mathematicians from Egypt, and astronomers from Babylon all found refuge in Rome, bringing with them the seeds of knowledge that would blossom into a golden age of innovation and learning.

The streets of Rome grew wider and more vibrant as the city's boundaries stretched to accommodate the influx of new inhabitants. The clamor of construction filled the air, the smell of freshly cut stone and sawdust mingling with the aroma of exotic spices from distant lands. New neighborhoods arose, each with its own unique character, as people from every corner of the empire brought their customs and cuisines to the capital. The whispers of a united Rome grew stronger, as the diverse population found common ground in their shared love for the city and its newfound spirit of enlightenment.

Artists painted frescoes that depicted scenes from Homer and Virgil, their brushstrokes capturing the very essence of human experience. The Colosseum, once a symbol of brutality and power, now hosted grand theatrical performances that drew upon the rich tapestry of the empire's cultures. Actors from Egypt recounted tales of Cleopatra, while poets from Spain sang ballads of their homelands. The air was thick with the scent of exotic spices, as the city's markets grew to reflect the diversity of its inhabitants.

The chariot games, too, evolved. The factions still competed with fervor, but now their rivalries were tempered by a shared respect for the sport. The whispers of corruption were replaced by the clanging of smithies forging new, innovative designs for chariots, their wheels spinning with the promise of a fair contest. The races became a showcase of human potential, a reflection of the city's newfound spirit of competition and progress.

In the shadow of the great libraries, scholars from across the empire gathered to share their findings. The whispers of discovery grew to a crescendo as they debated the mysteries of the cosmos and the nature of existence. The city's streets were lined with schools, their windows thrown open to let in the light of knowledge. Children played games that taught them the principles of mathematics and philosophy, their laughter echoing through the alleyways.

And amidst this cultural renaissance, the whispers of the old guard grew faint. The Senate, once a bastion of corruption, was now a place where ideas were tested and refined. New laws were proposed, and old ones discarded, as Rome sought to become a beacon of justice and enlightenment. The people, once divided by factions and whispers of political machinations, now gathered in the forums to debate the merits of stoicism and epicureanism, the poetry of Ovid and the history of Livy.

The influx of people from all corners of the empire brought with it a kaleidoscope of cultures, each adding its vibrant accent and unfamiliar tongues, all while merchants from Egypt, Greece, and beyond plied their wares in the bustling markets. The city grew not just in size but in spirit, its boundaries expanding to encompass the diverse tapestry of its inhabitants.

Neighborhoods once defined by the colors of their factions now boasted the vibrant hues of diverse cultures, as immigrants brought with them the richness of their homelands. The city's population swelled, stretching the ancient walls, which were soon replaced by grander structures to enclose the burgeoning metropolis. New districts grew like stalwart trees in a forest, each with its unique charm and bustling marketplaces where exotic goods and ideas were exchanged.

The cultural renaissance touched every aspect of Roman life. In the atriums of grand villas and the modest homes of the plebeians, the whispers of philosophical debates and the recounting of epic tales filled the air. Artisans from Greece painted frescoes that captured the essence of human emotion, while sculptors from Egypt chiseled the likenesses of gods and heroes into marble so lifelike that they seemed to breathe. The city's theaters echoed with the applause of audiences enraptured by the works of playwrights who dared to explore the complexities of the human condition.

The libraries, once the exclusive domain of the elite, threw open their doors to the masses. The whispers of scholars and scribes were replaced by the murmur of eager readers and the rustle of pages as the city's citizens devoured the works of Aristotle, Plato, and Virgil. The Colosseum, a monument to Rome's military might, now hosted gladiatorial contests that were less about bloodshed and more about the display of skill and discipline. The chariot races remained a spectacle of speed and strategy, but the air of corruption had lifted, and the cheers of the crowd were genuine expressions of excitement and camaraderie.

In the city's schools, children of all classes studied together, learning the principles of mathematics, rhetoric, and civic duty. The whispers of the streets were now the lessons of great philosophers, their words inspiring a new generation of Romans to dream of a world governed by reason and virtue. The air was alive with the chatter of students and the shushing of stern tutors, a stark contrast to the clandestine whispers of yesteryear.

Artisans from Greece painted frescoes that brought the stories of Homer to life on the walls of public buildings, while poets from Egypt recited verses that made the heart swell with the grandeur of the Nile. The city's streets were a living museum, with sculptures from every corner of the empire standing proudly alongside the stoic visages of Roman gods. The whispers of cultural exchange grew into a symphony of diverse voices, each contributing to the vibrant tapestry of Rome's identity.

The scientific inquiry that had once been stifled by the whispers of corruption now flourished under the bright light of Augustus's rule. In the shadow of the great library of Alexandria, Roman scholars pored over scrolls and tablets, eager to expand the boundaries of human understanding. The city became a bastion of knowledge, drawing in thinkers and innovators from across the empire, and as the city streets grew more erudite, as the people of Rome discussed the heliocentric theories of Aristarchus and the geometric brilliance of Archimedes.

In the hallowed halls of the newly founded academies, the clank of metal and the hiss of steam announced the birth of new inventions. The smell of hot iron and burning coal mingled with the scent of parchment and ink, as engineers and architects worked alongside scribes and philosophers. The city's streets were transformed into a living laboratory, with aqueducts snaking through the hills to provide clean water for drinking and bathing, and new roads laid to connect the growing neighborhoods. The progress grew into a cacophony of hammers and chisels, as Rome embraced innovation with open arms.

The chariot races themselves became a showcase of human ingenuity. Designers and craftsmen competed to create the fastest, most durable chariots, pushing the boundaries of what was thought possible. The Circus Maximus, once a stage for political maneuvering, now echoed with the roar of the crowd as they cheered for the daring innovations that sped across the track. The air was thick with the smell of burning wood and the sound of chariot wheels slicing through the dirt, a testament to the city's newfound spirit of competition and progress.

Amidst this intellectual awakening, a clandestine undercurrent began to form. Secret societies of scholars and thinkers, seeking refuge from the political machinations of the Senate, gathered in hidden chambers beneath the city's streets. They developed their own coded languages and symbols, a means of communicating and protecting their ideas from those who would seek to suppress them. These societies grew in number and influence, their members drawn from every corner of the city. They met in the dead of night in clandestine locations, the whispers of their debates and discoveries carrying through the shadows like a secret pulse beneath the city's vibrant surface.

Aurelius, ever curious and seeking truth, found himself drawn to the defiance of the underground. A powerful, shadowy organization whispered of in the back alleys and clandestine meetings—the Illuminati. He had heard rumors of their existence, of their pull on the strings of power, and of the coded languages they used to shield their secrets from the prying eyes of the Senate.

One evening, as he walked through the moonlit streets, he stumbled upon a gathering of cloaked figures in the shadows of an ancient aqueduct. Their hushed tones spoke of knowledge beyond the reach of the common man, of experiments in alchemy and astronomy that could reshape the very fabric of the world. Intrigued, Aurelius approached, his heart racing with a mix of excitement and fear.

The leader of the group, a man with piercing eyes and a gentle smile, took notice of him. He spoke in a cryptic tongue that Aurelius could not understand, but the message was clear: they had been watching him. They knew of his valor in the chariot games and his burgeoning reputation as a man of honor. They o ered him a choice: join them in their quest for knowledge and power, or return to the superficial glamour of the racetrack.

The whispers grew louder as Aurelius delved deeper into the world of the Illuminati. He attended secret gatherings in hidden chambers beneath the city's bustling streets, where the air was thick with the scent of incense and the faint hum of alchemical reactions. He met with scholars and philosophers who spoke in hushed tones of the cosmos, of the secrets of the ancients, and of the power that lay in understanding the very fabric of existence. His curiosity grew into fascination, and soon he found himself caught in the web of their clandestine world.

The Illuminati's influence was vast, stretching from the Senate to the darkest corners of the city. They sought to guide Augustus's hand, to ensure that Rome's newfound enlightenment served not just the people but the pursuit of an ancient, secret knowledge. Aurelius, torn between his love for the chariot games and his thirst for truth, found himself drawn into their world.

He attended their clandestine meetings, his curiosity piqued by their whispered debates and the tantalizing glimpses of arcane texts they allowed him to see. The scholars spoke in a coded language that was as intricate as it was mysterious, and Aurelius felt the thrill of being part of something larger than himself, something that could change the very course of history.

The Illuminati's goals were as ambitious as they were enigmatic. They sought to harness the power of the cosmos, to unlock the secrets of the ancients, and to reshape the very fabric of Roman society. Aurelius, once a simple charioteer, now found himself a key player in a game of shadows and whispers, his heart torn between the camaraderie of the racetrack and the seductive allure of secret knowledge.

As an information broker, Aurelius's role grew increasingly complex. He used his network of former drivers and mechanics to gather intel on the city's political landscape, information that was as valuable as gold in the right hands. His new identity was a tightrope walk between the glitz of the chariot games and the murky depths of Rome's underbelly.

One night, after a particularly grueling practice session, Aurelius found an anonymous message tucked under his chariot's seat. It was a simple, yet intricate, symbol drawn in a fine, almost imperceptible hand—a circle with an eye at its center, surrounded by a triangle. He knew the emblem well; it was the mark of the Illuminati. His heart raced as he followed the instructions within the scroll to a nondescript tavern in the shadow of the Colosseum.

The tavern's interior was dimly lit, the air thick with the scent of ale and roasting meats. But the whispers in the corner, where the shadows danced on the walls, spoke of matters far more profound. A figure, cloaked and hooded, gestured for him to approach. The voice that emerged from the shadows was cultured, a blend of Roman eloquence and a hint of something more exotic. The figure spoke of the Illuminati's quest for knowledge and power, and how Aurelius could be instrumental in shaping Rome's destiny.

Aurelius felt the weight of the decision before him. He knew the risks of such an alliance—betrayal, discovery, perhaps even death. Yet, the allure of the hidden truths and the chance to be part of something greater than himself was irresistible. He agreed to join their ranks, and the figure handed him a scroll, explaining that it contained the first lesson in their sacred tongue.

The weeks that followed were a blur of clandestine meetings and secret rituals. Aurelius learned the intricate web of symbols and codes that bound the Illuminati together, a language that allowed them to communicate their most dangerous ideas without fear of detection. He met with scholars who spoke of the cosmos and the power of the stars, of the alchemical secrets that could transmute base metals into gold, and of the ancient texts that contained the keys to eternal life.

As he delved deeper into their world, Aurelius found his role in the Illuminati expanding. His fame and connections within the chariot world made him a valuable asset. He became a courier of sorts, delivering messages and information between the various cells of the society, using his knowledge of the city's back streets and his reputation as a racer to move unnoticed through the bustling city.

The Illuminati's influence grew, on the citizens as well. After all they haven't seen such abundance their whole lives, Augustus was making it good for everybody why complain about some underground story tellings.

The clandestine meetings grew more frequent, and the whispers grew bolder. Aurelius found himself torn between his new life of secrets and the roar of the Circus Maximus. His skills as an information broker grew, and his network expanded to include not just the chariot factions, but also the whispers of the Senate and the murmurs of the city's elite. The chariot games, once the epicenter of his world, now felt like a stage-managed distraction from the real battles being waged in the shadows.

The Illuminati's leaders spoke of a grand design where knowledge is free and the people are one. Everyone is a brother or sister with their own light.

Aurelius's curiosity grew into obsession. He found himself spending more and more time with the Illuminati, his nights consumed by whispers of ancient secrets and clandestine rituals. His chariot racing days grew numbered as his dedication to the secret society grew stronger. The thrill of the race was replaced by the rush of uncovering hidden truths and the potential to shape Rome's destiny.

The underground community thrived in the shadows, their goals as varied as the stars in the night sky. Some sought the power to challenge the gods themselves, while others pursued knowledge that could unite the empire under a single, enlightened rule. Their experiments in alchemy and astronomy were whispered about in hushed tones, the fruits of their labor displayed only to the most trusted members. Symbols began showing up across the city. They were always watching, like they had said.

Aurelius's transition from charioteer to information broker was swift and seamless. His days of battling on the sands of the Circus Maximus were replaced by covert missions through the winding streets of Rome. The skills he honed on the racetrack—quick reflexes, sharp instincts, and the ability to read his opponents—served him well in the shadowy world of espionage. His network grew to encompass not just the factions of the games but the whispers of the Senate and the murmurs of the city's elite.

The Illuminati's whispers grew bolder as their influence spread. They recruited the brightest minds of Rome, promising them the keys to the universe in exchange for their allegiance. Aurelius found himself in the company of philosophers, mathematicians, and alchemists, all driven by a singular quest for knowledge. The clandestine meetings grew more frequent, their locations shifting like the shadows of the city at dusk. He was fascinated by the breadth of their ambition, the depth of their secrets, and the power they wielded.

Yet, as he ascended the ranks of the Illuminati, the weight of their goals grew heavier. The pursuit of forbidden knowledge was a double-edged sword, one that could either enlighten or destroy. The whispers of their experiments grew more alarming—of alchemical concoctions that could reshape the very fabric of reality, of astronomical observations that hinted at a cosmos far more complex than the simple celestial dance taught in the city's schools.

Aurelius found himself torn between his love for the chariot games and his newfound role. His skills in the arena had made him a hero to the masses, but his clandestine activities had turned him into a pawn in a much larger game. He was the conduit between the secret society and the factions, the bridge between the shadowy whispers of power and the roar of the crowd. His every move was scrutinized by both his Illuminati handlers and the watching eyes of his former comrades.

The Senate, once a bastion of corruption, now faced a new challenge: the young emperor's vision of progress. Augustus balanced his reforms with a careful hand, aware that too much change too quickly could topple the delicate structure of power. He faced resistance from those who clung to the old ways, whispering in the marble halls about the dangers of too much freedom and the need for order. Yet, the public's hope grew stronger with each new law, each public work completed. The whispers of skepticism were drowned out by the promise of a better life.

Rome's streets grew crowded as people from across the empire flocked to the city, drawn by the allure of opportunity and the emperor's promise of a better life. The whispers of the Illuminati grew louder amidst the din of the marketplace, their ideas of knowledge and power resonating with the ambitious and the disillusioned. The Senate, once the epicenter of power, now found itself a stage for heated debates between the progressive ideals of Augustus and the stubborn traditionalism of its most conservative members.

Aurelius watched as the Senate's marble halls echoed with the clash of new and old. The air was thick with the scent of ambition and the acrid stench of fear. Augustus's reforms had brought hope to the masses, but the elite felt the earth shift beneath their feet. The talks grew more intense, with rumors of wealth redistribution leaving the Senate's wealthiest members paler than their togas.

The city swelled with new arrivals seeking fortune and knowledge, their languages and customs painting a vibrant tapestry across the city's fabric. Yet, the whispers grew louder in the narrow alleys where long-time residents felt the pinch of change. They spoke of the strain on the city's resources, the struggle for work, and the fear of losing their identity in the flood of new faces. The whispers grew into grumbles, hinting at the tinderbox of tension that lay beneath Rome's surface.

The Illuminati saw opportunity in this chaos. They whispered of a new order, one where knowledge and enlightenment could replace the old ways of power and greed. They spoke of a Rome where the Senate's whispers of corruption were silenced by the collective voice of a learned populace. Aurelius felt the pull of their vision, but the whispers of doubt grew louder in his mind. Could such a society truly exist? And at what cost?

Augustus's reign was a dance of shadows and light. The Senate's traditionalists watched his every move with suspicion, their whispers of dissent echoing through the marble corridors. Yet, the emperor remained steadfast in his vision for Rome, balancing his progressive reforms with the need to maintain the status quo. The Senate's power structures, so intricately woven into the fabric of Roman life, resisted his e orts like a stubborn mule.

The hardships grew, as the consequences of wealth redistribution became clear. The elite, accustomed to their opulent lifestyles, found their co ers growing lighter. Their whispers of dissent grew into grumbles, then into shouts of protest. They feared that Augustus's reforms would strip them of their power, leaving them no better than the plebeians they had long held sway over. Yet, amidst the complaints of the wealthy, the city's poorer residents saw glimpses of hope in the form of new job opportunities and improved living conditions.

The tension between long-time residents and the influx of newcomers grew palpable. The streets, once a place of unity under the banner of Rome, now whispered with the tension of competition and fear of the unknown. The new arrivals brought with them a rich tapestry of cultures and languages, challenging the traditional Roman way of life Fights broke out in the crowded marketplaces, and the city's infrastructure groaned under the weight of the burgeoning population The wisest men all gathered and proposed elections for the king, and power coming to the senate. The new law was passed and election day was set in Rome.

The Colosseum, once a place of brutal entertainment, was now the stage for a battle of ideologies. Augustus and Aurelius stepped into the arena, not to fight with swords or chariots, but with words and visions. The air was electric, charged with the hopes and fears of the citizens who had gathered to hear their pleas. Augustus, with his steady gaze and the confidence of a man who had seen Rome through fire and ash, spoke of a Rome united under a single, enlightened rule. His voice boomed through the amphitheater, a promise of stability and prosperity.

Aurelius, the former charioteer turned information broker, stepped into the Colosseum with a sense of déjà vu. The sands had once been his battleground, but now, the arena hosted a di erent kind of contest. The air was electric with the anticipation of the impending debate between him and Augustus. Thousands of spectators packed the stands, their whispers echoing through the grand space, each one a vote in the battle of words that would shape Rome's future.

Augustus spoke first, his voice a sonorous symphony of hope and promise. He painted a picture of a Rome where the people thrived, where the harvests were bountiful, and the empire's borders stretched further than any had dared to dream. His words were like a warm embrace to the common folk, who had su ered under the heavy hand of corruption for too long. The Senate, once the epicenter of power, now found itself in the uncomfortable position of listening to the whispers of a leader who o ered not just wealth, but a vision of growth that transcended their grasping hunger for more.

Aurelius took a deep breath, his heart racing. He knew that his words must be chosen with the precision of a master charioteer navigating the tightest turn. He promised the people knowledge, the greatest treasure of all, whispering of the Illuminati's quest to unlock the secrets of the universe and to share them with the world. He spoke of a Rome where schools were open to all, where the pursuit of wisdom was not a privilege of the elite but a birthright of every citizen. His voice resonated with the promise of prestige and power that came not from wealth or birth, but from the enlightenment of the mind and the freedom of thought.

The Senate watched with a mix of intrigue and suspicion. Some saw in Aurelius's words the seeds of a revolution that could topple their own practices.

The Illuminati's structure was as complex as the city's labyrinthine streets. At its core was an inner circle of scholars, philosophers, and politicians, men who whispered of a world where power lay in the hands of the enlightened few. Their meetings were held in the shadows, their discussions veiled in the language of the ancients. They sought not just to understand the cosmos, but to harness its power. Theirs was a quest that transcended the mortal realm, a pursuit of knowledge that could make them gods among men.

Aurelius, once the hero of the chariot games, now found himself in the inner sanctum of this clandestine society. His valor and honor had not gone unnoticed, and his swift rise through their ranks had earned him a place at their table. Yet, even as he sat among them, he knew that he was not fully one of them. He was an asset, a weapon in their arsenal of whispers and secrets. His fame allowed him to navigate the city's social strata with ease, gathering information that could shift the balance of power in their favor.

The Illuminati's influence grew like a vine through the city, its tendrils reaching into every corner of Roman society. The inner circle, a congregation of scholars and philosophers, met in the most secret of locations, the whispers of their debates echoing through the shadows. They were the thinkers, the dreamers, the ones who sought to bend the very fabric of the universe to their will. Their agenda was ambitious: to usher in a new age of enlightenment where the Senate's whispers of corruption were drowned out by the collective wisdom of an informed populace.

The outer rings of the Illuminati were composed of operatives and informants, men and women from all walks of life, each with a unique role to play in the society's grand design. They gathered in the city's darker recesses, trading secrets and intelligence like coins in the marketplace. Aurelius, the former charioteer turned information broker, was a valuable asset among them. His fame and connections allowed him to navigate the city's social strata with ease, collecting whispers of political intrigue and the Senate's clandestine machinations.

The Illuminati's agenda was as vast as the empire itself. They sought not only to guide Rome towards a new age of enlightenment but to amass knowledge and artifacts of power that could reshape the very fabric of the world. Their long-term plans stretched beyond the city's walls, dreaming of a day when their influence would be felt in every corner of the known world. The whispers grew louder, their meetings more frequent, as they plotted the next phase of their grand strategy.

Aurelius's role grew more complex with each passing day. He was no longer just an information broker but had become a trusted advisor to the inner circle. He found himself privy to secrets that could topple empires, whispers of ancient artifacts and forgotten knowledge that could grant them unimaginable power. The chariot games now felt like a distant memory, a child's plaything compared to the intrigues and machinations that filled his waking hours.

The inner circle of the Illuminati was a gathering of the most brilliant minds Rome had to o er. They spoke in hushed tones of the cosmos, of alchemy and the transmutation of matter, of the power of the stars to foretell the future and the possibility of bending fate to their will. Aurelius was in awe of their wisdom, yet he could not shake the feeling that their thirst for power was insatiable. Each new discovery, each ancient scroll unfurled, brought them one step closer to their ultimate goal—a Rome where knowledge was power, and they were the sole arbiters of truth.

The whispers grew more intense as the Illuminati's influence spread. They had infiltrated the Senate, the military, even the emperor's own household. Yet, for all their cunning and wit, they remained a shadowy presence, their existence known only to a select few. The Senate, ever wary of threats to their power, grew suspicious of the sudden surge in progressive reforms and the whispers of a society that operated beyond their control. The stage was set for a clash of ideologies, a battle that would determine the fate of Rome and the future of the empire.

The final debate in the Colosseum was a spectacle that would be remembered for generations. Augustus and Aurelius faced each other, their words a dance of strategy and ideology. The crowd was a sea of faces, some hopeful, others fearful, but all hungry for change. The air was thick with anticipation, the whispers of the Illuminati resonating in the minds of their countless members who had gathered to witness the dawn of a new era.

The day of the elections arrived, and with it, the first people's vote for a king. The city buzzed with excitement and trepidation. The Senate watched from their lofty perches, their eyes narrowed with suspicion as the ballots were cast. The Illuminati had mobilized their vast network, their whispers echoing through the streets, urging their members to stand united behind Aurelius.

As the votes were counted, the whispers grew to a crescendo. The air was thick with tension, the very stones of the Colosseum seeming to hold their breath. And when the results were finally announced, the roar of the crowd was deafening. Aurelius had won, thanks in no small part to the Illuminati's influence. The Senate's whispers of protest were lost in the din as the former charioteer was crowned king, a symbol of the new Rome they had dreamt of.

The Illuminati's triumph was palpable, their whispers of power now a shout that could not be silenced. Aurelius felt the weight of their expectations upon his shoulders, the burden of leading a city that was both hopeful and afraid. He knew that his victory was not just his own but a victory for the society that had shaped his destiny. Yet, he could not ignore the nagging doubt that gnawed at his conscience—what price had he paid for this power?

In the days following the election, the city remained a tinderbox of emotions. The Senate, though begrudgingly, recognized Aurelius as the rightful ruler, their whispers of dissent now a mere murmur in the grand scheme of things. Yet, the whispers grew louder in the shadows, a testament to the Illuminati's continued work behind the scenes. The society's grip on Rome tightened, their members infiltrating every aspect of the city's life, ensuring that their agenda of enlightenment was carried out to the letter.

Aurelius faced his new role with a mix of excitement and dread. He knew that the path ahead was fraught with challenges, that the whispers of corruption had not disappeared but merely retreated to the darkest corners of the city. Yet, he was determined to honor the trust placed in him by the people and the Illuminati. He would rule with wisdom and justice, ushering in an era of knowledge and unity. The whispers of the streets had chosen him, and he would not let them down.

The Senate's whispers grew more frantic as they realized the depth of the Illuminati's infiltration. The society had become a force to be reckoned with, their influence reaching into the very heart of the city, its new king. And a third of the population as members. Symbols had become roadways to various points of interest across the city.

Aurelius's days as a charioteer were now behind him, his identity as a political operative taking precedence. He found himself navigating the city's social circles with a new purpose, using his charm and wit to extract information that could swing the balance of power. His visits to the stables had become less about the horses and more about the whispers of strategy and alliances that flowed as freely as the wine at the elite's banquets.

The Illuminati had given him missions that tested his mettle. He had infiltrated the most secure of political meetings, the sweat on his brow the only evidence of his racing heart. He had retrieved documents that could topple dynasties, his hands trembling with the weight of their secrets. And he had manipulated the outcomes of votes so subtly that even the Senate's most seasoned politicians had no inkling of his influence. Yet, with each victory, Aurelius felt a pang of loss for the simplicity of his former life.

The stables had been his sanctuary, the chariots his chariots his steeds of war, and the sands of the Colosseum his battleground. Now, the whispers of power and the intricate dance of political maneuvering had replaced the roar of the crowds and the thunder of hooves. He struggled with his new identity, torn between the thrill of his clandestine work and the nostalgia for the days when honor and valor had been the measures of a man's worth.

Aurelius moved with the grace of a charioteer through the city's social circles, his fame a shield that allowed him to glide unnoticed through the most exclusive gatherings. His ears were tuned to the whispers of conspiracy and the flutter of secret alliances. His eyes searched the shadows for the flicker of recognition from his Illuminati brethren. Each piece of information he gathered was a victory, a thread in the vast tapestry of Rome's fate that he hoped to weave to their advantage.

The missions grew bolder, the stakes higher. He found himself infiltrating the Senate's most guarded meetings, his heart pounding in his chest as he listened to the whispers of treachery and greed. He retrieved documents that could shake the very foundations of the Republic, his hands trembling with the weight of their secrets. His nights were spent in the Illuminati's hidden chambers, poring over ancient texts and artifacts that whispered of power beyond imagination.

Yet, amidst the whispers of power and the intoxicating scent of influence, Aurelius could not ignore the toll his new life was taking on his soul. The camaraderie of the charioteers, the roar of the crowd, and the simple thrill of the race now felt like a distant memory. In its place was a world of shadows and whispers, where the price of victory was paid in the currency of deceit and manipulation.

One evening, as he moved through the grandiose halls of a Senate gathering, Aurelius's gaze fell upon a tapestry depicting a chariot race from a time long past. The vivid colors and dynamic scene spoke to him in a way that the political machinations never could. He was struck by the stark contrast between the purity of the sport and the twisted game of politics he now played. With a heavy heart, he realized that the Colosseum had become a metaphor for his life—once a place of honor and valor, now a stage for hidden agendas and treacherous alliances.

A pivotal mission for the Illuminati soon presented itself, one that would test Aurelius's loyalty and skill to their breaking point. They had learned of a secret pact between a powerful senator and a foreign king, one that threatened the very sovereignty of Rome. The stakes were higher than ever before—the fate of the city rested in his hands. The whispers grew more urgent, the tension palpable as he prepared to infiltrate the senator's private chambers.

The night of the operation was moonless, the shadows of the city cloaking his movements as he scaled the senator's palatial walls. His heart hammered in his chest, a rhythm that competed with the distant echoes of his past glories. Inside, the air was thick with the scent of incense and the murmur of conspiracy. He searched the opulent rooms, his eyes adjusting to the dim light, until he found the scrolls detailing the treacherous agreement. With trembling hands, he rolled them up and secured them within his tunic, feeling the weight of Rome's future pressing against his chest.

The escape was a blur of adrenaline and silent footsteps, the whispers of his pursuers growing louder with each passing moment. Aurelius's heart pounded in his chest as he navigated the shadowy streets of Rome, the stolen scrolls a secret burden that could either save or doom the city. His mind raced with the faces of his comrades in the Illuminati, their trust in him unwavering, their whispers of encouragement echoing through his thoughts.

He delivered the scrolls to the inner circle, his hands shaking with the gravity of his actions. Their eyes widened with a mix of amazement and fear as they read the incriminating evidence. Aurelius had become more than just a charioteer turned spy; he was now a linchpin in the grand design of the Illuminati's power play. The society's leaders strategized, their voices a symphony of urgent tones in the dimly lit chamber. The whispers grew into a crescendo as they plotted their next move, their sights set on dismantling the corrupt alliance before it could come to fruition.

Aurelius felt a sense of pride swell within him, yet it was tainted by the bitterness of his deception. Each mission, each whispered conversation, brought him further from the light of his former life. He found himself lying to old friends, using his charm to coerce information from those who had once looked up to him. His every move was calculated, his smile a mask that concealed the turmoil within. Yet, he knew that this was the price of his new role, the cost of fighting for a brighter future for Rome.

The whispers grew into a storm as the Illuminati's plans unfolded. Aurelius watched as the society's influence spread through the city, their ideals of knowledge and enlightenment taking root in the minds of the people. He could feel the tide of change, a current that washed away the detritus of the old world, leaving behind a landscape ripe for rebirth. Yet, the shadows grew darker, the whispers of danger louder. He knew that his actions had not gone unnoticed by those who would seek to preserve the status quo.

One night, as he made his way home from a clandestine meeting, the whispers grew too loud to ignore. He felt the cold steel of a blade at his throat, the hot breath of an assailant in his ear. He acted instinctively, his charioteer's reflexes taking over. He disarmed the attacker and disappeared into the night, the adrenaline coursing through his veins.

The Illuminati's underground network was a marvel of ingenuity. Hidden beneath the cobbled streets of Rome, their secret libraries and laboratories were a bastion of knowledge and innovation. The air was thick with the scent of parchment and the faint hiss of steam engines that powered their experiments. The catacombs served as both a sanctuary and a conduit for their operations, the shadowy corridors connecting them to the heart of the city.

In these hallowed halls, scholars and philosophers debated the nature of governance, their voices echoing o the ancient stone. They discussed the merits of a society where power was not derived from birthright but from intellect and wisdom. The whispers of their debates reverberated through the catacombs, a testament to their conviction that knowledge was the true path to enlightenment.

The secret locations of the Illuminati were ingenious, a labyrinth of hidden chambers and tunnels that crisscrossed beneath the bustling city. The catacombs served not only as a means of covert movement but as a bastion of knowledge, a sanctuary where ideas could flourish beyond the stifling grasp of the Senate's control. Here, in the bowels of Rome, they cultivated a garden of innovation that threatened to uproot the very foundations of the Republic.

The society's use of the extensive sewer system was a masterstroke of strategy. It allowed them to move unseen, to deliver messages and supplies, and to escape the prying eyes of their enemies. The very veins of the city had become their ally, a silent testament to the ingenuity that powered their quest for a new Rome.

In the hidden laboratories beneath the city, the Illuminati's scholars worked tirelessly, their eyes straining by the flickering light of candles as they poured over ancient texts and drew intricate diagrams. The air was thick with the scent of herbs and metal, a testament to their pursuit of knowledge that defied the Senate's rigid laws. Here, in the heart of Rome's underbelly, they cultivated ideas that could reshape the world—if only they could be brought to light.

The catacombs were a sprawling network of secret passages and hidden chambers, a silent witness to the whispers of rebellion that echoed through the city. Aurelius knew these tunnels like the back of his hand, using them to navigate the political maze above. The society had mastered the art of leaving coded messages at designated drop points, a silent symphony of communication that kept their operations running smoothly.

Their experiments with steam power were a marvel to behold, the hiss and clank of machinery a stark contrast to the soft murmur of philosophical debates that often filled the air. The Illuminati sought not just to understand the world but to bend it to their will, to harness the power of creation itself.

In one such chamber, a group of scholars huddled around a table, their eyes glued to a series of brass tubes and gears. Sweat beaded on their brows as they discussed the potential of this new force. "Imagine," said one, his voice filled with wonder, "the day when Rome's legions march not on the backs of horses, but on machines powered by the very breath of Vulcan himself!"

Aurelius watched them, his heart torn between awe and fear. The knowledge they sought was intoxicating, the promise of a world where Rome's might knew no bounds. Yet, the whispers of caution grew louder in his mind, reminding him of the potential for such power to be wielded against the very people he sought to protect.

The Illuminati's experiments with steam power had already borne fruit, their ingenious contraptions a testament to the human spirit's insatiable curiosity. They had built prototypes of chariots that moved without the need for horses, the hiss of steam and the clank of metal replacing the familiar thunder of hooves. These machines were not just for show but for war, a revolutionary force that could shift the balance of power in an instant.

The scholars spoke of healing arts that could mend the most grievous of wounds, of potions that could grant a man the strength of Hercules. The potential to alleviate su ering and extend life was a siren's call that resonated deeply within Aurelius. Yet, he knew that such power could also be weaponized, the very essence of humanity itself distorted in the quest for dominance.

The philosophical debates on governance were the lifeblood of the Illuminati. They discussed the merits of monarchy, republic, and democracy, their whispers echoing through the catacombs. Aurelius found himself drawn to these conversations, his mind racing with the implications of each argument. The Senate's whispers of corruption had once seemed omnipotent, but now, the society o ered a tantalizing alternative—a Rome ruled by enlightenment and wisdom.

In the medical chambers, the air was thick with the scent of herbs and the faint metallic tang of blood. Here, physicians pushed the boundaries of healing, developing serums that could mend bones and elixirs that could restore vitality. They spoke of a world where disease was a memory, where the poorest citizen could live a life free from pain and su ering. Aurelius watched as a young girl, her arm crushed in an accident, was treated with a steaming concoction that had her wounds knit themselves before his very eyes. The whispers of hope grew louder, drowning out the shadows of doubt that had plagued him since he had first donned the robes of the Illuminati.

Yet, as he emerged from the catacombs and into the bustling streets of Rome, the whispers of reality were unavoidable. The Senate's power was waning, but it was not yet broken. They watched him with suspicion, their whispers of distrust following him like a shadow. The Senate had its own secret societies, its own agents of influence. The struggle for Rome's soul had become a silent war, waged in whispers and shadows, with the Illuminati and their rivals each vying for dominance.

One evening, as Aurelius walked through the market, a cloaked figure stepped from the shadows. The whispers grew still as the man spoke, his voice a harsh contrast to the gentle chatter of the traders.

"Aurelius," the figure said, his voice low and urgent. "Your work for the Illuminati has not gone unnoticed. There are others who seek to shape Rome's destiny, and they do not appreciate your interference."

Aurelius's hand instinctively moved to his dagger, his eyes scanning the area for any signs of danger. "Who are you?" he demanded, his voice steady despite the fear that knotted his stomach.

The man's smile was cold. "I am a servant of the Iron Hand," he said, revealing a tattoo of a clenched fist on the back of his hand. "Our society seeks to preserve the traditional ways, to prevent the Illuminati from plunging Rome into chaos with their dangerous ideas."

The Iron Hand was a rival secret society, rumored to be just as influential and ruthless as the Illuminati. Their loyalty lay with the Senate, and they would stop at nothing to maintain the status quo.

Aurelius knew that this was not an empty threat—his life was now in danger from two fronts.

The whispers grew tense as Aurelius reported this encounter to the Illuminati's inner circle. They knew of the Iron Hand, had even infiltrated their ranks, but had underestimated their reach. The Senate's whispers of fear and anger had given rise to a monster that threatened to devour the very society that sought to save Rome.

The Illuminati's inner circle was alarmed by the revelation of the Iron Hand's overt threat. Their whispers grew frantic as they debated how to respond to this emerging danger. The room was alive with the crackle of tension, each member leaning in to hear the latest piece of information, to o er a strategy or to voice a concern. Aurelius felt a cold dread seep into his bones as he realized the full extent of the web he had become entangled in.

Aurelius was tasked with gathering intel on the Iron Hand, using his position in the Senate to uncover their plans without alerting them to the Illuminati's interest. He mingled with the city's elite, his smile as bright as the gleaming bronze of the Senate House, while his thoughts churned with the whispers of his true allegiance. The weight of his newfound power was a constant presence, a reminder of the fine line he tread between the light of enlightenment and the shadow of betrayal.

The Iron Hand, though a formidable opponent, was not the only challenge Aurelius faced. The religious tensions in Rome had reached a boiling point. Conservative factions, fearing the spread of the Illuminati's progressive ideals, accused scholars and scientists of heresy. The whispers grew darker as priests and zealots called for the heads of those who dared question the gods' dominion over the mortal world. Augustus, ever the pragmatist, sought to balance the scales, advocating for tolerance and unity.

Amidst this turmoil, spies from foreign lands flooded the city, drawn by the scent of change. Their whispers of intrigue and deceit wove through the fabric of Roman society, carrying tales of gold-laden lands and powerful artifacts that could shift the balance of power. Aurelius found himself caught in the crossfire, as emissaries from distant empires sought his ear, hoping to sway him to their cause. He knew that the Illuminati's reach was not infinite, and the threat of external forces seeking to manipulate Rome's transformation for their own ends was very real.

One night, as he strolled through the moonlit Forum, Aurelius stumbled upon a clandestine meeting between the Iron Hand and Nero's Gold Faction. The whispers grew frenzied as he realized the extent of their alliance—the Senate and the Colosseum's corrupt elite had united to crush the Illuminati's influence. He retreated into the shadows, his heart racing with the urgency to warn his comrades.

The Illuminati's response was swift and decisive. They leaked damning information about the Gold Faction's illegal activities to the public, sparking a wave of outrage that shook the city. The Senate, fearing a backlash, was forced to disavow Nero and his ilk, weakening their grip on power. The elites introduced gold juice to its members. Promising wealth and prestige to those who drink it.

Aurelius was called to a meeting in the heart of the Illuminati's catacomb network, the whispers of the city's secrets echoing around him as he descended into the chamber. The grand master revealed their ultimate plan: to create a network of enlightened cities across the empire, each a bastion of knowledge and power, each governed by a member of the society. The whispers grew louder as the implications of this grand scheme filled the air.

He was assigned a pivotal mission: to infiltrate the Senate and ensure that key positions were filled with Illuminati loyalists. His role as a charioteer turned spy had prepared him for this moment, but the weight of the responsibility was almost too much to bear. The whispers of doubt grew louder in his mind, his every move scrutinized by the society's leaders.

As Aurelius prepared for his mission, he stumbled upon an ancient scroll, hidden away in a forgotten corner of the catacombs. It spoke of a celestial event that would soon befall the city, a threat from the stars that only the Illuminati's enlightened rule could prevent. The whispers grew hushed as he read, the gravity of the revelation sinking in.

The scroll spoke of a time when the heavens would open and chaos would reign, a time when only those with the knowledge to harness the power of the cosmos could save humanity. The Illuminati believed that they were the chosen guardians of this knowledge, that it was their destiny to prepare Rome for the coming cataclysm.

Aurelius felt the tension coil within him, his heart torn between his loyalty to the society and the whispers of doubt that plagued him. The

Illuminati's ambition was vast, reaching beyond the confines of Rome to encompass the entire empire—and perhaps even the stars themselves. Yet, as he read the cryptic texts, he could not shake the feeling that there was something more, something that even the Illuminati's all-seeing eye had not foreseen.

The tension grew as he grappled with the decision before him. Would he fully commit to the cause, becoming an architect of Rome's rebirth and the empire's salvation?

Aurelius knew that the Illuminati's grand scheme was more than a mere political maneuver—it was a call to arms for humanity's future. The scroll spoke of ancient prophecies, celestial omens, and the power that could be harnessed from the very fabric of the cosmos. He felt a tremor of excitement, the whispers of destiny calling him to a higher purpose.

Yet, as he contemplated the scroll's ancient wisdom, he could not ignore the nagging feeling that there was a piece of the puzzle missing. The gold juice. What was this new elixir they were giving out? It seemed to make the old young again, and the promise of wealth and prestige behind it Aurelius was not sure if it was for him or not.

Aurelius found himself drawn to the company of a brilliant scholar within the Illuminati, named Claudia. Her sharp intellect and fiery spirit had captured his attention, and their shared passion for knowledge had blossomed into something more. Their whispers of love grew stronger with each clandestine meeting, a beacon of light in the shadowy world he now inhabited. But the love was haulted, as he knew that their union could complicate his already precarious situation.

One fateful evening, Aurelius encountered Castor and Pollux, his former rivals and colleagues from the Colosseum. Their eyes held a mix of anger and betrayal, their whispers of accusation cutting through the air like knives. They had heard of his rise within the Illuminati and the Senate, and they could not fathom how he had abandoned the life they had once shared.

The confrontation stirred up a tempest of emotion within Aurelius. He felt the pull of his past, the camaraderie and passion of the races that had once defined him. Yet, the whispers of his new life grew louder, reminding him of the promise of a better Rome, of the love that had blossomed in the shadows with Claudia. The tension between his old loyalties and his new path was a constant storm within him, a battle between the comfort of the familiar and the call of destiny.

The whispers grew more insistent as Aurelius approached Augustus, now his mentor and ally. Their relationship had evolved from one of distant admiration to a complex dance of trust and manipulation. As they strategized in the emperor's private chambers, Aurelius could not help but feel the weight of his deception. He knew that the Illuminati's ultimate goal was to surpass the Senate and even the emperor, yet here he was, advising the very man he was destined to overthrow.

Augustus, ever the astute politician, sensed the shift in the air. His eyes searched Aurelius's, seeking the truth behind the polished facade. The bond they had forged in the wake of Nero's downfall was being tested by the whispers of a revolution that grew louder each day.

"Your loyalty is not in question," Augustus said, his voice a mix of warmth and steel. "But I feel the tides of change shifting beneath us. Tell me, Aurelius, are you still with me in this quest for a new Rome?"

Aurelius took a deep breath, the scent of incense and the crackle of the burning candles a stark reminder of the gravity of his words. "I am," he replied, the whisper of doubt echoing faintly in his voice.

The romance with Claudia had become a beacon of light in the shadowy labyrinth of his life. Her intellect and passion were a balm to his weary soul, a reminder of the purity of their shared vision. Yet, their love grew in the shadows, a secret whisper amidst the cacophony of political maneuvering and the Illuminati's grand designs. Aurelius knew that their union was fraught with danger, that the discovery of his divided loyalties could shatter the fragile trust he had built with Augustus and the society.

The whispers grew more urgent as the nights grew longer. The clandestine meetings with Claudia grew more frequent, their conversations a mix of passionate whispers and furtive glances. Her eyes held the same fire that had once burned in his heart when he raced in the Colosseum, the same desire for truth and justice that had led him to the Illuminati. In her arms, he found solace from the storm of doubt that plagued him.

The encounter with Castor and Pollux had left him shaken. Their accusations of betrayal resonated in his ears, a haunting echo of the camaraderie they had once shared. He knew that his new path was a treacherous one, that he had turned his back on those who had once been his brothers in arms. Yet, the whispers of the Illuminati's purpose grew louder, drowning out the cries of his past.

Aurelius's relationship with Augustus had grown into a complex tapestry of trust and deceit. They had forged an alliance in the aftermath of Nero's fall, but the whispers of revolution had changed the fabric of their bond. Augustus had become more than just a leader to him—he was a mentor, a friend, and a symbol of the Rome he had sworn to protect. Yet, the Illuminati's whispers of a greater destiny called to him, a destiny that required him to stand against the very man he had vowed to serve.

In the quiet of his chambers, Aurelius often found himself torn between his love for Claudia and his duty to the Illuminati. Her passion for knowledge and her unyielding spirit had captured his heart, but her allegiance to the society was unwavering. Their stolen moments together were a stark contrast to the shadowy world they navigated, the whispers of their love a stark reminder of the humanity they sought to preserve amidst the political maelstrom.

As he sat with Augustus, the whispers of their shared history mingled with the tension of their unspoken future. The emperor's gaze was knowing, as if he could hear the silent confessions that danced on the edge of Aurelius's lips. Their bond had grown stronger, forged in the crucible of change, yet the whispers of the Illuminati's ultimate goal remained a barrier between them. Aurelius felt the weight of his deception, a heavy stone pressing upon his chest, threatening to crush the fragile trust that had been built.

In the quiet sanctity of their hidden chamber, Claudia's eyes searched his, her love a beacon in the darkness. Her warmth was a stark contrast to the cold steel of the Illuminati's grand scheme, a whisper of tenderness in a world of shadows. Yet, her unwavering dedication to the society served as a constant reminder of the path he had chosen. The whispers of their love grew more complex, intertwined with the whispers of his conflicted loyalties.

The encounter with Castor and Pollux had been a stark reminder of the life he had left behind. Their anger was a mirror reflecting the betrayal he felt in his own heart. The whispers of their accusations echoed through the catacombs, haunting Aurelius as he walked the shadowy corridors of power. He knew that his path with the Illuminati was a solitary one, fraught with danger and deceit. Yet, he could not ignore the whispers of his past, the bonds of friendship and camaraderie that had been forged in the dust of the Colosseum.

His relationship with Augustus grew more complex with each passing day. The whispers of their shared history were a double-edged sword, forging a bond while simultaneously driving a wedge between them. Aurelius found himself torn between his loyalty to the emperor and his allegiance to the Illuminati. The whispers of his secret life grew louder, a constant reminder of the treacherous tightrope he walked.

The romance with Claudia had become the one bright spot in his tumultuous world. Her passion for knowledge and justice was a balm to his weary soul, a whisper of hope amidst the chaos. Their love was a secret shared only in the safest of confines, the walls of their hidden chamber echoing with the whispers of their love and fear. Yet, even in the sanctity of their stolen moments, Aurelius could not shake the feeling that their union was a ticking time bomb, ready to explode at the first sign of discovery.

The whispers grew more insistent as he approached Augustus, the man who had once been a distant hero, now a confidant and potential adversary. The emperor's eyes searched his own, seeking the truth behind the facade. Aurelius felt the weight of his deception, a heavy stone threatening to crush the fragile trust that had been built between them. The line between mentor and foe grew thinner with each whisper of revolution that danced through the air.

One evening, as the whispers grew to a crescendo, Aurelius made a decision that would change the course of his life. He would tell Augustus of the Illuminati, lay bare the whispers that had consumed him. The air was thick with anticipation as he approached the emperor, his heart racing like the chariots of his youth.

Augustus's chamber was a study in opulence, the flickering candlelight casting shadows on the gilded walls. The emperor looked up from his scrolls, his eyes reflecting the same curiosity that had driven Aurelius to seek the society's embrace. The words tumbled out of Aurelius, a confession whispered into the heart of power.

Augustus was stunned into silence, his gaze unwavering as he digested the revelation. Then, to Aurelius's astonishment, a slow smile spread across his face. "I have felt the whispers of change," he said, his voice low and filled with intrigue. "I wish to join your society, to be part of this grand vision for Rome's future."

Aurelius felt a rush of relief, but also a new burden of responsibility. He knew that the emperor's involvement could either cement the Illuminati's power or lead to their downfall. The whispers grew louder in his mind as he weighed the consequences of his words. "Your place is not guaranteed," he warned. "The Illuminati demand absolute loyalty and adherence to our principles."

Augustus nodded solemnly. "I am aware of the risks," he said. "But I believe that together, we can create a Rome that stands as a beacon of enlightenment for all the world to see." His eyes shone with the same passion that had once burned in Aurelius's own heart.

The emperor's interest in the Illuminati was not entirely unexpected. His own reign had been marked by a hunger for knowledge and innovation, a desire to elevate the empire beyond the grasp of the traditional Senate. The whispers of the Illuminati's grand scheme resonated with his own vision for Rome's future, and the prospect of an alliance was tantalizing.

Aurelius shared the details of the Illuminati's most secretive ritual: the Game of Shadows. A contest of wit and strategy, and pure luck, ran by the society's elders, where the players are put to life of death stakes and voluenteer to play for a prize of 5 million dollars. The games range from simple rock paper scissors and marbles to land or fall, a bridge game where one side is safe and the other leads to your falling death 50/50 shot and total chance. They devise an o er for the elders. One game, 2 players, Augustus wins the he is made a brother in the organizations ranks. If Aurelius wins, then his work with the illuminiti is complete his oath dissolved and his romance is allowed to continue. If he looses he is exiled from the brotherhood and slandered to the point of shame, ripped of all legacy and prestigue. And Augustus would step up and fill his role in both rome and the organization. Maybe not life and death stakes but definately worth the approach to the elders.

Aurelius and Augustus approached the chamber of the Illuminati elders. The gold juice was in a huge golden trophy at the center of the round table with 12 cups circled around. The air was thick with anticipation and the whispers of the catacombs grew still. The elders, their faces obscured by hoods, listened intently as Aurelius laid out the terms of the proposed alliance, their eyes gleaming with the light of the flickering torches. The room grew tense, the whispers of their collective power a palpable force that seemed to press against the very walls.

The elders retreated to a chamber shrouded in darkness, leaving Aurelius and Augustus to wait in the candlelit silence. The shadows danced on the walls, whispering secrets of their own, as the minutes stretched into an hour. The air grew heavy with the scent of incense, mingling with the faint metallic tang of the hidden mechanisms that powered the society's many innovations.

When they emerged, one elder took the trophy and filled each of the 12 cups. Another elder had two goblets and handed them to Aurelius and Augustus as the other filled their cups. "Life is a maze traveled backwards to get to your final destination, now drink to the unity of the brotherhood and the powers we all yeild." Exclaimed the elder. Drink to sanction this one of a kind game more exciting then anything they had the pleasure of running in a long time. Some excited for Aurelius to win and get the life he wants, and the happinesslove brings. Or for Augustus to step into some big shoes to fill, a major player from the start within the illumaniti and the skills to guide the people forward with the agenda at work. A chance to unify rome and possibly the world.

Aurelius took a deep breath and raised the cup to his lips, the whispers of his future swirling like the liquid gold within. The taste was unlike anything he had ever experienced—sweet and potent, a promise of power and knowledge that sang through his veins. Augustus followed suit, his eyes never leaving Aurelius's as they both drank deeply. The room fell silent as the whispers of the gold juice took hold, a shared bond forged in the heart of the Illuminati's most sacred rite.

The date was set—a month hence, under the auspices of the new full moon. Also a time where orians belt was aligned with the pyramids of giza. a special moment in the cosmos is the perfrct time to hold such a game.The whispers grew to a crescendo as the elders departed, leaving Aurelius and Augustus alone with their fates. The emperor's gaze was filled with a mix of excitement and trepidation, the whispers of ambition and hope mingling with the ancient secrets that now flowed through them both.

The silence grew in intensity as the days passed, the anticipation of the Game of Shadows a constant presence in Aurelius's thoughts. His training with Castor and Pollux had honed his skills, but the whispers of the Illuminati's grand scheme filled him with a newfound purpose. The society's vision of a Rome governed by wisdom and enlightenment, rather than greed and corruption, was intoxicating.

Yet, the shadow of doubt lingered, whispering that power could so easily corrupt even the noblest of intentions.

The Illuminati's master plan was indeed a grand one, a vision that stretched beyond the city's walls to encompass the entire empire. A network of enlightened cities, each a bastion of knowledge and power, governed by reason and science. Their goal was to prepare humanity for a cosmic event foretold in ancient prophecies, an event that could either signal Rome's rise to greatness or its ultimate doom. The whispers of destiny grew louder as Aurelius contemplated the stakes.

The stages of implementation were meticulously laid out. First, they would consolidate their power within Rome, ensuring that the Senate and the emperor were under their influence. Then, they would expand their reach to the key provincial capitals, planting the seeds of enlightenment across the empire. Finally, they would reshape the very structure of governance itself, guiding the Roman world into a new era of wisdom and progress.

The Illuminati's grand scheme was a complex web of strategies and contingencies, a series of interlocking wheels that would turn the gears of history. Their long-term vision was nothing less than the creation of a utopian society, one that would stand as a beacon of knowledge and reason in a world mired in superstition and darkness. They believed that by controlling the flow of information and guiding the hands of the powerful, they could steer the empire away from the path of destruction that seemed ever more likely.

Aurelius found himself drawn further into the society's intricate machinations, his role as a double agent growing more critical with each passing day. He whispered in the ears of the Senate, advocating for the Illuminati's interests while simultaneously feeding them just enough rope to hang themselves. His relationship with Augustus grew stronger, the emperor's curiosity about the society's capabilities a double-edged sword that could either secure their alliance or lead to their downfall.

The whispers grew louder as the day of the Game of Shadows approached. The stakes were high—his love for Claudia, his loyalty to the Illuminati, and the fate of Rome itself all hinged on the outcome. Aurelius knew that he was playing a dangerous game, one that could end in triumph or tragedy. Yet, the whispers of destiny called to him, urging him to press onward despite the risks.

The grand hall of the Illuminati was a study in opulence and secrecy. The walls were adorned with tapestries that whispered of ancient knowledge, and the air was thick with the scent of incense and the anticipation of the grand scheme unfolding. The elders had gathered to reveal the intricate tapestry of their master plan to Aurelius and Augustus.

The long-term vision was a breathtaking tapestry of enlightenment. A network of gleaming cities, each a bastion of wisdom, stretching across the vast expanse of the Roman Empire. The whispers of science and reason would replace the cacophony of superstition and ignorance, a beacon to guide humanity through the tumultuous night of the coming cosmic event. The whispers grew stronger as Aurelius envisioned the world the Illuminati sought to create—a new order, where knowledge was power, and power was wielded by the just.

The first stage of their plan was to consolidate their influence within Rome. They would weave a web of alliances and manipulations, ensnaring the Senate and the emperor in their grasp. The whispers grew more insistent as Aurelius contemplated the delicate dance he would need to perform—his public loyalty to Augustus, and his clandestine service to the Illuminati. It was a dangerous game, but one he knew he must play to ensure the society's vision became a reality.

The second phase would see the Illuminati extend their reach to the provinces, planting the seeds of enlightenment in the very hearts of the empire's diverse cities. Aurelius knew that this would not be an easy task—each region had its own entrenched power structures and traditions, and the whispers of change would not be welcome by all. Yet, the promise of progress and prosperity was too tempting to resist, and the whispers of a brighter future grew louder in his mind.

The final stage was the most audacious of all—reshape the very fabric of the empire's governance. The Illuminati dreamed of a world where the Senate was but a shadow of its former self, and the emperor a figurehead guided by the wisdom of the enlightened few. This was the ultimate goal, the culmination of their grand scheme—to create a utopia where the whispers of knowledge and reason drowned out the cries of superstition and fear.

As Aurelius listened to the whispers of the elders, he felt the weight of his decision grow heavier. The love of Claudia and the friendship of Augustus whispered one truth, while the all or nothing shadow game decidijg it all. Such things like shaping rome and the world we tree all left up to a game. The elders talk and talk about what game will be played. After heavy discussion it is said, "red light, geen light. Some skill needed but simple enough to not give an advantage to any one player." The game was kept hidden until the day of the event.

The first phase of the Illuminati's grand scheme was already in motion. The whispers grew louder in the corridors of power as Aurelius worked tirelessly to win over the Senate and consolidate the society's influence in Rome. Each whispered conversation, each subtle nudge of political maneuvering brought him closer to the heart of the empire's governance. The Senate grew more and more divided, with whispers of reform and accusations of heresy echoing through the marble halls.

In the provinces, the whispers of change grew stronger. The Illuminati's emissaries, cloaked in the guise of philosophers and engineers, had infiltrated the courts of the regional governors. They whispered of new technologies and enlightened governance, promising a future that could not be ignored. The whispers of the society's influence grew into a soft murmur that resonated through the empire's very bones, a gentle reminder of the tides of change that were approaching.

The second phase of the Illuminati's grand scheme began in earnest. Aurelius and Claudia traveled to the distant capitals, bringing with them the whispers of revolution. They demonstrated the wonders of steam engines and advanced medicine, o ering the governors a taste of the power that could be theirs if they embraced the society's vision. One by one, the key cities of the empire began to lean towards the Illuminati's cause, their leaders seduced by the whispers of progress and enlightenment.

Yet, as the whispers grew louder, so too did the rumbles of dissent. The Iron Hand, a rival secret society dedicated to the preservation of traditional Roman values, had not been idle. They watched the Illuminati's rise with suspicion, their own whispers of fear and anger spreading through the city. Led by the charismatic and ruthless Caius, the Iron Hand sought to crush the Illuminati's influence before it could take root.

The whispers of conflict grew to a crescendo as the two groups' agendas collided. The Illuminati, driven by their vision of a new world order, were forced to defend their ground against the Iron Hand's fervent nationalism. Aurelius found himself in the center of this storm, his loyalty to the Illuminati's grand scheme clashing with his friendship with Castor and Pollux, who had pledged themselves to the Iron Hand's cause.

The stage was set for the Grand Scheme to unfold. The Illuminati's elders had whispered the details of their ambitious plan into the eager ears of Aurelius and Augustus. A vision of a Rome reborn, casting o the shackles of ignorance and corruption to embrace a future of enlightenment and progress. The whispers grew more urgent as the day of the fateful game approached, each detail of the plan a carefully laid stone in the foundation of their new world order.

Aurelius knew his role was pivotal. He would serve as the liaison between the di erent factions that made up the intricate tapestry of Roman society. His connections in the racing world had given him a unique insight into the hearts and minds of the people, and he would use that knowledge to spread the whispers of change. He leveraged his growing political influence to sway the opinions of resistant senatorial families, weaving the threads of the Illuminati's vision into the fabric of their daily lives.

His assignments were clear and critical. Infiltrate the households of those who clung to the old ways, seeking out the curious and the ambitious. Identify those who could be molded into the new guardians of Rome's destiny, recruiting them to the Illuminati's cause with whispers of power and knowledge. Oversee the implementation of key technologies that would revolutionize the city, each whisper of innovation a step closer to the ultimate goal.

As the whispers grew stronger, so too did the opposition. The Iron Hand watched the Illuminati's progress with a wary eye and set out to expose the secret society.

Aurelius's role grew increasingly complex as he juggled his public persona as a champion of the people with his clandestine duties to the Illuminati. His nights were spent navigating the shadowy alleys of Rome, whispering sweet nothings of enlightenment to those who had the ear of the Senate. His days were a masquerade of political theater, where every gesture and word was calculated to sway the city's elite towards the society's grand design.

The whispers grew more urgent as the day of the Game of Shadows approached. Each meeting with Claudia was a stolen moment, but this meeting was of passion amidst the chaos of their double lives. Their love was a beacon of light in the shadowy world of conspiracy and intrigue, a whisper of hope that seemed to grow fainter with each passing day.

Aurelius's role as liaison between the Illuminati and the city's factions grew more vital than ever. He used his racing connections to navigate the city's social circles, whispering the society's ideals into the ears of the curious and the disenchanted. His public persona as a champion of the people was a mask that allowed him to infiltrate the very households of those who stood in the way of progress. With each whispered conversation, he planted the seeds of doubt and the promise of something greater.

Leveraging his newfound political influence, Aurelius worked tirelessly to sway the Senate's more progressive members to the Illuminati's cause. He painted vivid pictures of a Rome where science and knowledge ruled, where the whispers of the ancients guided them towards a future that could not be contained by the old ways. His words were like whispers of the wind, slipping through the cracks of their traditionalist walls, carrying the scent of change.

The Illuminati had given him specific assignments that required all his skill and cunning. He had to identify potential recruits among the city's elite, those whose thirst for power could be channeled into the society's grand scheme. His eyes searched the crowded halls of the Senate, looking beyond the masks of loyalty to the hunger that lay beneath. And he found them—young men and women with the spark of curiosity and ambition that could be fanned into the flames of enlightenment .

The implementation of key technologies was a delicate dance. Each whisper of innovation had to be introduced with care, a slow crescendo that built anticipation without causing alarm. Aurelius oversaw the construction of new aqueducts and roads, marveled at the implementation of steam powered trains.

Amidst the bustle of the city, he would meet with Castor and Pollux in the shadows, sharing whispers of the Illuminati's progress and receiving their own reports from the Iron Hand's ranks. The tension between their allegiances was palpable, the whispers of their conversations charged with the electricity of their shared destiny. Yet, their friendship remained steadfast, a silent testament to the bonds that had been forged in the fires of their youth.

As the day of the Game of Shadows approached, the city was abuzz with excitement and apprehension. The game was said to be a gentlemans bet put on stage. They knew the real implications the outcome delt.

The Illuminati had orchestrated a series of chariot races that coincided with pivotal political events, using the roar of the crowd and the thunder of hooves to mask their clandestine meetings. Aurelius found himself at the center of this elaborate dance, his every move calculated to sway public opinion. He whispered to the jockeys and the race organizers, ensuring that the outcomes served the society's purposes. Some races were rigged to boost the popularity of certain senators, while others were staged to discredit their enemies.

One such event was a race scheduled to coincide with the opening of the Senate's debate on religious reforms. Aurelius had worked tirelessly behind the scenes, whispering in the right ears and placing the right wagers. The outcome was a foregone conclusion—a victory for the charioteer who supported the Illuminati's progressive views on the gods. The crowd roared its approval, the whispers of the society's influence echoing through the grand stands.

As the chariots thundered around the track, Aurelius slipped away to a hidden chamber beneath the arena. There, he met with a group of influential senators who had been swayed by the Illuminati's whispers. Their conversation was hushed, but the air was thick with the scent of ambition and the promise of power. They discussed the reforms in detail, the whispers of their voices weaving a tapestry of political strategy that would shape the very fabric of Rome's future.

Meanwhile, in the city's streets, a series of "accidents" occurred—wagons overturned, fires that seemed to spring up from nowhere.

Aurelius watched as the whispers grew to a murmur, then a roar. Each incident was meticulously planned, a masterstroke of the Illuminati's hand. They knew the value of chaos in shaping public opinion, and they wielded it with precision. Each disaster served a purpose, a carefully crafted narrative that painted their opponents in a harsh light. The people of Rome grew restless, their chants of fear and anger a siren's call for change.

One such incident involved a high-profile senator, a vocal critic of the Illuminati's influence. His carriage was set upon by a group of "thieves" in the dead of night, his guards mysteriously ine ective. The next day, the —his gold had been stolen, but not his scrolls, which contained damning evidence of the society's existence and true intentions. The public, fed a story of divine intervention, whispered of the gods' protection for the chosen ones.

The chariot races continue, each victory was meticulously orchestrated to align with the Illuminati's objectives, each loss a strategic sacrifice that pushed their enemies further into the shadows. The society's influence grew like a vine, entwining itself around the city's power structures, squeezing out the old and making room for the new.

The day of the grand finale dawned, a race that would not only decide the fate of the season but also the political landscape of Rome. Aurelius knew that the Illuminati had their hand in this, he strategized with Claudia, the tension between them palpable as they worked to ensure the outcome served their society's grand design.

The Colosseum was a hive of activity, the air thick with the scent of sweat and anticipation. The chariots were prepared, each team adorned with the colors of their sponsoring senators. The race was scheduled to coincide with the climax of the Senate's debate on religious reforms—a debate that had grown increasingly heated in the face of the Illuminati's growing influence.

The rivalries between the teams were as intense as the political machinations that played out in the shadows. As the charioteers took their places, Aurelius could feel the energy of the crowd, a living, breathing entity that could be shaped and directed by the right person. The Iron Hand had caught wind of the Illuminati's plan and had placed their own pawns in the race, hoping to disrupt the society's grand scheme.

The signal was given, and the chariots thundered forward, a cacophony of hooves and wheels that drowned out the whispers of the conspirators. Aurelius watched with a mix of excitement and trepidation, his heart racing as much from the danger of his secret mission as from the thrill of the race itself. The chariots weaved and clashed, their drivers' faces a blur of determination and fear. Each victory was a hint of power, each loss a strategic sacrifice to keep the larger narrative on track.

As the chariots rounded the final turn, the outcome of the race was still uncertain. Aurelius's heart pounded in his chest, not just for the thrill of the competition, but for the fate of Rome that hung in the balance. He had worked tirelessly to ensure that the Illuminati's chosen racers would prevail, o ering instructions and bribes where necessary. The race was more than just a spectacle—it was a battleground for the city's soul.

The crowd roared as the chariots thundered towards the finish line, the air charged with the energy of the unfolding drama. Aurelius's eyes darted between the racers, his heart racing in time with the pounding hooves. This was no mere spectacle—it was a battle for the very soul of Rome, and the Illuminati had placed their pawns with care. Each victory ushered in a promise of a new era, each loss a calculated setback to keep the game in play.

As the dust settled and the winners were crowned, the croud grew louder. The Senate's debate on religious reforms had reached its peak, and the Illuminati's plans had become a deafening success. The victorious charioteers, unknowing pawns in a grander game, were showered with garlands and adoration. Each victory had been carefully orchestrated to sway the public's mood in favor of the society's progressive ideals, turning the race into a living symbol of the change they sought.

The staged incidents had served their purpose well. With each "accident," the Iron Hand's credibility had been chipped away, their true colors revealed to the people of Rome. The Illuminati's power and hold grew bolder, weaving a tale of destined greatness and divine favor. Aurelius had orchestrated each event with precision, ensuring that the whispers of the society's enemies were drowned out by the cheers of the manipulated masses.

The grand finale of the chariot season was upon them, the final race that would serve as a beacon of hope for the Illuminati's vision. As the chariots raced through the dusty arena, the cheers grew louder. Aurelius had worked tirelessly to ensure that the outcome of this race would resonate through the halls of power, a declaration of the society's dominance. The Iron Hand had tried to counter their moves, but the Illuminati's web of influence had stretched too wide, too deep. The hopes of their grand scheme had become a gale force wind, carrying the scent of revolution through the city.

As the chariots approached the final stretch, Aurelius felt a knot in his stomach. This was it—the moment that could either solidify the Illuminati's grasp on Rome or see their downfall. The chariotee representing their faction was in the lead, but a rival racer, backed by the Iron Hand, was gaining ground. The crowd's roar grew deafening as the chariots thundered closer to the finish line.

The Illuminati had meticulously timed the race to coincide with a crucial Senate vote on religious tolerance. A victory here would sway public opinion in their favor, granting them the momentum needed to push through the reforms that were central to their vision for an enlightened empire. The society had used the chariot races as a tool for social engineering, their whispers of strategy and manipulation echoing through the very fabric of the city's entertainment.

Aurelius had arranged for the races to serve as covers for their clandestine meetings. As the city held its breath for the outcome, he and his fellow Illuminati would slip away into the shadows, their work continuing unseen. The staged incidents had been a masterstroke, each "accident" carefully orchestrated to discredit their enemies and test the city's emergency response systems. The chaos had been a canvas upon which they painted their narrative of change, a narrative that grew more convincing with each passing day.

The chariots reached the final turn, and the tension in the air was almost tangible. The racer from the Iron Hand's faction made a daring move, cutting o the Illuminati's charioteer. The crowd gasped as the chariots clashed, sending splinters of wood flying into the air. Aurelius's heart skipped a beat, his mind racing through the consequences of failure. If their man did not win, the Senate would not be swayed, and their grand scheme could unravel.

But the Illuminati's driver was a master of his craft. He regained control of his chariot, his eyes focused on the finish line. The Iron Hand's driver pressed on, his chariot a mere horse-length behind. The crowd was on its feet, screaming, their emotions a tumultuous sea that could tip the scales of power in Rome.

The Illuminati's chariot surged ahead, the roar of the crowd swelling as the racer's horses responded to their driver's desperate cries. The finish line loomed closer, and Aurelius could almost taste victory. This was not just a race—it was a battle for the hearts and minds of Rome, and the Illuminati were poised to win.

As the chariots crossed the line, the crowd erupted in a frenzy of cheers. The Illuminati's charioteer had won! Now only to carry this luck into the game of shadows. But it wasnt luck, it was percise planning, and yielding the power with all the pieces in place. Well played. One more game left.

The Illuminati's moves grew bolder as they turned their attention to recruitment. Aurelius, with his charismatic presence, became the society's poster boy. He identified key individuals across various sectors, those whose talents could serve the grand scheme. Scholars and scientists with ideas that could revolutionize Rome were approached with the promise of funding and protection, their curiosity piqued by the whispers of ancient knowledge that lay within the society's vaults. Influential political figures were drawn in by the allure of power and the chance to shape history. Skilled artisans and engineers were sought after for their ability to bring the Illuminati's vision to life, crafting the tools of the future with their calloused hands.

The vetting process was rigorous and shrouded in secrecy. Prospective members were subjected to a series of tests, designed to prove their worthiness and loyalty. They were led through a labyrinth of challenges, each more cryptic and demanding than the last. Only those who demonstrated an unwavering commitment to the cause were granted the honor of knowing the Illuminati's true nature. The initiation was a sacred rite, a whispered promise of enlightenment and power, sealed with an oath of secrecy that bound them tighter than the chains of fate.

Aurelius felt the weight of his new responsibilities as he ventured into the city's intellectual circles. His talks grew more frequent, his eyes searching for the spark of curiosity that marked a potential recruit. The Senate's hallowed halls echoed with the footsteps of those who had come before, their legacies now mere shadows in the grand tapestry of Rome. Yet, amidst the dusty scrolls and marble statues, he found them —the dreamers and the doers, those who yearned for a Rome that could reach for the stars.

The light grew more insistent as the day of the final Game of Shadows approached. Each recruit was a thread in the Illuminati's grand tapestry, each oath a stitch that bound them closer to their goal. Yet, as the network expanded, so too did the potential for betrayal. The Iron Hand had not been idle, their own whispers spreading like a plague through the city's underbelly. They watched, they waited, and they plotted. Aurelius knew that the final game was not just about winning a race, but about securing the very future of the society he had come to believe in.

He walked the cobblestone streets of Rome, his eyes scanning the bustling marketplaces and the scholars' quiet sanctums. Each person he met was a puzzle piece, a potential ally or enemy. His charm was a tool, his words a key to unlock the doors of their minds. He whispered of ancient wisdom and the promise of a brighter future, of a Rome that could stand tall amidst the shadows of ignorance.

The vetting process grew more intense as the Illuminati's influence spread. Each candidate faced a series of trials that tested their mettle, their wits, and their resolve. They were led through the city's hidden chambers, their eyes blindfolded, their senses assaulted by whispers of knowledge and power. Only the worthy were allowed to see the truth, drink the gold juice. While their hearts pounded in their chests as the veil lifted and the society's true nature was revealed.

Aurelius felt the burden of his role as recruiter and mentor. The fate of the Illuminati rested on his ability to discern friend from foe, to see beyond the masks of ambition and fear. He knew that the Iron Hand had its own agents, their ideals just as persuasive as his own. The stakes were higher than ever, each recruit a potential double agent, each alliance a dance on the razor's edge of treachery.

In the heart of the city, where the scent of ink and parchment mingled with the aroma of roasting meats, he found a young scholar named Tiberius. His mind was a sponge, eager to soak up the whispers of the Illuminati's knowledge. Aurelius recognized the spark in his eyes, the same hunger for truth that had drawn him to the society. He brought Tiberius into the fold, whispering of the cosmos and the secrets of the ancients, watching as the young man's imagination caught fire.

Within the shadowed corridors of the Senate, Aurelius encountered a seasoned politician named Seneca. His eyes held the weight of a thousand compromises, his smile a veil over a sharp intellect. Aurelius knew that Seneca could be a powerful ally, his influence stretching further than most. Through careful dialogue and strategic whispers, he revealed the Illuminati's vision of a Rome that transcended the squabbles of the old guard. Seneca was intrigued, his curiosity piqued by the tantalizing promise of power and progress.

The vetting process was a delicate art. Aurelius had to navigate the murky waters of ambition and greed, seeking out those whose hearts burned with the fire of knowledge and the desire to serve a higher purpose. The Illuminati's reach grew large in the city's intellectual circles, drawing in the curious and the ambitious. Among them was a young scholar named Tiberius, whose insatiable thirst for knowledge made him an ideal candidate. Aurelius approached him with the promise of secrets lost to time, the whispers of the ancients that could reshape the very fabric of Rome.

Tiberius was a natural fit for the Illuminati. His curiosity was a beacon that could not be ignored, his intellect a sharp tool ready to be honed. Aurelius mentored him closely, teaching him the subtleties of political maneuvering and the art of whispered persuasion. Together, they moved through the city's academic circles, identifying other scholars who were ripe for the society's message.

Among the influential political figures, Aurelius found a kindred spirit in Seneca. The seasoned politician's hunger for power was matched only by his love for Rome. Through shared whispers of the Illuminati's grand design, they forged a bond that would stand firm in the storms to come. Seneca's support in the Senate was invaluable, his silver tongue turning potential enemies into allies and his tactical mind weaving a web of protection around their cause.

The artisans and engineers were the lifeblood of Rome's transformation. Aurelius sought them out in the dusty workshops and bustling markets, speaking to them of wonders that could only be dreamt of, of machines that could tame the very elements. The promise of a city where innovation was celebrated and not feared and punished.

One such encounter was with a blacksmith named Vulcan. His forge was a sanctum of steel and fire, the air thick with the scent of metal and soot. Aurelius spoke to him of inventions that could revolutionize warfare and construction, of a Rome where such innovation was not just accepted but revered. Vulcan's eyes lit up with a fiery passion as he listened, and he agreed to join the Illuminati's cause, his hammer becoming an instrument of change.

The initiation process was a delicate dance, a series of trials that tested the limits of the candidates' resolve. They were led through the catacombs beneath the city, the echoes of their footsteps mingling with the whispers of the dead. Each test grew more perilous, each revelation more profound. The final act was the most sacred—the consumption of the golden elixir that promised enlightenment and power.

Tiberius took the elixir, his eyes widening as the ancient knowledge flooded his mind. The viocesbgrew louder, the secrets more tantalizing. He emerged from the shadows a changed man, his eyes alight with the fire of the Illuminati and the power of the gold juice. His loyalty was unshakeable, his commitment to the cause absolute.

Seneca, too, passed through the trials with surprising ease. His oath of secrecy was a solemn promise, his gaze steady as he took his place among the society's ranks. His influence grew, his words carrying the weight of an oracle's. The Senate began to lean towards the Illuminati's cause, the chance of reform growing louder with each passing day.

The Iron Hand watched from the shadows, their grip tightening around the city's throat. Their leader, Caius, had become a thorn in Aurelius's side, his presence a constant reminder of the danger that lurked in the dark. Yet, amidst the growing tension, Aurelius remained steadfast in his mission.

The Illuminati's network grew, a web of light in the shadowy corridors of power. Their hand spread through Rome, reaching even into the distant provinces. Aurelius had become the society's beacon, drawing in the brightest minds and strongest wills. Each recruit was a victory, each oath sworn a step closer to their ultimate goal.

The process of recruitment was meticulous. Aurelius identified potential members with a keen eye for ambition and a thirst for knowledge. They were approached with whispers of secrets long buried, of a world beyond the confines of the known. In quiet corners of the city, they gathered, their eyes alight with curiosity as they listened to the promise of a new Rome.

The grand event of the shadow game approached, to be held in the colosseum. The air was charged with anticipation, the very stones of the ancient arena seemed to hum with excitement. The main event was set to be a race of champions, but the evening began with a dance battle, a display of grace and skill that transcended the ordinary. The colosseum's torches cast a warm glow over the contestants as they moved with the fluidity of water, their every step a silent declaration of allegiance to the Illuminati's cause.

Following the dance was a jousting tournament, a relic of the past that had been reimagined with a futuristic twist. The knights, bedecked in

gleaming armor, rode horses bred for speed and strength. Their lance:
were tipped with a mysterious metal that glowed faintly, hinting at th
society's advanced knowledge. The crowd roared as the champion:
clashed, each impact resonating through the very foundations of th
Colosseum. The Illuminati's influence was clear in the high-tecl
weaponry and the precise, almost mechanical precision of the knights
movements.

Before the final race, a short play was performed, a cautionary tale of
the dangers of ignorance and the importance of enlightenment. The
actors moved with a grace that belied the gravity of their words, their
faces painted with the colors of the society's emblem—the all-seeing
eye. The story unfolded, a tapestry of shadows and light, a subtle
allegory of the struggle between the Illuminati and the Iron Hand. The
crowd watched, rapt, as the plot unfolded, their hearts beating in time
with the rhythm of the society's message.

The Colosseum's grandeur served as the backdrop for the evening's
events. Torches cast flickering shadows across the stands, and the air
was thick with the scent of incense and the murmur of hushed
conversations. The Illuminati had transformed the ancient arena into
a stage for their grand design, a place where the whispers of the
future could be heard loud and clear.

As the final act of the play concluded, the tension grew palpable. The
main event was about to begin—a race, red light green light, that
would not only determine the fate of two men but also the balance of
power in Rome itself. The bag of gold, a symbol of wealth and power,
sat gleaming at the finish line, bathed in an otherworldly light that
washed over the Colosseum in an emerald hue. The air was electric

with anticipation, the very stones of the ancient arena seeming to hold their breath.

The dance battle had showcased the grace and poise of the Illuminati's champions, their movements a silent testament to the society's belief in the harmony of mind and body. The jousting tournament had demonstrated the society's mastery of technology, the glowing tips of the lances a stark contrast to the ironclad tradition of Rome's past. The play had woven a narrative of enlightenment and the perils of ignorance, leaving the audience pondering the implications of the society's growing influence.

Now, Augustus and Aurelius took the stage, the air charged with the silent challenge between them. The race was more than just a contest of speed and strategy; it was a proxy battle for the soul of Rome. Aurelius, with his charismatic allure and tactical mind, was the embodiment of the Illuminati's promise of a brighter future. Augustus, on the other hand, represented the stability of the old guard, the wisdom of tradition and the power of established order.

The crowd held its collective breath as the starting signal was given. The two men stopped and stared each trying to outpace the other— the bag of gold that gleamed under the ethereal emerald light, a symbol of the empire's wealth and power, but they knew the real prize, control over everything that was about to become.

They both lurched forward as the light turned green, and the race was on. The thunder on green light and the roar of the crowd melded into a symphony of passion and determination.

The race was tight, the two men neck and neck, their eyes locked in silent stares. Each knew that victory would be pyrrhic if it came at the cost of the other's friendship. Yet, the stakes were too high to hold back. The fate of Rome hung in the balance, and the deal of destiny called for a winner to emerge from the shadows.

In a flash of brilliance, Aurelius saw an opening. He darted to the side, his sandals barely touching the ground as he sprinted towards the gleaming bag of gold. His heart pounded in his chest, not just from the exertion but from the weight of his decision. He knew that by winning, he could free himself from the Illuminati's grasp and finally claim the love of Claudia, who watched from the stands with bated breath.

The green light flickered and changed to red, but Aurelius did not stop. He could feel the power of the society surging through him, urging him onward. His legs burned, his lungs screamed for air, but his resolve was unshakeable. With a final burst of speed, he reached the bag and grabbed it, the emerald light enveloping him in a warm embrace.

The crowd erupted into a frenzy of cheers and applause, the Colosseum trembling with the force of their collective excitement. Aurelius looked up to find Claudia rushing towards him, her eyes shining with hope and love.

Her embrace was like a warm sunrise, banishing the shadows that had plagued him for so long. He knew that in this moment, he had won more than just a race; he had won a future with her. The kiss they shared was a declaration of freedom, a silent rebellion against the Illuminati's control.

The green light had turned to red, and with it, the tide of fate had shifted. The bag of gold in his grasp was a symbol of their victory, not just over Augustus but over the very society that had sought to manipulate him. The cheers of the crowd were a cacophony of liberation, echoing through the ancient stones.

Their eyes met, and in that moment, Aurelius knew that they were no longer pawns in the Illuminati's grand game. They had played their roles to perfection, and now it was time to step away from the shadows.

The final meeting with the elders was held in a chamber deep beneath the Colosseum, illuminated by the flickering flames of ancient torches. The air was thick with incense, the scent of power and secrets long held. The gold juice was passed around the circle, each sip a silent a rmation of their bond, a final communion before the ties that bound them were severed.

The elder spoke in a hushed tone, the words ancient and powerful. "Your oaths are burned, your duty to the brotherhood fulfilled. The whispers of the ancients have been heard, and Rome has taken the first steps towards enlightenment. Your service to the Illuminati is at an end."

Aurelius felt the weight of his oath lift from his shoulders as the parchment blackened and curled in the flame. The gold juice was bittersweet on his tongue, a reminder of the path he had walked, the battles he had fought. Yet, as he drank, he knew that he was not just being released from his obligation; he was being set free.

He looked around the chamber, at the faces of the men and women who had once been his brothers and sisters in the shadows. Some were proud, others wary, but all bore the marks of the path they had chosen. As the flames consumed the parchment, the whispers grew softer, the all-seeing eye's gaze less intense.

The elder's voice was solemn as he spoke the final words of the ceremony. "Your oaths are now as ash upon the wind, your deeds recorded in the annals of our society. You have served well, and your debt to the Illuminati is paid."

Aurelius felt the weight of his decision, the gravity of his newfound freedom. He had given his all to the society, had danced the shadow game with the best of them. Yet, as the gold juice warmed his veins for the last time, he knew that his heart belonged elsewhere.

Their parting was bittersweet, a tapestry of whispered goodbyes and the clinking of glasses filled with the elixir that had once bound them. The emerald light grew dimmer, the whispers fading into the very fabric of the air. As they emerged into the night, the Colosseum loomed over them, a silent sentinel of the battles they had fought and the battles yet to come.

Their final act as Illuminati agents was to burn their robes, the garments that had marked them as part of the elite. The flames licked at the fabric, sending tendrils of smoke into the night sky. It was a symbolic cleansing of this life, and a clean start of a new.

The elder's words hung in the air, a benediction that released them from their sacred vows. Aurelius felt the tension ease from his body, his soul no longer chained to the whispers of the ancients. The gold juice flowed through him one last time, a warm embrace that bid him farewell.

The stables of the Illuminati's hidden compound was a sanctuary of sorts. It was there that Aurelius had found solace amidst the political maelstrom. The scent of horses and hay, the soft whickers in the quiet night, grounded him in reality, reminding him of the world beyond whispers and shadows. He had always loved horses, their power and grace a mirror to his own spirit.

Now, as he stepped into the cool embrace of the stables, the scent of horses and hay washed over him, a welcome respite from the heavy air of the Illuminati's underground chamber. The soft nickering of the animals comforted him, their gentle eyes reflecting the torchlight in the dim space. He had always found peace here, a quiet corner of the world where the whispers of the ancients ways helped him connect with the animals spiritually.

Aurelius approached his favorite steed, a majestic black stallion named Apollo. He had raised Apollo from a foal, and the bond between them was unbreakable. The horse's warm breath on his hand was a reminder of the simple joys in life, the kind that didn't require the cloak of secrets or the pursuit of power. He stroked the stallion's neck, feeling the tension in his own muscles ease away.

Augustus, too, had found refuge in the stables, his mind racing with the events of the night. He had lost the race, but he had won something far more valuable—his friendship with Aurelius and a place in the Illuminati. The loss had stung, but the society's acceptance filled him with a newfound purpose. He watched Aurelius from a distance, his thoughts a tumult of questions and excitement.

As Aurelius turned, he caught Augustus's gaze, and a silent understanding passed between them. Despite their rivalry, they had become bound by a shared destiny. With a nod, Aurelius just passed the reigns over to Augustus, his role in the illuminati etched in the records for the ages. Responsible for growing exponentially, spreading the light into new cities, paving the way for whats to come.

———————————————————————————————. —————————————————

The city of Rome buzzed with niose of the impending elections. The air was thick with the scent of ambition and the clatter of political machinations. The Senate was ablaze with debates, the once-steady rhythm of tradition now a cacophony of new ideas and alliances.

In the heart of the city, the Illuminati's influence grew stronger. The Senate was a chessboard, and they had placed their pawns with precision. Augustus, now openly backed by the society, stepped forward as a candidate for king. His youthful vigor and vision for a new Rome resonated with the people, his every word echoing with the promise of change.

Against him stood a formidable opponent—a long-time senator named Gaius, a man of stoic demeanor and unyielding tradition. His silver hair and stern gaze spoke of a time when Rome was unchallenged, his every step a reminder of the old ways, before the orginization had its hold in everything.

The debate in the Colosseum was fierce, each man's words echoing o the ancient stone walls. Augustus spoke with the passion of a man who had seen the future, his eyes alight with the promise of progress. His words painted a picture of a Rome where knowledge was power, where the people were lifted from the shackles of ignorance and fear. The crowd was spellbound, their eyes reflecting the emerald light that su used the arena.

Gaius countered with the wisdom of the ancients, his voice a solemn warning against the dangers of change. He spoke of the gods' wrath and the sanctity of tradition, his words resonating with those who clung to the familiar. Yet, the whispers of the Illuminati were stronger, the promise of a new dawn too tempting to resist.

As the final words were spoken, the air was still, the only sound the flutter of banners in the breeze. The crowd held its breath, waiting for the verdict. The roar that followed was deafening—Augustus had won the debate, his vision for Rome capturing the hearts and minds of the people.

The election was a mere formality. Augustus's victory was as certain as the sunrise. The ballots were cast in his favor, the Senate's nod a mere formality. His rise to power was swift and decisive, a testament to the Illuminati's influence and the people's hunger for change.

The night of the election, the Colosseum was alight with celebration. Torches and candles cast a warm glow over the city, their flames flickering like the stars above. The Illuminati had emerged from the shadows, their society's emblem—the all-seeing eye—now proudly displayed on banners that flutter throughout the city. And why not they always had the puzzle figured out, each piece working with perfection like it was meant to be.

In the heart of this new Rome, Seneca stood tall, the mantle of power fitting him like an ancient tunic tailored by the gods themselves. He had been chosen by Augustus as his second-in-command, a trusted advisor and the guardian of the society's influence in the Senate. His mind raced with the weight of his new responsibilities and the challenges that lay ahead.

The Iron Hand had not disappeared, their presence a persistent thorn in the side of the Illuminati's new order. They watched from the shadows, biding their time, waiting for the perfect moment to strike. The balance of power was fragile, a house of cards that could topple with the slightest breeze.

Seneca knew that to maintain the Illuminati's grip on Rome, they needed a new guard—a legion of men and women who were as skilled in the art of war as they were in the subtleties of political intrigue. He called for tryouts, inviting the strongest and the most cunning from across the empire to prove their worth.

The trials were rigorous, a series of challenges that tested not only their physical prowess but also their wit and loyalty. Senators whispered about the mysterious group of elite soldiers that would soon stand beside the new king. The tryouts were held in a vast training ground on the outskirts of Rome, a place where the whispers of the ancients were as faint as the distant echoes of battles long past .

Warriors from every corner of the empire had come to prove themselves, their eyes gleaming with ambition and hope. They faced a gauntlet of trials—archery, hand-to-hand combat, and puzzles that would make even the most seasoned strategist pause. Each challenge was designed to weed out the weak, to find those who could be trusted to guard the light of knowledge and enlightenment that the Illuminati sought to spread across the empire.

Seneca observed from a raised platform, his gaze sharp and discerning. He had studied the art of war and statecraft under the greatest teachers Rome had to o er, and he knew what it took to forge a group that could stand against the Iron Hand. He watched as they competed, their muscles gleaming with sweat under the relentless sun. Yet, it was not just their skills that interested him, but the fire that burned within their hearts—a desire to protect the future of Rome from the shackles of ignorance and fear.

The final challenge was a test of stealth and cunning. The hopefuls were sent into the heart of the city, tasked with retrieving an artifact from the Iron Hand's stronghold without being detected. Among them was Vulcan, a burly man with a gentle touch and an unrivaled skill in the forge. His fiery eyes and coal-stained skin were a stark contrast to the refined marble structures of Rome, yet his demeanor spoke of a wisdom that belied his origins.

Vulcan moved through the city like a shadow, his steps silent on the cobblestone streets. His journey took him past the gleaming temples of the gods and into the labyrinthine alleys of the city's underbelly. His hands, though calloused from a lifetime of shaping metal, were nimble as he scaled the walls and slipped through the shadows.

When he reached the stronghold, the air was thick with the scent of burning incense and the murmur of hushed conversations. The Iron Hand was ever vigilant, their eyes peeled for any sign of infiltration. Yet Vulcan's talents had not gone unnoticed. His unassuming nature and his ability to manipulate the very metal that made up the city's defenses had earned him a place in the Illuminati's ranks.

With the artifact in hand, Vulcan slipped away, his heart racing with the thrill of victory. The Iron Hand had not seen him come, nor had they seen him go. He returned to the training ground, the artifact held tightly against his chest, a trophy of his cunning and skill.

Seneca's eyes lit up as he approached, the flames of the nearby torches casting an orange glow upon his face. "Well done," he said, his voice deep and measured. "Your place in the guard is secured." Vulcan nodded, his eyes never leaving the prize. He knew that this was only the beginning.

In the days that followed, Vulcan distinguished himself not only as a fierce warrior but also as a master blacksmith. His hands, once used to forge weapons for the common soldier, now crafted the finest instruments of war for the Illuminati's elite guard. The metal sang beneath his hammer, each strike a declaration of his loyalty to the cause of enlightenment.

The weapons he forged were not just tools of destruction but symbols of the society's power. Emerald-studded swords that gleamed with the light of knowledge, shields adorned with the all-seeing eye, and chariots that whispered of speed and precision. Each piece was a masterwork, a testament to the society's commitment to exelence.

As the guard grew in numbers and skill, so did the whispers of their existence. The Iron Hand took notice, their leaders sensing the shift in the balance of power. They knew that the Illuminati had always been more than just a rumor, and now they had the means to act against them.

The tension grew palpable, the air in Rome thick with the scent of impending conflict. Yet, amidst the vioces in the shadows, a spark of hope flickered to life. The people had seen the guard in action, had felt the protection of the Illuminati's light. They whispered stories of Vulcan and his band of elite warriors, their tales growing with each retelling.

The city was a tinderbox, waiting for a spark to set it ablaze. And when the moment came, it was not in the Senate or the Colosseum, but in the quiet sanctity of a scholar's study. An attack by the Iron Hand, swift and brutal, left a trail of blood and fear in its wake. The Illuminati's response was swift and decisive—the guard, led by Vulcan, descended upon the assailants, their emerald-hued weapons cutting through the shadows like beams of light.

Vulcan's place in the king's guard was no longer a secret. His valor in the face of danger had earned him the respect of the Senate and the adoration of the people. They saw in him a protector, a champion of the new Rome that Augustus and the Illuminati promised to build. His name became a rallying cry, a symbol of the society's power and the threat they posed to those who would stand in the way of progress.

The guard grew stronger, their numbers swelling with each victory. They patrolled the streets, their emerald insignia striking fear into the hearts of the Iron Hand's agents. The rival secret societies had become more than just whispers in the night; they were now two sides of a coin, each fighting for the soul of the eternal city.

As the days turned to weeks, the Iron Hand grew bolder, their attacks more frequent and daring. The Senate was in an uproar, demanding action against the shadowy threat that loomed over the city. In response, Augustus called for a grand spectacle at the Colosseum, a show of force that would serve as a prelude to the Game of Shadows and a declaration of the Illuminati's intent to protect Rome.

The tradition of gladiatorial combats was reborn with a twist—now these pre-race battles were not merely entertainment but a display o the guard's might. The Colosseum roared with excitement as the firs gladiators took the sand, their emerald armor glinting in the sun. The crowd was a sea of faces, each one hungry for the thrill of combat, the taste of victory on their lips.

Vulcan emerged as the king's champion, a silent sentinel who had never known defeat. His background was shrouded in mystery, whispers of his past a mere smoky veil that hinted at his true lineage. Some said he was the son of a god, others a former gladiator who had earned his freedom and chosen to serve the Illuminati. Yet all agreed, his fighting style was unmatched, a dance of steel and shadow that had earned him the respect of friend and foe alike.

The Colosseum's grand spectacle grew in grandeur with each passing day. The air was thick with the scent of blood and the thirst for wisdom. The pre-race gladiatorial combats were no longer just a prelude to the main event but had become a battleground for political posturing and public adoration. The Senate looked on with a mix of excitement and trepidation, their whispers hinting at the power play unfolding before their eyes.

The day of the pivotal battle dawned hot and heavy, the sun a fiery disk in the cloudless sky. The Colosseum was packed to the brim, the cries of the crowd a deafening roar that seemed to shake the very foundations of the ancient arena. Vulcan strode into the sand, his emerald armor gleaming, his eyes as cold and unyielding as the steel he wielded. His opponent, a towering brute named Titan, was a formidable challenger, his reputation for savagery preceding him.

Their clash was a symphony of steel and fury, a dance of death that had the crowd on the edge of their seats. Titan was brutal and relentless, his blows like the hammer of the gods themselves. Yet Vulcan, with his agility and precision, parried each strike with ease, his blade a serpent darting through the air. The battle raged on, each warrior pushing the other to the brink of defeat.

But fate had a twist in store. In the heat of battle, Titan's blade found its mark, a glancing blow that sent Vulcan to his knees. The crowd gasped, their cheers turning to a collective intake of breath. For a moment, the Colosseum was silent, the only sound the ringing of steel and the pounding of hearts.

Vulcan's eyes narrowed, his breath shallow. This was not the end he had envisioned. With a roar that seemed to shake the very air, he surged to his feet, his sword flashing in an arc of emerald light. The crowd erupted, their cries of disbelief morphing into a fervent chant of his name.

The battle raged on, each blow more fierce than the last. The sand grew crimson with their mingled blood, a grim testament to the price of power. Yet Vulcan, driven by a fierce determination, parried and thrust, his movements a blur of emerald and steel. Titan, unaccustomed to such resistance, began to tire, his swings growing sloppy, his breath ragged.

The crowd watched in rapt silence, the air thick with tension. Each clang of their swords was a toll that echoed through the Colosseum, a reminder of the stakes—knowledge, freedom, and the very soul of Rome. The Illuminati's emerald banners fluttered above, a stark contrast to the Iron Hand's crimson emblems that dotted the stands.

In a flash of emerald, Vulcan struck a final, decisive blow. Titan fell, his lifeless body a grim exclamation to the end of the bout. The crowd erupted in a frenzy of cheers, the Illuminati's symbolic victory reverberating through the city. The Senate looked on, their faces a mix of awe and fear. They had seen the guard's might and knew that the society's influence was not to be underestimated.

The grand spectacle at the Colosseum had served its purpose—it had shown Rome that the Illuminati were not just scholars and thinkers but a force to be reckoned with, willing to spill blood for their cause. Yet, amidst the jubilation, a shadow fell upon the city. The Iron Hand had been humiliated, and their thirst for vengeance grew stronger.

Rumors of an impending clash between the two societies grew louder, each whisper more urgent than the last. The Senate was a powder keg of tension, with factions forming around the new guardians of knowledge and the traditionalists who feared the Illuminati's power. Yet, amidst the political posturing and shadowy maneuverings, the Colosseum remained a beacon of unity, its grand spectacles drawing the masses together under the guise of entertainment.

The gladiatorial combats grew in complexity, each battle a microcosm of the larger struggle for Rome's future. The Senate had unwittingly become a stage for the Illuminati's power play, as Augustus and Seneca used the games to showcase their society's might and garner public support. The people, ever eager for the spectacle, were drawn to the emerald-clad champions, their hearts beating in time with the clang of steel and the roar of victory.

Vulcan, the king's champion, had become a legend in his own right. His background remained shrouded in mystery, but his prowess was undeniable. Was he a demigod sent to protect the city of Rome? Or perhaps a former gladiator whose valor had earned him the favor of Augustus? The truth remained elusive, a secret guarded by the Illuminati.

The day of the pivotal battle dawned, the air heavy with the scent of anticipation. The Colosseum's arches loomed over the city, casting long shadows over the crowded streets. The newly instituted tradition of pre-race gladiatorial combats had become the talk of the town, a clever ploy by Augustus to showcase the Illuminati's power and win the hearts of the people. The Senate had sanctioned the event, but the whispers grew louder of the political machinations behind the scenes.

Vulcan, the king's champion, was a man of enigma. His emerald armor shimmered in the sun, a stark contrast to the crimson banners of the Iron Hand that were noticeably absent from the arena. His background was a tapestry of rumors and legends—some said he was the son of a god, others whispered that he was a former gladiator plucked from obscurity by Augustus himself. Yet, his prowess was undeniable. The crowd's excitement grew palpable as he entered the arena, his very presence a declaration of the Illuminati's might.

The grand spectacle began with the clang of swords and the roar of the crowd. Each combat was a choreographed dance of death, the gladiators' movements precise and deliberate. Yet, as the battles unfolded, it became clear that these were not mere entertainments—they were a showcase of power, a declaration of the Illuminati's influence over the city.

Vulcan, the king's champion, emerged into the arena to a crescendo of cheers. His eyes, cold and unyielding, scanned the stands as he searched for any sign of Iron Hand interference. His reputation had grown with each victory, his name whispered in the same breath as the gods of old. Yet, his true identity remained a closely guarded secret, known only to the Illuminati's inner circle.

His opponent today was the fearsome Vigo, a brute of a man whose very presence sent shivers down the spines of the lesser gladiators. The two warriors circled each other, their blades glinting in the sun, each waiting for the perfect moment to strike. The crowd held its breath, the anticipation a living thing that seemed to pulse in the very air.

Their battle was an epic saga played out in the sands of the Colosseum. Vulcan's emerald blade was a blur as it parried Vigo's relentless attacks. The king's champion was a maestro of the sword, his movements a symphony of grace and power. Yet, Vigo was no ordinary opponent. His sheer strength and ferocity made each clash a battle of wills, a struggle that tested Vulcan's limits.

As the combat raged on, the crowd grew ever more frenzied. The air was thick with the scent of sweat and blood, the cries of the spectators a constant backdrop to the clanging of steel. The Senate watched from their lofty perches, their eyes gleaming with the light of political ambition. They knew that the outcome of this battle would have far-reaching implications, that the fate of Rome hung in the balance.

Vigo, a beast of a man with a reputation for mercilessness, fought with a ferocity that seemed almost inhuman. Yet Vulcan, with his emerald blade, met each attack with a grace that seemed almost supernatural. The sun glinted o their armor, casting a kaleidoscope of light across the sand. The battle was a dance of death, a ballet of blood and steel that had the audience transfixed.

Suddenly, Vulcan's blade slipped, and Vigo's sword sliced through the air, aimed straight for his heart. Time seemed to slow as the crowd watched in horror. Yet, with a speed that seemed impossible, Vulcan twisted away, the blade grazing his armor. His counterattack was swift and precise, his emerald sword finding its way to Vigo's throat. The Iron Hand's champion fell, the sand staining red beneath his body.

The Colosseum buzzed with excitement as the gladiators took a momentary pause. In the shadows of the royal box, Aurelius, now a mentor to the young Tiberius, watched the unfolding spectacle with a keen eye. His pupil, a promising young man with a thirst for knowledge and an unrivaled ability to read the unspoken, had caught his attention during the early days of the Illuminati's rise to power.

Tiberius's background was one of curiosity and natural talent. Raised in a household of scholars, he had always questioned the established order, seeking the truth beyond the veil of religion and politics. It was this insatiable hunger for understanding that had led him to the Illuminati's doorstep. His sharp intellect and intuitive nature had not gone unnoticed by Aurelius, who recognized in him a potential equal.

Their relationship began with a series of tests, Aurelius probing the depths of Tiberius's resolve and intellect. The young man passed each challenge with flying colors, his mind a sponge eagerly absorbing the ancient wisdom that Aurelius o ered. Finally, with a firm hand on Tiberius's shoulder, Aurelius declared him worthy of the Illuminati's teachings, marking the start of their bond as master and apprentice.

In the dimly lit chambers of the Illuminati's secret library, Aurelius shared the society's most sacred texts, their pages whispering of lost civilizations and forgotten truths. Tiberius's eyes lit up with each revelation, his curiosity insatiable. They discussed the "Light," the ancient force that the Illuminati sought to harness for Rome's enlightenment. It was a power that required understanding and discipline, a dance of shadows and whispers that could shape the very fabric of reality.

Aurelius taught Tiberius the art of observation, showing him how to read the unspoken language of power that flowed through the city's veins. They strolled through the bustling markets, their eyes peeled for signs of political maneuvering and hidden alliances. Each gesture, each subtle shift in tone, became a puzzle piece in the grand mosaic of Rome's intrigues.

Their lessons grew more intense as they ventured into the practical application of their newfound knowledge. Aurelius guided Tiberius through the art of manipulation, demonstrating how a single word, a strategic silence, or a well-placed question could sway the course of a conversation. It was a heady power, one that Tiberius found both thrilling and terrifying.

The philosophical discussions that followed were equally as challenging. They grappled with the nature of power and the weight of responsibility that came with it. Aurelius spoke of the delicate balance between guiding and controlling, of leading by example rather than by fear. Tiberius, ever the eager student, absorbed these lessons with a fervor that was both inspiring and slightly unsettling. His mind raced with the implications, the potential for good and the temptation of power.

Their bond grew stronger as the days turned to weeks, the cobwebs of knowledge stretching from the dusty tomes to the gleaming emerald weapons of the Illuminati's guard. Aurelius saw in Tiberius a reflection of his younger self—a hunger for truth, a desire to reshape the world. Yet, he knew that this path was fraught with danger and moral quandaries that would test the young man's resolve.

The time came for Tiberius's final test. Aurelius sent him into the city to uncover a rumor of an Iron Hand infiltration within the Senate. His mission was simple—find the truth without revealing his a liations. Tiberius moved through the marble halls of power with the grace of a cat, his eyes and ears tuned to the whispers of conspiracy.

The young apprentice faced his challenge with a mix of excitement and dread. Each step he took through the grand halls of the Senate was a silent testament to his newfound place in the Illuminati's grand design. Tiberius had always felt a sense of otherness, a pull towards the shadows that lay just beyond the surface of the world. Now, with Aurelius as his guide, he was beginning to understand the true extent of that power.

Their relationship grew deeper as Aurelius shared the ancient wisdom of the "Light" with his pupil. The texts spoke of a force that could reshape the very fabric of reality, a force that had been lost to time and greed. Tiberius's mind raced with the possibilities, his thoughts a tumultuous sea of wonder and fear. Yet, as he delved deeper into the society's teachings, he found that the "Light" was not just a tool for power—it was a responsibility, a burden that weighed heavily on those who sought to wield it.

Aurelius watched Tiberius from the shadows as he navigated the corridors of the Senate, his heart swelling with pride. His pupil had come far, his mind a blade sharpened by the ancient wisdom of the Illuminati. The young man had an uncanny ability to unravel the complex webs of power that wove through Rome's political fabric.

In the public eye, Seneca's influence grew like a mighty oak. His appointment as Augustus's chief advisor was met with a mix of admiration and skepticism. His philosophical musings and eloquent speeches had earned him a devoted following among the citizens, who saw in him a beacon of wisdom in a city fraught with turmoil. Yet, the Senate's traditionalists whispered of his foreign ways, his Stoic beliefs a stark contrast to their own entrenched dogmas.

Seneca's public persona was one of calm and reason, a bastion of enlightenment amidst the chaos. His writings, which touched on the nature of power and the responsibilities of leadership, sparked heated debates in the city's forums. Some hailed him as a prophet of a new age, while others feared his ideas were a Trojan horse for the Illuminati's hidden agenda. Yet, amidst the clamor of public discourse, the true extent of his influence remained shrouded, known only to those who sat in the inner sanctum of power.

Behind the scenes, Seneca's counsels to Augustus were invaluable. His insights into human nature and his understanding of the delicate dance of governance allowed the young king to rule with a firm yet fair hand. Yet, the shadows of the Senate were thick with tension, as the old guard eyed the newcomer with suspicion. The whispers grew louder—Seneca was a puppet master, a sly fox whispering heresies into the king's ear.

Augustus, however, trusted his advisor implicitly. In the quiet of the night, when the burden of rule weighed heavy upon him, it was Seneca's voice that o ered guidance and solace. The two men had become a formidable duo, a yin and yang of power and wisdom that had transformed the very essence of Rome.

But even as Seneca's star rose, so too did the whispers of his true loyalties. His a liation with the Illuminati was known only to a select few, and even they could not guess the extent of his knowledge or his intentions. The Senate had a chair open updue to a death. Augustis is swayed to fill it with tiberius. The favor is quickly done puttin another member of the illuminati in a senate chair.

The Senate's traditionalists watched with wary eyes as the philosopher's influence grew. They murmured of his "foreign" ways and his "dangerous" ideas, fearing that the very fabric of Roman society was at risk. Yet, their words fell on deaf ears as Augustus stood firmly by his side, the wisdom of the Illuminati shaping his rule.

One fateful night, a covert operation led by the Illuminati's newest recruit, Tiberius, resulted in the capture of a high-ranking Iron Hand member. The man was caught red-handed, attempting to bribe a senator with information that could topple the precarious balance of power. His initial resistance to interrogation was fierce, but the Illuminati were notorious for their ability to coax the truth from even the most stoic of adversaries.

In the bowels of the Colosseum, where the screams of the damned had once echoed, the captured Iron Hand member faced his inquisitors. Aurelius, his face a mask of cold resolve, led the questioning. The man was a seasoned warrior, his body scarred from countless battles, yet he had never faced a mind as sharp as Aurelius'. The air grew thick with tension as the interrogation began.

The Iron Hand member spat in defiance, his eyes glinting with the fire of his convictions. Yet, the Illuminati were notorious for their patience and methods. They had honed the art of extracting information from the most stoic of adversaries. Slowly, with a combination of psychological prowess and subtle physical coercion, the man's resistance began to crumble. His secrets, once tightly held, began to spill forth like wine from a shattered amphora.

The revelations were damning. The Iron Hand's reach extended far beyond the gladiatorial games, their tentacles coiled around the very heart of Roman society. The Senate's whispers grew to shouts as the public announcement was made—Rome had been infiltrated by a secret society bent on chaos and destruction. The city was gripped by fear, the once-proud citizens now looking over their shoulders praying to the gods that harm not come their way. Soon they had plenty of information, the identities of members, where the base camps were, the daily operation, their mumbers, and future plans of sabatoge.

Aurelius and Tiberius stood before the Senate, the captured Iron Hand member at their feet, his face a twisted mask of pain and anger. They recounted the details of their daring operation, their voices calm yet firm, the very embodiment of the Illuminati's stoic resolve. The Senate erupted in outrage, the air thick with the scent of fear and accusation. The Illuminati had not only exposed the Iron Hand but had captured one of their leaders, a man who had once wielded significant power in the shadows.

The interrogation had been methodical and brutal. The Iron Hand member had been subjected to a series of psychological and physical torments, his will broken layer by layer. Yet, it was not just the pain that made him talk—it was the promise of the "Light," the whispered promise of knowledge and power that had eluded his grasp for so long. In the end, he had revealed everything, his voice a broken reed in the storm of Roman politics.

The public announcement of the Iron Hand's existence sent shock waves through the city. The Senate's marble halls echoed with the cries of disbelief and outrage. The Illuminati's triumph was complete, their enemy's secrets laid bare for all to see. Augustus took to the podium his face a mask of righteous anger, and announced the capture of the Iron Hand's leader. The crowd, once divided, now stood united in fear and anger. The Iron Hand had been exposed, their plot to sow chaos and seize power in tatters.

Caius, the Iron Hand's leader, watched the unfolding events from the shadows. His mind raced, weaving new strategies, new plans. He knew that the game had changed, that the Illuminati had played a masterstroke. Yet, he was not one to be easily deterred. The society had been built on the bones of adversity, its very existence a testament to the resilience of its members. He vowed to strike back, to show Rome that the Iron Hand could not be so easily vanquished.

The city of Rome, once a bastion of order and stability, descended into a maelstrom of paranoia. Every corner whispered of conspiracy, every shadow a potential threat. The Senate called for heightened security, the city's guard was at high alert. The king's guard gather at

100 men. The time to stomp out the last issue in the great city, the Iron Hand.

Agustus knew that the Iron Hand would not go quietly into the night. They were a hydra, each head cut o only to be replaced by two more. The Illuminati had to act swiftly and decisively. He gathered his most trusted agents, a group of elite warriors and scholars, to embark on a covert mission through the city. Their goal was clear—to root out every member of the Iron Hand, to bring them to justice or to turn them into loyal servants of the "Light."

The Illuminati's hundred-man force moved through the city like a silent storm, their emerald armor gleaming in the moonlight. They struck without warning, apprehending Iron Hand members who had once strutted the streets with arrogant confidence. The once-feared warriors were now little more than cattle herded into the light, their fates sealed by the swiftness and precision of their captors.

Vulcan, the enigmatic champion of the Illuminati, led the charge. His blade sang a song of dominance, and with each strike, another Iron Hand member fell, their crimson emblems of rebellion staining the cobblestones. Those who resisted capture met a swift and brutal end, their lifeblood mingling with the shadows as Vulcan's legend grew. Yet, amidst the chaos and fear, vulcan's heart was heavy. He knew that every life taken was a tragedy, a testament to the depths to which Rome had descended.

The captured Iron Hand members were not executed but instead were given a choice—swear fealty to the Illuminati and work to rebuild Rome, or face a fate worse than death. The society had no use for mindless violence, preferring instead to bend the wills of their enemies to their cause. They were rebranded as the "Builders of the New Dawn," their hands bound in chains of enlightenment as they toiled under the watchful eyes of their new masters.

The city's construction projects grew at an unprecedented pace, fueled by the relentless labor of the repurposed Iron Hand members. The once-crumbling infrastructure was revitalized, a gleaming testament to the Illuminati's power and vision. The people of Rome watched the transformation with a mix of awe and dread. They knew that the city was changing, that the very air they breathed was su used with the "Light."

Each dawn saw the Builders of the New Dawn marching through the streets, their once-crimson armbands replaced with emerald shackles that marked them as servants of the Illuminati. They worked tirelessly their newfound loyalty enforced by the ever-watchful eyes of their captors. The clang of hammers and the scrape of chisels against stone became the rhythm of the city, a constant reminder of the society's dominance.

Vulcan and his guards patrolled the city, a silent vigil against any who would dare to oppose the Illuminati's grand plan. Their presence was a stark reminder of the new order that had been established—one of knowledge and enlightenment, but also of absolute power. It was during one such patrol that they received word of Caius's whereabouts—his hiding place had been uncovered by a traitor within his own ranks.

The Illuminati descended upon the ramshackle tavern where Caius had sought refuge. His desperate pleas for mercy fell on deaf ears as the emerald-clad warriors closed in. Augustus stepped forward, his gaze cold and unyielding. "Caius," he said, his voice echoing through the room, "you have been found guilty of treason against Rome. You shall pay the price for your actions against Rome."

The once-proud leader of the Iron Hand was dragged out into the street, his once-fiery spirit now extinguished. His eyes searched the crowd for a shred of mercy, but all he found was a sea of fearful faces. The people had turned against him, their trust shattered by the revelations of his treachery. He knew that his fate was sealed, that his name would be etched into the annals of history as a traitor.

Augustus stood tall, his gaze never wavering from Caius's broken form. "Your treachery will serve as a lesson to all who dare to oppose the "Light," he declared, his voice carrying through the hushed whispers of the gathered citizens. "You shall face the beasts of the Colosseum, a public spectacle to remind Rome of the price of betrayal."

In the shadow of the Senate House, Seneca watched the procession, his mind racing with the implications of Caius's capture. His influence within the Illuminati had been unknowingly significant, his philosophical teachings and strategic insights shaping the society's approach to governance. The city was changing, and with each new dawn, the "Light" grew stronger. Yet, even as the Iron Hand was brought to heel, he felt a growing sense of unease. The whispers of the Ottoman Turks' rise to power grew louder, their ambitions casting a long shadow over the Mediterranean.

Tiberius, once a curious scholar, now stood as a formidable force within the Illuminati. His rapid ascent through the ranks had not gone unnoticed, and his potential as a key player in the unfolding events was clear. His cunning and his dedication to the "Light" had earned him the trust of Aurelius and Augustus alike. As they observed the city from their vantage point, they knew that the time for subtlety was coming to an end.

Seneca, whose philosophical teachings had unwittingly become the bedrock of the Illuminati's strategy, watched the city's transformation with a mix of pride and trepidation. He had always sought to uplift humanity through wisdom, but the power of the "Light" was not something to be wielded lightly. The society's rise had been swift and decisive, but he feared the consequence of expansion.

One evening, Augustus summoned Aurelius to a private chamber within the Senate House. The air was thick with the scent of burning candles and the weight of unspoken words. The king's eyes bore into Aurelius, reflecting the gravity of the o er he was about to make. "My friend," he began, his voice low and measured, "Rome is changing, and we must adapt. We need a bastion of our ideals, a place where the "Light" can shine without the shackles of this city's politics."

Aurelius, his curiosity piqued, leaned forward. "What do you propose, my king?"

Augustus unfurled a parchment map of the Mediterranean, his finger tracing the outline of a distant island. "Crete," he said, his eyes alight with ambition. "We shall make it a beacon of enlightenment, a place where the Illuminati can shape the world without the corruption of the Senate's shadow." He o ered the scroll to Aurelius. "I want you to be the first mayor of Crete. Only answering to me back here in Rome. You run the territory and spread the light there like you did here. He accepted under one condition, Tiberius come with him and handle the illuminati side of things, and Claudia would be able to accompany him. Aurelius would not join the brotherhood again or leave her behind. The deal is struck sending Aurelius back into politics.

The news of Aurelius's new role spread through the city like wildfire, igniting a spark of hope in the hearts of the people. Many saw in him a leader who could bridge the gap between the Illuminati's ideals and the Senate's old guard. His reputation as a fair and just man grew, and his unconventional approach to governance had the potential to usher in a new era of peace and prosperity.

Meanwhile, in the dusty arena of the Colosseum, a new charioteer had captured the public's imagination. Marcus, a young man of mysterious origins, had emerged as a racing sensation. His unorthodox style, a blend of speed and precision, sent the crowds into a frenzy. His dark hair whipped in the wind as he steered his chariot with a confidence that seemed almost supernatural. His eyes, a piercing blue, seemed to see through the very fabric of the games, hinting at secrets yet to be revealed.

The season-opening spectacle had been arranged with great care to showcase the Illuminati's might. Vulcan, now a legend in his own right, was set to face three of the Iron Hand's most formidable gladiators, all once elite members of the society they had sought to destroy. The tension in the air was palpable as the gladiators took their positions, their chariots poised like predators ready to pounce.

The crowd held its collective breath as the signal was given, and the chariots surged forward. The battle was fierce, a dance of steel and strategy that had the spectators on the edge of their seats. Vulcan's emerald armor flashed in the sunlight as he parried and struck, his every move a testament to his mastery of the arena. The Iron Hand gladiators fought with a desperation born of their impending doom, yet it was clear that Vulcan was in a league of his own.

As the dust settled, Vulcan stood triumphant, his enemies vanquished. The crowd erupted in a cacophony of cheers, their adoration washing over him like a wave. Yet, his gaze remained fixed on the king's box, his mind racing with the knowledge of the true battle that lay ahead. The Iron Hand had been dealt a severe blow, but Caius had yet to be executed.

Romulos, the new racing sensation, watched from the sidelines, his eyes narrowed in concentration. His heart pounded not with fear but with the thrill of competition. He had seen much in his short life, and he knew that the games of Rome were not merely a spectacle but a stage for power and intrigue. His unorthodox style was not just for show—it was a declaration of war against the stagnant traditions that had ruled the city for too long.

As Vulcan stepped into the arena, the crowd's roar grew deafening. The Iron Hand gladiators, once feared as the untouchable elite, were now mere pawns in the Illuminati's grand scheme. Their eyes burned with a fierce hatred, a silent promise of vengeance that Vulcan knew all too well. Yet, as the battle commenced, it was clear that the "Builders of the New Dawn" had been stripped of their former might.

Their skills had been honed by desperation, but it was no match for the methodical precision of the Illuminati.

Vulcan fought with a grace that belied his brutal e ciency, his blade a blur as it danced through the air. Each strike was calculated, each movement a testament to his mastery. The three Iron Hand gladiators fell at his might.

Romulos watched the display with a keen eye, his mind racing. He knew that the games were a microcosm of the city's power struggles, and the Illuminati's victory here was a clear message to all who would oppose them. Yet, there was something more to Vulcan than mere strength and skill—there was a quiet intensity that spoke of a deep personal vendetta.

The moment of truth arrived as Caius was led into the arena, his once-proud visage now a twisted mask of terror. The great white lion, symbol of the Illuminati's purity, stalked towards him, its eyes gleaming with an eerie intelligence. The crowd fell silent, their breaths held in anticipation of the gruesome spectacle.

The creature pounced, and Caius's screams were lost in the roar of the beast. His body was torn apart, a gruesome reminder of the fate that awaited those who dared to challenge the new order. The crowd's initial horror gave way to a morbid fascination, then a cathartic cheer. The Iron Hand had been vanquished in the most public and humiliating manner possible.

The execution served as a turning point, the public's fear of the Iron Hand transformed into a fervent support for the Illuminati. The Senate, though wary, could not deny the stability that Augustus's reign had brought to the city. The "Builders of the New Dawn" were now hailed as heroes, their emerald emblems a symbol of hope in the eyes of the people.

The city buzzed with excitement and fear as rumors spread of Aurelius's new role in Crete. His departure from Rome was met with a mix of sorrow and anticipation, for many knew that his presence there meant that the Illuminati's influence was growing beyond the city's walls. The Senate's power was waning, and in its stead arose a new breed of leaders, guided by the "Light" of knowledge and wisdom.

Romulos's victory in the chariot race had been nothing short o spectacular, his unconventional tactics leaving the seasoned racers ir his dust. The crowd's adoration grew with each race, and soon he was hailed as the "Dark Horse of Rome," a symbol of hope in the shadow o the Illuminati's emerald reign. Yet, the society's elders saw in him a potential threat, an unknown quantity that could not be allowed to disrupt their grand design.

Tiberius and his duty to the Illuminati, approached Romulos with an o er to join their ranks. He knew that the young racer's talents could be harnessed for the greater good, to spread the "Light" through the games. Yet, Romulos's heart was unyielding. His own code of honor and his suspicion of the society's true intentions made him immune to their allure.

The Illuminati's elders, displeased by Romulos's refusal, saw in him a dangerous wildcard that could undermine their control over the city. They decided to eliminate the threat. During the celebratory feast following his victory, a slyly administered poison found its way into Romulos's goblet. His subsequent illness was swift and severe, his body wracked with pain and convulsions.

The city mourned the sudden demise of their new champion, but the Illuminati moved swiftly to ensure that his death was not in vain. His tragic end served as a warning to others who might dare to oppose them. His legacy, they would claim, was the very embodiment of the "Light" they sought to spread. Yet, whispers of foul play began to circulate, casting a pall over the Illuminati's victory.

Vulcan, torn between his duty to the society and his growing respect for Romulos, took it upon himself to investigate the circumstances of the young man's death. His inquiries led him to the shadowy figure of Tiberius, whose hand had been behind the poisoning. The revelation shook Vulcan to his core, and he began to question the "Light" he had sworn to uphold.

The Illuminati, undeterred, turned their attention to the upcoming races. Aurelius knew that the people needed a new hero to rally behind, a figure that could be controlled and manipulated to serve their purposes. Thus, they turned their sights on the young and ambitious Sextius a stable hand, grooming him to become the face of the society's power within the arena.

Under Vulcan's tutelage, Sextius trained relentlessly, his skills honed to perfection. The society's gold faction invested heavily in advanced chariots, crafted with the same technology that had made Vulcan an unstoppable force. The designs were ingenious, incorporating hidden weapons and mechanical enhancements that would ensure victory.

The day of the next great race dawned, and the Colosseum once again echoed with the roar of the crowd. Sextius took his place, his emerald armor gleaming in the sun, his heart a tumult of excitement and fear. He knew that this race was not just about entertainment—it was a declaration of the Illuminati's dominance over Rome.

The chariots thundered forth, and the battle for supremacy began. Sextius, driven by a mix of ambition and fear, pushed his steeds to their limits, weaving through the chaos with the grace of a dancer and the ruthlessness of a predator. The advantage proves to be too much and Sextius wins his first race with ease.

The Illuminati's influence grew stronger with each victory, and the Senate's power waned. Yet, as the society's tentacles stretched further, so too did the whispers of dissent. In the shadows, a new faction began to form, one that saw the "Light" not as a beacon of hope but as a harbinger of tyranny.

On the distant shores of Crete, Aurelius, Claudia, and Tiberius arrived under the cover of night. The island was a stark contrast to the bustling metropolis of Rome, its rugged beauty a stark reminder of the challenge ahead. They surveyed the landscape, noting the ancient ruins that spoke of civilizations long forgotten, and the potential for a new order to rise from the ashes. Their mission was clear: to establish an Illuminati stronghold and spread the "Light" of knowledge across the Mediterranean.

Their first act was to locate a suitable base of operations. Tiberius, ever the strategist, had his eyes on an old church that had once been a bastion of power for the Iron Hand. It lay in ruins, a testament to the society's decline. With the help of the repurposed Builders of the New Dawn, they set to work renovating the structure, transforming it into a beacon of Illuminati influence. It would serve as their headquarters, a place where they could safely communicate with Augustus and the society's leaders in Rome.

Their arrival had not gone unnoticed. The Cretan elite, a mix of old-world tradition and nascent curiosity, watched the newcomers with a blend of suspicion and intrigue. Tiberius knew that to conquer hearts and minds, he must tread carefully. He set out to identify those who might be swayed by the Illuminati's ideals, crafting his recruitment strategies around the island's cultural fabric.

The first to join were the scholars and philosophers, men and women whose thirst for knowledge had long been stifled by the Iron Hand's oppressive rule. They saw in the Illuminati a chance to breathe new life into their studies, to explore the world beyond the confines of their island. Through clandestine meetings and the promise of access to the society's vast archives, Tiberius grew the ranks of the Illuminati in Crete, one mind at a time.

The public relations campaign orchestrated by Aurelius and Claudia was a masterstroke. They spoke of Rome's grandeur, its innovations in engineering and governance, painting a picture of a city bathed in the "Light" of enlightenment. Their words resonated with the Cretan populace, weary of the Iron Hand's tyranny and eager for change. They promised a new age of prosperity and understanding, one where the "Builders of the New Dawn" would remake the world in the image of their enlightened city.

Yet, not all were swayed by their oratory. Some, clinging to the old ways, saw the Illuminati as a foreign invader, a threat to their traditions. But so many had gone without their whole lives, abundance like they have in Rome was too inticing.

In the heart of Crete, a clandestine assembly of Iron Hand loyalists plotted their counterattack. The ruins of their former stronghold had been defiled by the Illuminati's touch, and they vowed to reclaim what was once theirs. Their leader, a stoic Cretan named Ariadne, had studied the art of war and knew that the society's power was not invincible. Her eyes gleamed with a fierce determination as she rallied her followers, speaking of the "Shadow" that had once protected the island and could do so again.

Meanwhile, in Rome, the Senate grew increasingly nervous of the Illuminati's growing influence. They watched the society's expansion to Crete with a mix of fascination and dread. Some saw it as a power play, an attempt to create a new Rome beyond their control. Others, like Seneca, feared that the Illuminati's hunger for power could consume them all, and that the Senate's days as Rome's true rulers were numbered.

Seneca approached Augustus with his concerns, urging caution. "Your Highness," he said, his voice low and measured, "the Illuminati's power is like a river. It can bring life to the parched earth, but if unchecked, it can also flood the lands and destroy what we hold dear." Augustus, ever the pragmatist, nodded thoughtfully. He knew that the Senate was a fickle beast, but he also knew that their fear could be used to his advantage.

In response to the Senate's unease, Augustus announced a series of public works projects, funded by the Illuminati's wealth. The city's crumbling infrastructure would be repaired, new schools and libraries built, and the arts would flourish. It was a shrewd move, one that placated the Senate and won the hearts of the people. Yet, it was clear that this was not enough to sate the Illuminati's ambition. They needed a grander stage, a new frontier to conquer.

And so, with the Senate's reluctant blessing, Augustus dispatched a delegation to the distant lands of Egypt. Their mission: to establish trade routes, forge alliances, and spread the "Light" of the Illuminati. Tiberius, ever eager to prove his worth, was placed in charge of this ambitious endeavor. His cunning and diplomatic skills would be tested to the limits as he navigated the complex web of Egyptian politics.

The journey to Egypt was fraught with danger, the deserts and seas teeming with bandits and pirates. Yet, Tiberius and his entourage pressed on, driven by the promise of wealth and power that awaited them.

Once in Egypt, Tiberius quickly established a base of operations within the bustling city of Alexandria. The grandeur of the ancient world's greatest library inspired him, and he vowed to surpass it with an Illuminati archive that would rival the ancients'. His charm and wit won over the local scholars and o cials, who were eager to ally themselves with the enigmatic society that had transformed Rome.

Aurelius and Claudia, however, found the Cretan landscape less welcoming. The scars of the Iron Hand's rule were still fresh, and the people were wary of outsiders. They set to work rebuilding the old church with a mix of excitement and trepidation. The structure, once a bastion of darkness, would now be a beacon of the Illuminati's "Light." The labor was backbreaking, but the promise of a new dawn spurred them on.

Under Aurelius' watchful eye, the church began to take shape, its stones rearranged by the skilled hands of the Builders of the New Dawn. The once-mighty edifice stood as a stark reminder of the Iron Hand's fall and the Illuminati's rise. The labor was grueling, but with each passing day, the structure grew more magnificent, a beacon of the society's influence over the island.

Tiberius, ever the tactician, worked tirelessly to establish a network of safe houses and secret meeting spots throughout the Alexandria. His charm and cunning won over the local elite and intellectuals, who saw in the Illuminati a chance to break free from the Iron Hand's yoke. He spoke to them of the "Roman model," a society built on knowledge and innovation, where freedom of thought reigned supreme. His words resonated with the Cretan scholars, who had long su ered under the Iron Hand's oppressive regime.

The public relations campaign spearheaded by Aurelius and Claudia was a masterful display of oratory and diplomacy. They traversed the island, speaking to the masses of Rome's grandeur and the wonders that awaited Crete under the Illuminati's guiding hand. They promised an era of prosperity and enlightenment, where the "Shadow" of the Iron Hand would be replaced by the "Light" of the Illuminati. Their message was met with both hope and skepticism, yet the allure of Rome's advancements was undeniable.

As the society's influence grew, so too did the whispers of a "new age." The Cretan economy began to shift, with trade routes opening and goods flowing in from across the Mediterranean. The ports welcomed the new goods and people to the now alive island.

The Senate in Rome watched these developments with a mix of pride and trepidation. The Illuminati's power had been a double-edged sword, bringing both stability and fear. Some whispered of a Rome that had strayed too far from its roots, others saw it as a natural evolution. Yet, all knew that the society's influence was expanding beyond their control.

The public relations campaign continued with Aurelius and Claudia at the forefront. They traversed the island, their words weaving a tapestry of hope and progress. They spoke of the "Roman model," a society where knowledge was power, and freedom of thought was the cornerstone of governance. Their eloquence painted a picture of a world where the "Shadow" of the Iron Hand had been vanquished by the light of the brotherhood.

Their speeches resonated with the Cretan scholars, who had su ered under the Iron Hand's oppressive regime. These intellectuals saw in the Illuminati the potential for a renaissance of their own culture. Yet, the local traditions ran deep, and not all were willing to embrace the change. The Senate, though skeptical, recognized the value in an alliance with Crete and allowed the society to operate with a degree of autonomy.

The spread of the Illuminati's influence was not without its challenges. While some Cretan elite were eager to align themselves with the society's ideals others refused to join and didnt welcome change.

Tiberius knew that to truly conquer Egypt, he had to win the hearts and minds of its people. He tailored his recruitment methods to appeal to the local culture, hosting grand feasts and scholarly debates that showcased the Illuminati's wealth and knowledge. His charm and wit disarmed even the most skeptical of Egyptians, and soon enough, he had gathered a following of influential thinkers and politicians. These new recruits were eager to bring the "Roman model" to their own lands, seeing it as a path to prosperity and enlightenment .

Aurelius and Claudia, on the other hand, faced a more formidable challenge in Crete. The Iron Hand's legacy had left deep scars, and the Cretan elite was divided. Some were drawn to the Illuminati's promises of knowledge and power, while others clung to the traditional ways. They knew that the key to their success lay in identifying potential members among the elite and intellectuals, those whose influence could sway the tide of public opinion.

They tailored their approach, hosting discreet gatherings in the newly restored church. The walls echoed with debates on philosophy, science, and governance, the air thick with the scent of ink and parchment. Aurelius and Claudia listened intently, identifying those who thirsted for a new order, who were tired of the Iron Hand's tyranny. They spoke of Rome's advancements in art and engineering, of the Senate's wisdom and the "Light" that guided the Illuminati.

Their words were met with a mix of awe and skepticism, but the seeds of curiosity had been sown.

The public relations campaign grew in sophistication, with Aurelius and Claudia crafting speeches that resonated with the Cretan elite and intellectuals. They spoke of a world where knowledge and innovation reigned supreme, where the "steam horse" would connect distant lands as never before. The concept of a train and rail system, powered by steam, was a marvel that captured the imagination of those who yearned for progress. They painted a picture of a future where goods and ideas traveled swiftly, knitting the empire closer together.

Tiberius's success in Egypt was not lost on the Illuminati elders in Rome. They recognized the strategic importance of the region and its riches. With the Senate's blessing, they began to plan the construction of a grand library in Alexandria, one that would surpass even the great library of their sister city. This would serve as a bastion of Illuminati power, a beacon of the "Light" that would draw scholars from across the known world.

Back in Crete, the Illuminati's presence grew more pronounced. The once-desolate streets now bustled with the sounds of construction and the chatter of eager minds. Aurelius and Claudia had identified several influential Cretans who shared their vision for a new age. These new recruits were influential in their own right, bringing with them networks of supporters and resources that bolstered the Illuminati's cause.

The public relations campaign grew bolder with each passing week. Aurelius and Claudia traveled from city to city, speaking to crowds that grew larger with every visit. They regaled the people with tales of Rome's grandeur and the wonders of steam power. The concept of a train, a "steam horse," that could pull heavy loads and travel at unprecedented speeds captured the imagination of the Cretan populace. They painted a vivid picture of a future where the island was connected to the vast Roman world, where goods and ideas flowed freely, and where the "Shadow" of ignorance had been vanquished by the "Light" of progress.

The Illuminati's influence grew stronger as they recruited more members from the Cretan elite. Each new recruit brought with them a wealth of knowledge and connections, further entwining the society into the fabric of the island's power structure. Yet, for every victory, there were challenges. Resistance grew among those who feared the loss of traditional Cretan culture and the Senate's grip on power. They saw the "Roman model" as a Trojan horse, threatening to overshadow their own traditions and autonomy.

Their speeches grew more nuanced, weaving the threads of Roman innovation with the rich tapestry of Cretan heritage. They assured the crowds that the "steam horse" was not a tool of subjugation but a bridge to a brighter future. The concept of a train and rail system, powered by steam, was a revelation that piqued the interest of many. It promised to revolutionize trade and travel, bringing the distant lands of the empire closer together.

The Illuminati's plan to introduce the steam powered train was met with a mix of amazement and skepticism. Some in the Cretan elite were intrigued by the prospect of modernization, seeing it as a way to secure their own power and wealth. Others, more cautious, feared that such advancements would only serve to tighten Rome's grip on their island.

Aurelius and Claudia identified these potential allies through meticulous social engineering. They hosted opulent banquets and intellectual soirees, using their charm and wit to seduce the curious and the ambitious. They tailored their message to each guest, speaking of the "Roman model" as a means to revitalize Crete's ailing economy and restore its cultural luster. The concept of a steam-powered locomotive, a "steed of iron and fire," that could race across the land faster than any horse, captured the imagination of those who yearned for progress.

Their public relations campaign grew more sophisticated with each passing day. They took to the streets, delivering speeches that showcased Rome's advancements in technology and governance. They promised that the "steam horse" would not only revolutionize trade but also bring the enlightenment of Rome to the farthest reaches of the empire. The crowds grew larger, drawn by the allure of a world where knowledge and power were intertwined, and where progress was a tangible, attainable goal.

But the path to power was not without its thorns. An old Cretan senator, Demetrius, emerged as their most vocal critic. He clung to the traditional ways, fearing the Illuminati's influence would erode the very essence of Cretan identity. His words resonated with those who were wary of the "Shadow" that had once plagued them, now dressed in the guise of the "Light."

In response to the growing resistance, Aurelius called for the first public debate. He knew that his eloquence and the power of his vision could win over the undecided. The event was held in the heart of the city, where the ruins of the old Iron Hand stronghold now stood as a testament to the Illuminati's triumph. The air was electric with anticipation, the crowd a sea of faces, some hopeful, others skeptical.

Demetrius, a Cretan senator, stepped forward as the voice of tradition. His deep, resonant voice spoke of the "Shadow" that had once been their oppressor and the "Light" that now threatened to consume them. He warned of the dangers of embracing the unknown, of the potential loss of Cretan identity in the face of Roman progress.

Aurelius listened, his eyes never leaving Demetrius' face. When it was his turn to speak, he approached the podium with a calm resolve. He acknowledged the fears of the crowd but spoke passionately of the "steam horse," the locomotive that would unite Crete with Rome, bringing wealth and knowledge to their shores. He promised that the Illuminati's "Light" would not destroy but enhance Cretan culture, creating a new era of prosperity and understanding.

The debate was a turning point for the Illuminati's cause in Crete. Aurelius's words, filled with passion and a clear vision for the future, resonated with the people. They saw in him not just a Roman envoy, but a leader who understood their struggles and aspired to uplift them. The concept of the "steam horse" became a symbol of hope and progress, and the once skeptical crowd began to murmur in approval.

In the wake of the debate, the Illuminati's popularity grew. Cretans flocked to their meetings, eager to hear more about the "Roman model" and the wonders it could bring. Aurelius and Claudia worked tirelessly, addressing local concerns and emphasizing the society's commitment to preserving Cretan culture. They promised that the steam train would not just be a tool for Roman domination but a bridge connecting Crete to the wider world, bringing with it the riches of knowledge and trade.

The economic and cultural shifts began to take shape as the Illuminati's influence grew. The city bustled with new construction projects, and the ports saw an influx of goods and ideas from across the Mediterranean. The local economy boomed, and the once-impoverished populace saw their fortunes rise. Yet, the whispers of a "new age" brought with them a sense of unease. Some Cretans feared that their ancient ways would be lost in the rush to embrace the modern world. But welcomed the abundance flowing in.

The first election for the position of Crete's mayor was a tense a air. Aurelius faced a stoic opponent, Philoctetes, a man whose gray hair and furrowed brow bore the weight of years spent upholding the old ways. His voice trembled with the passion of a man fighting to preserve the very essence of his homeland. Yet, Aurelius's oratory shone with the promise of a future that would not only preserve but elevate Cretan culture.

The crowd listened intently as Aurelius laid out his vision for Crete's integration into the Roman world. He spoke of the "steam horse," a marvel of engineering that would transform their lives, bringing goods and ideas from distant lands. His words painted a picture of a Cretan renaissance, a rebirth fueled by the Illuminati's "Light." The air was thick with anticipation as the people weighed the potential gains against the fear of losing their identity.

The election was a pivotal moment for Crete. The ballots were cast, and the results were tallied under the vigilant eyes of both the Illuminati and the Iron Hand loyalists. The tension was palpable as the town crier announced Aurelius as the new mayor, a victory won not just by his eloquence but by the promise of progress that the steam train represented. The crowd erupted in cheers, drowning out the whispers of the old guard.

The economic and cultural shifts that followed were undeniable. The Illuminati's influence spread like wildfire, bringing with it a wave of innovation and prosperity. Yet, the whispers of a "new age" were met with a mix of excitement and apprehension. Some Cretans embraced the change eagerly, eager to leave the shadow of the Iron Hand behind and step into the "Light" of progress. Others clung to their traditions, fearful that the very fabric of their society was being torn apart by the relentless march of "Romanization."

Under Aurelius's leadership, the construction of the steam train's infrastructure began. The sight of the great iron beasts grew more frequent, their fiery breath and mechanical roars a testament to the power of human ingenuity. The project was a monumental task, requiring the labor of hundreds and the cooperation of the entire island. Yet, the promise of prosperity and progress was a siren's call that few could resist.

The economic boom brought on by the Illuminati's initiatives was undeniable. The ports of Crete grew busier than ever before, filled with ships from distant lands eager to trade with the enlightened island. The streets were lined with new shops and markets, and the clang of hammers and the whirl of machinery became the island's new heartbeat. The people of Crete, once mired in poverty, now had a glimpse of a future filled with wealth and opportunity.

Culturally, the shifts were more subtle but equally profound. The Illuminati sponsored schools and academies, filling the minds of the young with the wisdom of Rome. The arts flourished under their patronage, with new sculptures and frescoes adorning the city walls. Yet, the old ways were not entirely forgotten. The society's leaders, including Aurelius, were careful to blend Roman innovation with Cretan tradition, creating a unique fusion that was both a source of pride and a point of contention.

The news of Aurelius' victory in Crete reached Rome's ears with a mix of excitement and skepticism. Augustus, ever the strategist, saw the potential in the island's resources and its strategic location. Yet, he was wary of the Illuminati's growing power and the burden it placed on Rome's stretched resources. He knew that the Senate would be watching closely, their concerns about the society's ambitions and influence growing with each new victory.

Seneca, the wise and cautious adviser, urged Augustus to tread carefully. He reminded the king that the Illuminati's true strength lay in their secrecy and unity. To expand too quickly, to overreach, could expose them to dangers they had not anticipated. Augustus, however, saw the potential in Aurelius' victory. He knew that to secure Rome's future, they must expand their influence, and Crete was but the first stepping stone in a grander vision.

In the Senate, some were thrilled by the prospect of a stronger, more prosperous empire, while others feared the Illuminati's growing power. They debated late into the night, their voices echoing through the marble halls. The Senate was divided, and the tension was palpable. Some questioned the cost of such rapid expansion, while others saw the strategic advantage of controlling the Mediterranean's vital trade routes. Yet, amidst the discord, a consensus grew that the Illuminati's influence must be monitored.

On Crete, the completion of the "Steam Horse" project was met with awe and anticipation. The gleaming locomotive, a testament to Roman engineering, stood proudly on the newly laid tracks, its metallic body reflecting the Cretan sun. The air was filled with the scent of coal and oil, a stark contrast to the olive groves and sea breeze that once dominated the landscape. The local population gathered around the train, whispering in hushed tones about the magic that would soon move them faster than any horse had ever dreamed.

The inaugural journey of the first train on Crete was an event of unparalleled excitement. Aurelius, as mayor, presided over the ceremony, his heart swelling with pride as the engine roared to life. The crowd watched in amazement as the "steam horse" began to move, chugging steadily along the track, leaving a plume of smoke in its wake. The train's whistle pierced the air, and children cheered, running alongside as it picked up speed. The sight was nothing short of a marvel, a symbol of the Illuminati's promise made real before their eyes.

The Grand Celebration that followed was a spectacle that drew visitors from far and wide. The city was adorned with banners and lights, and the air was filled with the scents of roasting meats and exotic spices. Senators and dignitaries from Rome had made the journey to witness the unveiling, and their speeches were filled with praise for the society's ingenuity and foresight. Among them, Tiberius had arrived from Egypt, bringing news of his own successes and o ering his congratulations to Aurelius and Claudia.

The festivities were a showcase of Roman culture and Cretan hospitality. Musicians played lively tunes as acrobats danced and twirled through the streets. The people of Crete mingled with the Romans, sharing stories and laughter, their fears of the "Shadow" momentarily forgotten. The Illuminati's influence was clearly in the island.

Local leaders took the stage, their words interwoven with subtle nods to the society's philosophy. They spoke of unity and progress, the "steam horse" as a symbol of a shared destiny. Among them, Aurelius and Claudia's voices were the loudest, praising the Illuminati's guidance and the wisdom of Augustus. Their speeches were met with applause and cheers, the crowd captivated by the promise of a better tomorrow.

The celebrations were not just for show; they were a declaration of intent. The Illuminati had planted its flag on Crete, and their sights were set on the rest of the island. The influx of curious visitors from other lands brought a buzz of excitement and a blend of diverse cultures. Envoys from distant lands came to marvel at the "steam horse" and to seek alliances with the society that had brought such a marvel to life. They saw in the Illuminati not just a political force but a catalyst for change that could reshape the world.

The local leaders took to the stage, their speeches a harmonious blend of Cretan pride and Roman ambition. They talked of unity, of the "steam horse" as a symbol of their shared destiny. Among them, Aurelius and Claudia's voices were the most persuasive, praising the Illuminati's enlightenment and the wisdom of Augustus. Each word was carefully chosen, each gesture deliberate, as they wove a narrative of hope and progress that resonated with the gathered crowd. The applause and cheers that followed were not just for the show but for the promise of a brighter future.

With the successful debut of the "Steam Horse," the local leaders of Crete, many of them secretly sworn to the Illuminati's cause, took to the stage. Their speeches, resonating with the spirit of the society's enlightenment, painted a picture of a united future. They outlined ambitious plans to lay down a sprawling network of railways that would crisscross the entire island, connecting its distant corners and fostering a new era of prosperity. The economic impact was clear; goods would flow more freely, trade would flourish, and opportunities would abound.

But the true intent of these speeches went beyond mere infrastructure. They were a declaration of the Illuminati's hidden hand in shaping Crete's destiny. Each word was chosen to instill a sense of awe and loyalty towards the society and its Roman benefactors. The speakers spoke of unity, progress, and the power of knowledge— themes that were the very essence of the Illuminati's doctrine. The crowd, intoxicated by the grandeur of the moment, hung on every syllable, their hearts swelling with hope for the future.

The Illuminati's influence grew more pronounced as the railway system expanded. The once-remote regions of Crete were now within reach, and with each new stretch of track, the society's "Light" pushed back the shadows of ignorance and superstition. The economic impact was immediate and profound. Goods that once took weeks to transport by sea or donkey could now be shipped across the island in a matter of hours. The prices of commodities dropped, and the markets swelled with exotic goods from Egypt and beyond.

Society was transformed as well. The "steam horse"

The construction of the railway system across Crete was a herculean task, but one that Aurelius and Claudia approached with unbridled enthusiasm. The Illuminati had laid the groundwork for a network that would not only unite the island under their banner but also serve as a beacon of progress to the wider world. As the iron tracks stretched from the coastal cities into the heart of the island, so too did the society's influence. The once-distant regions of Crete grew closer, their cultures intertwining as people from all walks of life boarded the trains to explore the new opportunities that lay before them.

But the Illuminati's ambitions did not stop at the island's shores. During the height of the celebrations, Aurelius made a stunning announcement that sent ripples through the Mediterranean. He declared their intention to build a bridge connecting Crete to Africa, a monumental feat of engineering that would stand as a testament to Rome's power and the society's ingenuity. The crowd gasped in amazement, their eyes wide with wonder as they imagined a world where the continents were no longer separated by vast stretches of sea.

The proposal was met with a mix of excitement and skepticism. The Senate in Rome was torn between admiration for the audacity of the plan and fear of the resources it would require. The Iron Hand loyalists, sensing a weakness in the Illuminati's grand narrative, began to spread whispers of madness and hubris. Yet, the people of Crete, having witnessed the "steam horse" come to life, dared to believe that even such an impossible dream could be realized under Aurelius' leadership.

The planning for the bridge was a monumental undertaking, requiring the finest minds of Rome and Crete to come together. Architects and engineers were summoned to Aurelius' side, and the great library of Alexandria was opened to them, o ering its vast wealth of knowledge to fuel their designs. The bridge was to be a marvel of the age, a fusion of Roman grandeur and Cretan innovation that would stand as a gateway to a new era of trade and cultural exchange.

The design that emerged was breathtaking: a colossal arch of gleaming stone and steel that would span the narrowest point between the two lands. It would be a symbol of Rome's dominion over nature itself, a bridge that would unite the continents and usher in a new age of prosperity for all who lived under the Illuminati's "Light." The project was to be named "The Bridge of Unity," a name that spoke to the hearts of many Cretans who yearned for a future free from the shackles of the Iron Hand's tyranny.

But as the excitement grew, so too did the whispers of dissent. Some Cretan elders, wary of the rapid pace of change, saw the bridge as an a ront to the gods, a challenge to the natural order of the world. They warned of divine retribution and the loss of their island's sacred autonomy. Others, influenced by the Iron Hand's rhetoric, feared that the bridge would be a gateway for Roman legions, and used as an avanue of war.

The Illuminati could not ignore these voices. The nights grew tense as whispers of dissent grew louder. Aurelius knew that if not addressed, the fear and mistrust could fracture the fragile alliances they had forged. He called upon his most trusted agents to identify the ringleaders of the opposition, those who sought to cast shadows on the society's grand design. One by one, these naysayers began to vanish, their fates unknown. The streets of Crete grew quieter, the talks of doubt were silenced by the cold hand of the night.

The sudden disappearance of the dissenters sent a clear message: question the Illuminati at your own peril. The methodical extermination of opposition was swift and merciless. Each dawn revealed a new absence, a reminder of the power that now ruled the island. The Cretan people looked over their shoulders, their whispers of doubt now replaced by hushed tones of fear. The "Light" of progress had a darker side, one that was willing to snu out any candle that dared to challenge it.

The Senate in Rome, hearing the chilling reports, debated the morality of Aurelius' actions. Some argued that the end justified the means, that a few sacrifices were necessary for the greater good. Others, like Seneca, voiced concerns about the society's descent into tyranny. Augustus, ever the pragmatist, recognized the need for swift and decisive action but also knew that fear could not be the foundation of their empire. He dispatched a letter to Aurelius, advising caution and reminding him of the delicate balance between power and consent.

The nights on Crete grew colder, the shadows darker, as the Illuminati's grip tightened. The once-lively streets now echoed with the clank of soldiers' armor and the hiss of torches. The citizens spoke in hushed tones, their eyes darting nervously as they went about their business. The "Bridge of Unity" had become a symbol of fear rather than hope, a stark reminder of the power that the Illuminati wielded.

Amidst this tension, a new player emerged. A charismatic young man named Theseus, claiming to be the voice of the Cretan people, began to rally the masses. His speeches were filled with tales of Minotaurs and labyrinths, of ancient heroes who had faced darkness and triumphed.

Theseus spoke of a di erent kind of unity—one that didn't require the imposition of foreign gods or the erasure of Crete's heritage. He called for elections, for a true voice of the people to be heard in the governance of their land. His words resonated with the traditionalists, who saw in him a champion against the Illuminati's relentless march towards a homogenized world.

The bridge's construction continued, a silent testament to the Illuminati's determination. Each stone laid, each rivet hammered into place, brought the two continents closer together, but it also seemed to widen the chasm between the society and the people they sought to enlighten. The once eager workers now toiled under the watchful eyes of Roman guards, their enthusiasm replaced by a grim sense of duty.

The Cretan people grew restless, their whispers of dissent swelling into a roar that could no longer be silenced. They demanded a say in their future, a voice in the halls of power that had been taken from them. The Illuminati's shadow had grown too long, and the light of democracy began to pierce through the cracks.

The Senate in Rome took note of Theseus' growing popularity, and whispers of rebellion reached Augustus' ears. He knew that to maintain their grip on Crete, they needed to act swiftly. Yet, he was torn between his faith in Aurelius and the fear of losing the very hearts and minds they sought to win.

The Senate dispatched a delegation to Crete, ostensibly to oversee the bridge's progress but primarily to assess the situation and quell the rising unrest. The delegation included influential figures from various factions, among them was Tiberius, who had grown wary of Aurelius' methods and wished to gauge the people's true feelings. As the "Steam Horse" chugged along the railways, ferrying the Roman o cials, the tension in the air was palpable.

Theseus, now a formidable force, capitalized on the discontent. His impassioned orations grew more frequent, his calls for elections resonating with the Cretan's desire for self-determination. The Illuminati's bridge, once a symbol of unity, now loomed as a harbinger of Roman dominance. The society's agents observed the swelling crowds with growing unease, their whispers of dissent now amplified into a collective voice demanding change.

Amidst the political maelstrom, the bridge's construction progressed at a glacial pace. Each stone laid was a silent negotiation, a testament to the Illuminati's steadfast belief in their vision. Yet, the Cretan workforce grew increasingly restless, their eyes drawn to the horizon where Theseus' flag fluttered proudly, a beacon of hope and resistance. The "Bridge of Unity" had become a battleground of ideologies, with every hammer stroke echoing the clamor for democracy.

As the delegation arrived in the heart of Crete, the tension boiled over. A public assembly was called, and Theseus stepped forth, his eyes ablaze with conviction. He addressed the people, speaking of the sanctity of their traditions and the importance of their voice in shaping their destiny. The crowd roared its approval, and the demand for elections grew into a deafening crescendo. The Illuminati's influence, once so pervasive, now faced a formidable challenge from a man who embodied the very spirit they sought to suppress.

The Roman o cials, caught in the crossfire, found themselves in a precarious position. To support Theseus was to defy the Illuminati, yet to silence the people's call was to invite rebellion. Tiberius, ever the pragmatist, recognized the shifting tides and the need to adapt. He approached Aurelius, his expression a mask of neutrality, and spoke of the inevitable: the Cretans' desire for a say in their own governance could no longer be ignored.

The Illuminati leaders gathered in a hushed chamber, the air thick with tension. The whispers of the Senate's concerns had reached their ears, and they knew they could no longer ignore the Cretan people's growing unrest. Reluctantly, they conceded to the idea of holding elections, a concept foreign to their manipulation-driven society. The decision was made: Tiberius, the voice of Rome and the Illuminati's chosen representative, would face Theseus, the charismatic leader of the Cretan uprising, in a bid to control the booming island hub.

The stage was set for a political showdown that would shake the very foundations of the Illuminati's dominion. The election campaigns were a flurry of passionate speeches and grand promises, each side vying for the people's trust. Tiberius, the stoic Roman with the Illuminati's backing, promised stability and protection under the society's enlightened rule. Theseus, the fiery Cretan, o ered the sweet taste of freedom and a return to the island's storied heritage.

The day of the elections dawned, the air thick with anticipation. The people of Crete gathered in the grand amphitheater, their voices a cacophony of hope and uncertainty. The Illuminati's agents were everywhere, their eyes watching, their ears listening, ensuring that the "correct" message was heard. Yet, the whispers of Theseus' words had spread like wildfire, and the air was electric with the scent of change.

The debate between Tiberius and Theseus was a spectacle that drew the eyes of the entire island. Each man stood tall, their words echoing through the ancient amphitheater, each seeking to sway the hearts of the Cretan people. Tiberius spoke of Rome's grandeur and the protection it o ered under the Illuminati's guidance, while Theseus painted a picture of a Crete that could stand proudly as an equal, not a conquered territory. The crowd listened with bated breath, their allegiances swaying like a ship on a stormy sea.

The day of the election was a tapestry of anticipation and suspense. As the sun dipped below the horizon, casting long shadows across the voting booths, the Illuminati elders gathered in an alcove, their faces a mix of excitement and trepidation. They knew the outcome could swing either way, and with it, the fate of their control over the island. The votes were counted with meticulous care, each tally whispered with the weight of destiny.

When the final count was announced, the crowd erupted. Theseus had won by a landslide, his message of freedom and cultural preservation resonating with the Cretan people. The Illuminati elders watched from the shadows, their faces a mix of surprise and dismay. The cheers grew louder as Theseus took the stage, his eyes shining with triumph.

The young leader raised his hands, and the crowd fell silent. He spoke of his vision for Crete, a place where the old and new could coexist, where the wisdom of the ancients would guide the innovations of tomorrow. His words were met with thunderous applause, the echoes bouncing o the amphitheater's stones.

But amidst the jubilation, a cold reality set in. The Illuminati had not lost without a fight. As Theseus' victory celebration reached its peak, a group of elders, their faces etched with the weight of their decision, approached the new leader. They led him to an empty chamber, the grandeur of the amphitheater giving way to the starkness of shadows and silence.

There, they o ered him a chalice filled with a golden liquid—the symbol of their power and the price of his newfound authority. The room grew tense as the elders explained the unspoken truth: while the people had chosen him, the Illuminati remained the puppeteers in the shadows. They o ered him a deal, one that would secure his rule but bind him to their will. Drink the "golden juice," they said, and he would have their support, ensuring stability and protection for Crete. Refuse, or he would face the same fate as the opposition they had so e ciently silenced.

Theseus's heart raced as he stared into the chalice. The taste of victory was bittersweet, and he knew the price of power all too well. Yet, he had not fought for personal gain but for the freedom of his people. He took a deep breath, his hand trembling slightly as he raised the chalice to his lips. The golden liquid, a symbol of the Illuminati's dominion, was both a promise and a threat.

The elders watched him intently, their expressions unreadable. As the chalice emptied, the room grew still. Theseus felt a strange warmth spread through his veins, a sensation that was both comforting and unsettling. He knew he had made a pact with the shadows, but for now, the cheers of the Cretan people drowned out any misgiving.

The Illuminati had underestimated Theseus. His victory was not a mere political triumph but a declaration of intent. He would rule Crete, not as their pawn but as a leader who would blend the society's ideals with the island's spirit. The whispers grew louder, the whispers of those who had been silenced, and Theseus knew that he had to tread carefully.

The days that followed the election were a dance of diplomacy and strategy. Theseus met with Tiberius, their conversations a delicate dance of words and unspoken threats. Each man knew the other's strengths and weaknesses, and both were acutely aware of the power dynamics that had shifted beneath their feet. The Illuminati had made their intentions clear: they would support Theseus's rule, but at a cost .

Tiberius, ever the strategist, had already begun laying the groundwork for the Illuminati's African foothold. In the newly conquered territories, he held covert meetings with influential figures, planting the seeds of their ideology in fertile minds. His approach was subtle yet persuasive, speaking of unity and enlightenment in a way that resonated with the local leaders hungry for power and knowledge. Meanwhile, Vulcan's military campaigns provided the perfect cover for Tiberius's clandestine operations, ensuring that the society's influence grew in lockstep with Rome's territorial gains.

Upon his appointment as Mayor of Cairo, Tiberius faced the challenge of balancing his o cial duties with his secret agenda. The city was a bustling metropolis, a tapestry of cultures and allegiances, and his every move was scrutinized by both the Roman authorities and the nascent Illuminati network. He worked tirelessly to implement subtle changes, weaving the society's threads through the fabric of the city without alerting the people of any danger. His main change was members being in the open wearin the badge of the illuminati with honor.

The Illuminati's influence grew steadily. Their symbols began to appear in local businesses, a silent declaration of allegiance to the society. Secret meeting places and safe houses were established, nestled within the city's ancient walls, a testament to their growing numbers and reach. New recruits were drawn in, their curiosity piqued by whispers of enlightenment and power. These were not just Romans but Africans too, eager to be part of a movement that promised a brighter future.

Tiberius, the Mayor of Cairo, walked the tightrope of his dual roles with finesse. His public persona was one of a benevolent leader, bringing order and Roman wisdom to the city. Yet, behind closed doors, he cultivated a network of like-minded individuals who shared his vision for a world guided by the Illuminati's light. His policies, while ostensibly for the city's good, were carefully designed to align with the society's goals, ensuring their influence remained unseen but deeply felt.

The Illuminati's African branch grew stronger, with Tiberius's strategic maneuvering laying the foundation for their foothold. His covert meetings with influential Africans bore fruit as they embraced the society's vision for a progressive future. He whispered sweet nothings of power and enlightenment into their ears, and they listened with rapt attention, hungry for a narrative that o ered them more than the Roman yoke.

In Cairo, Tiberius's appointment as Mayor was met with a mix of curiosity and suspicion. The people knew him as the stoic Roman who had stood by Augustus during the tumultuous times of the Game of Shadows. Yet, beneath his stern exterior, they sensed a di erent kind of fire, one that didn't burn with the same fervor for Rome's traditional values. He moved through the city with purpose, his eyes always watching, his mind always planning. The Illuminati's influence grew like a vine, wrapping itself around the ancient structures of governance, steadily entwining itself in the very fabric of Egyptian society.

As the society's power grew, so too did its visibility. Illuminati symbols began to appear in marketplaces and on the walls of wealthy estates, a silent declaration of the new order. Secret meeting places were established, hidden in plain sight among the ancient ruins and bustling bazaars. The whispers grew bolder, and the society's influence began to permeate the very essence of African culture.

Tiberius, now the Mayor of Cairo, was the linchpin of this burgeoning network. His public persona was that of a just and fair leader, implementing Roman law and order with a firm but kind hand. Yet, in the shadows, he worked tirelessly to ensure that the Illuminati's ideology took root. His appointments to key positions within the city were strategic, placing trusted members of the society in roles where they could subtly influence policy and perception.

The Illuminati's African branch grew in numbers and strength. Tiberius had a knack for finding young, ambitious leaders who were disillusioned with their traditional roles in society. He o ered them a path to power and knowledge, one that didn't require them to abandon their heritage but instead, to embrace it.

In the quiet of the night, Tiberius called together his most trusted African recruits. They gathered in a hidden chamber, the air thick with the scent of incense and the whispers of secrets. He spoke to them of the society's grand design, of how their continent could be the birthplace of a new era of enlightenment. They listened with rapt attention, their eyes reflecting the flickering candlelight, as he outlined a hierarchical structure that would mirror the Illuminati's Roman counterpart. Each was given a role, a title, and a mission to spread the society's ideals.

The African branch of the Illuminati grew in power and sophistication. Tiberius understood that to truly integrate the society into the fabric of African culture, he had to adapt their teachings. He blended Roman wisdom with local traditions, creating a synthesis that resonated with the people. Their symbol, the All-Seeing Eye, was incorporated into traditional art and architecture, becoming a beacon of progress and unity rather than a symbol of oppression.

Tiberius established a hierarchy that mirrored the Roman structure but allowed for local customs and practices. He appointed leaders from various African tribes and cities, ensuring that the Illuminati's influence stretched across the continent. These leaders were not just figureheads; they were true believers, chosen for their charisma and their ability to inspire change. They were the society's eyes and ears, reporting back to Rome through secure, encrypted messages.

Regular communication with the Roman headquarters was crucial for maintaining unity and strategic coordination. Messengers traveled along the expanding railway network, delivering dispatches filled with updates and requests for guidance. Financial support flowed from Rome through covert channels, funding infrastructure projects that not only improved the lives of Africans but also served as a showcase for Roman innovation and engineering prowess.

The society's investments in Africa were not just for show. Tiberius knew that a self-sustaining financial network was key to their long-term success. They funneled funds into agriculture, education, and technology, empowering the continent while subtly embedding their ideals. As the months turned into years, the Illuminati's presence in Africa grew stronger, a testament to Tiberius's leadership and the society's adaptability.

The Roman Senate, though aware of the Illuminati's growing influence, turned a blind eye to their activities. Their focus was on maintaining the peace and expanding their empire, and Tiberius had proven himself a capable and loyal servant of Rome. Yet, whispers of a new power began to reach the ears of the Senate, whispers of an enlightened order that transcended borders and traditional allegiances.

In Cairo, the Illuminati's African headquarters, the society's influence was palpable. Their leaders were revered, their meetings a mix of ancient ritual and futuristic strategy. They held the balance between Rome's iron grip and the continent's yearning for self-determination. The local leaders who had been handpicked by Tiberius grew in power and influence, their loyalty to the society unshakeable.

Vulcan's troops, once feared conquerors, had been rebranded as protectors of the peace, their red cloaks now a symbol of order and stability. Under Tiberius's command, they had become the Illuminati's enforcers, ensuring that the society's will was done without raising suspicion of Rome's true intentions. The conquered lands were transformed into showcases of Roman innovation and Illuminati enlightenment, with grand temples and gleaming palaces that served as beacons of a new, unified continent.

The society's reach stretched from the sands of Egypt to the jungles of Nubia, the hand of the Illuminati ever present in the lives of the conquered. Vulcan's legions, now back in Ciaro, marched under the banner of unity and progress. Their crimson cloaks had become a beacon of hope and order amidst the chaos of change. The continent was a chessboard, and Tiberius played his pieces with the precision of a grandmaster.

On a day that would be etched in the annals of history, Tiberius called for a grand ceremony in the heart of Cairo. The air was electric with anticipation as the legions gathered in the newly constructed

Illuminati fortress, a bastion of power and knowledge that dwarfed the ancient pyramids. The ceremony was not just a celebration of victory but a declaration of intent.

As the sun dipped low in the sky, casting long shadows across the gleaming armor and proud faces of the legionnaires, Tiberius took to the podium. His voice boomed across the square, a mix of Roman resolve and Illuminati vision. He praised the valor and discipline of his troops, awarding them with medals and promotions. The crowd roared with approval, their loyalty to Tiberius and Rome unshakeable.

Then, with a flourish of his hand, Tiberius called forth Vulcan, the hero of the Colosseum. The crowd fell silent, their eyes fixed on the legendary gladiator-turned-general. He strode into the center of the square, his steps echoing on the stone. The Mayor's smile was like the sun breaking through the clouds as he m. The armor, forged from the finest Roman steel and adorned with gold, was a testament to the society's wealth and the power it wielded.

The crowd watched in awe as Vulcan rose, his new rank etched upon his crimson cloak. His transformation from gladiator to general was complete, and he stood before them as the embodiment of the Illuminati's might. Tiberius spoke of his valor, of the battles won and the peace brought to the conquered lands. The people of Cairo cheered, their voices rising to the heavens, as Vulcan raised his sword in a salute to his new commander and the society that had elevated him.

The ceremony concluded with a grand procession through the city, the legions marching in lockstep with the Illuminati leaders. The golden light of the setting sun reflected o the gleaming armor, casting a warm glow over the ancient streets. The citizens of Cairo lined the roads, their faces a canvas of hope and trepidation. They had seen the power of Rome, and now they beheld the power of an invisible force that shaped the destiny of their land.

In the days that followed, Vulcan donned his new armor and took command of the African legions. His presence was felt across the continent, his name a whisper of change. He was the society's sword, cutting through the weeds of oppression and planting the seeds of enlightenment. The crimson cloak of the Illuminati fluttered behind him as he rode into the heart of Africa, his legions a testament to Rome's might and the society's vision.

The ceremony had served its purpose, bolstering the legions' morale and solidifying the Illuminati's grip on the continent.

The strategic importance of Africa was not lost on Tiberius. Its vast resources, rich culture, and geographic position made it a crucial piece in the Illuminati's grand vision of a world united under their enlightened rule. The society saw in the continent not just a source of wealth and power but a fertile ground for their ideology to take root and flourish.

The challenges of maintaining control over such vast new lands were manifold. The diverse cultures, languages, and traditions of the conquered territories presented a complex tapestry that required careful handling. Tiberius knew that brute force alone would not su ce; the Illuminati had to win the hearts and minds of the people.

To this end, the society had plans to introduce advanced Roman technologies to the Africans, a demonstration of the benefits of their enlightened governance. These innovations would not only improve the quality of life but also serve as a testament to the Illuminati's foresight and benevolence. The construction of aqueducts to bring water to the parched lands, the establishment of libraries filled with ancient knowledge, and the spread of medicine to conquer diseases that had plagued the continent for millennia were all part of their grand design.

The Illuminati's long-term strategy was to integrate Africa into a global network of knowledge and power, where the continent's vast resources and manpower would fuel the society's expansionist ambitions. Tiberius knew that to achieve this, he had to tread carefully, ensuring that the society's influence grew organically, like a plant seeking the sun. His approach was one of gradual assimilation, allowing the African leaders to maintain their cultural identities while subtly guiding them towards the Illuminati's vision.

The Roman Senate, though wary of the Illuminati's growing power, recognized the strategic importance of the African territories. The continent's wealth in gold, spices, and exotic animals could bolster Rome's co ers and secure its status as the dominant empire. Yet, the challenges of maintaining control over such diverse lands were not lost on them. The Senate watched Tiberius's moves with a mix of admiration and suspicion, their confidence in his leadership balanced by the fear of a shadowy force operating within their own ranks.

Amidst the grandeur of the new Roman-African capital, Tiberius worked tirelessly. His days were filled with meetings and strategy sessions, his nights with messages to Rome. His vision for Africa was clear: a continent united under the banner of enlightenment, a beacon of progress that would outshine even the glory of the Eternal City. He knew that the key to achieving this was to win the trust of the people, and so he turned his attention to the introduction of Roman innovations that would improve their lives.

The construction of aqueducts in the desert cities brought water to the parched lands, transforming the arid wasteland into lush oases. The Illuminati's engineers worked alongside African laborers, sharing their knowledge and forging bonds of mutual respect. The water flowed, and with it, the seeds of Roman innovation and Illuminati philosophy. The local leaders who had embraced the society watched their people's lives improve, and their loyalty grew stronger.

In the heart of Africa, the Illuminati established great libraries and schools, where scholars from across the empire gathered to share their wisdom. The continent's youth flocked to these institutions, eager to learn the secrets of the conquerors. They were taught the classics of Greek and Roman thought, but also of their own history and culture, a delicate balance that Tiberius knew was essential to maintaining peace. The society's scholars were careful to weave their ideology into the very fabric of education, ensuring that the next generation of leaders would be steeped in the values of the organization.

The introduction of Roman medicine was met with awe and gratitude. Diseases that had once ravaged the land were now treatable, and the society's healers became revered figures. They o ered cures and knowledge, and in return, the people o ered their allegiance. Yet, the Illuminati's intentions were not purely altruistic. With every life saved and every mind enlightened, the society's influence grew. Their presence was felt not just in the grand temples and gleaming palaces but in the very lives of the Africans they sought to uplift.

The Roman Senate watched the transformation of Africa with a mix of pride and unease. The wealth and resources flowing into the empire were a boon, but whispers of the Illuminati's true intentions grew louder. Some feared the society sought to replace Rome's traditional values with their own, more radical ideologies. Others, like Aurelius, saw the potential for a new kind of empire, one that transcended the petty squabbles and power grabs of the Senate.

Meanwhile, Rome was set to hold its next races.

The Colosseum buzzed with excitement as the grand event approached. The air was thick with the scent of roasting meats and the sweet aroma of exotic spices, mingling with the cries of merchants and the laughter of the crowd. The games had been revamped with a new twist, courtesy of the Illuminati's influence: a brutal combat between a lion and a bear, a spectacle that drew gasps and cheers from the bloodthirsty masses.

In the midst of this carnival atmosphere, jokers and fools danced among the spectators, their antics a stark contrast to the deadly seriousness of the battles to come. The Senate had sanctioned this new form of entertainment, bringing the people some smiles instead of just blood.

The crowd's anticipation grew as the lion was released into the arena. The great beast's mane fluttered in the breeze, its fiery eyes searching for its prey. The bear, chained and enraged, roared in defiance. The tension was palpable as the two beasts circled each other, their every move a dance of death. The crowd held their breath as the lion lunged, its teeth sinking into the bear's thick fur. The bear retaliated with a powerful swipe of its paw, sending the lion reeling.

Amidst the chaos, the gamblers had set up their tables, eager to capitalize on the spectators' passion. The introduction of this gambling addition to the races had been a stroke of genius, bringing in even more wealth to line the Senate's co ers.

Sextius, the Illuminati's new champion, sat astride his chariot, watching the brutal spectacle with a stoic expression. His eyes, once filled with the fire of competition, had grown cold and calculating. He knew that today's race was not just about victory; it was about power, and the stakes were higher than ever before.

The jokers and fools danced and cavorted, their laughter a stark counterpoint to the savagery in the arena. The crowd roared, their appetite for entertainment insatiable. Yet, amidst the revelry, a new element had been introduced: the scent of wealth and opportunity. The gambling tables had become the heart of the Colosseum, the lifeblood of the games.

Sextius's chariot thundered onto the sand, the gleaming wheels leaving trails in their wake. His opponents were mere shadows in his periphery, their desperate cries for victory lost in the deafening roar of the spectators. His eyes were fixed on the prize, his muscles taut with the promise of triumph. The chariots clashed and careened, a whirlwind of dust and steel, but Sextius remained unflappable. His whip cracked through the air, his horses responding with a surge of power that propelled him ahead of the pack.

As the race neared its end, the crowd's cheers grew deafening. The chariots hurtled towards the finish line, a blur of color and motion. Sextius leaned forward, his hand tight on the reins, his heart racing in time with his horses' hooves. And then, in a sudden, breathtaking surge, he broke free from the pack. The Illuminati banner fluttered in the wind as he crossed the line first, the dust of the arena swirling in his wake.

The crowd erupted into a frenzy of applause and jubilation. The gamblers' tables rattled with the exchange of coins and the shouts of triumph and despair. Sextius leaped from his chariot, the taste of victory sweet on his lips. He had not only won the race but had also secured a substantial sum from his own strategic bets placed through intermediaries. The winnings were a testament to his skill and the society's influence.

With the adrenaline of victory still coursing through his veins, Sextius made his way through the throngs of people, his eyes scanning the sea of faces for familiar ones. He found Aurelius and Claudia, who had traveled from Crete to witness the event. Their smiles were as bright as the gold coins that now filled his purse. They embraced him warmly, their laughter mingling with the celebratory din of the Colosseum.

The trio retreated to a private suite, where the air was thick with the scent of fine wine and roasting meats. The candlelight danced across the walls, casting flickering shadows that seemed to mirror their own jovial spirits. They sat around a table laden with delicacies, their plates filled with the finest dishes Rome had to o er. They drank deeply from goblets that shimmered with the reflection of the flames, their conversation a blend of joyous reminiscing and strategic musings.

Aurelius, his gaze lingering on the flickering candles, spoke of his time in Crete, of the challenges and triumphs of governing such a diverse land. He told tales of political alliances and cultural exchange, his voice filled with a passion that had not dimmed despite the distance from the island. Claudia, her eyes sparkling with mirth, recounted the tales of Cretan folklore that had become the bedtime stories of their daughters.

Sextius, his mood lighter than it had been in months, regaled them with stories of his own exploits in the gladiatorial games, of the fierce battles and the camaraderie found in the arena's sands. His laughter was deep and infectious, drawing smiles from the weary souls who had gathered to revel in the warmth of friendship.

The wine flowed freely, the amber liquid swirling in their cups as they raised them in toasts to each other, to Rome, and to the Illuminati. The music grew louder, the strings of a lyre plucked by a skilled musician echoing through the suite. The night was still young, and the festivities had only just begun.

Sextius, his victory still fresh in his mind, felt a restlessness stir within him. He excused himself from the table, the clinking of his coins a silent declaration of his intentions. The air outside was cool, a stark contrast to the heat of the Colosseum. He made his way through the crowded streets, the sounds of revelry a siren's call that grew louder as he approached the red-lit district.

The brothel was known as the House of Desire, its crimson walls a stark contrast to the cold cobblestone streets of Rome. Sextius pushed the heavy oak door open, the warm, spicy scent of incense enveloping him. The dimly lit interior was alive with the sounds of hushed whispers and soft laughter, the promise of pleasure lurking in every shadowy corner.

The madam, a heavyset woman with a knowing smile, greeted him with a nod of recognition. She led him to a private chamber where two beautiful women awaited, their eyes dark with kohl and their bodies adorned with gold. They were exotic, one with skin as dark as the Nubian night and the other with the pale glow of a Greek goddess. The room was a sanctuary of velvet and silk, the candles casting a warm glow that danced across their skin.

Sextius felt the weight of the day's tension melt away as they welcomed him into their embrace. Their hands were soft and skilled, their kisses sweet and fiery. The night was a blur of passion and pleasure, a celebration of life that transcended the brutality of the arena.

As dawn approached, Sextius bid the women farewell, his pockets lighter but his spirit lifted. He stumbled through the quiet streets, the cool air sobering him as he made his way home. His villa was a testament to his success, a bastion of Roman opulence nestled in the heart of the city. The marble floors were cool under his sandals, and the frescoes on the walls whispered of myths and legends. He collapsed onto his bed, the scent of the women lingering on his skin, and slept the deep, contented sleep of the victorious.

Meanwhile, Claudia and Aurelius had left the Colosseum, the sounds o the city's revelry fading behind them. They climbed into a luxuriou: carriage, the plush seats enveloping them in a cocoon of warmth anc comfort. The carriage rolled through the city, the hooves of the horse: clattering rhythmically on the cobblestone streets. Their conversatior grew quieter, the weight of the day's events pressing down upon them.

The cottage was a sanctuary from the chaos of Rome, nestled in a quiet corner of the city where the air was fragrant with the scent of blooming jasmine. Inside, the soft glow of oil lamps cast a warm light over the polished wooden floors and the rich tapestries that adorned the walls. The fireplace crackled, the embers casting a warm, flickering glow over the room.

They danced together, their bodies moving in perfect harmony to the music of a distant lute. The wine flowed freely, their laughter echoing through the quiet streets as they lost themselves in the moment. The burdens of governance and the shadowy dealings of the Illuminati were forgotten, if only for a night. The cottage was a haven of tranquility amidst the city's chaos, a place where they could simply be a man and a woman in love.

As they stepped inside, the warm embrace of the fireplace beckoned them closer. The flames danced in the hearth, casting shadows that danced playfully across their faces. They sat on the soft rug before the fire, their fingers entwined, and talked of dreams and the future.

The crackling of the firewood was the only sound that pierced the silence, a gentle reminder of the passage of time.

The flames grew low, the embers glowing a soft red, as the conversation drifted to a gentle lull. The candles flickered, their light casting a warm, intimate glow over the room. Aurelius leaned in, capturing Claudia's lips in a kiss that spoke of the depth of his love and the fierce protection he vowed to provide. She responded with a passion that ignited a fire within him, one that burned away the doubts and fears of the world outside.

Their love was a beacon in the shadowy world of political intrigue and power struggles. In the sanctity of their cottage, they found refuge from the storm that brewed in the halls of the Senate. The night grew late as their passion subsided. they check on baby taboulous and go to sleep.

As dawn broke over the Tiber, a new chapter in Rome's history was being written. A mysterious general had arrived on the docks, his ship cutting through the early morning mist. He was a man of imposing stature, his eyes the color of steel and his beard flecked with grey, a testament to his years of experience. His armor was unadorned, yet it bore the unmistakable marks of countless battles. The whispers among the dockworkers spoke of a leader who had risen from obscurity to conquer distant lands.

This new general, a man of few words and great presence, was to serve alongside Vulcan in the forthcoming campaign against the Ottoman Empire. His name was Julius, and his reputation had traveled the breadth of the Mediterranean. The Senate had called upon him to bolster their forces and bring a swift end to the looming threat. The Illuminati, ever watchful, had secretly orchestrated his arrival, recognizing the strategic importance of this alliance.

Julius's arrival brought a palpable tension to the city. His presence was a reminder of the wars that had forged the empire and the price of its power. Vulcan, the Illuminati's trusted general, met him with a mix of respect and wariness. The two men were as di erent as night and day yet they shared a common purpose: the expansion of Rome's influence and the protection of its citizens.

Together, they pored over maps and scrolls, their strategies a dance of steel and cunning. The Ottoman campaign was to be a showcase of Rome's might, a demonstration of the society's ability to protect and guide the empire. The Senate watched with bated breath as the legions marched forth, their banners fluttering in the wind. The Illuminati's hand was hidden, yet it was they who pulled the strings of this grand play.

The battles against the barbarian hordes were fierce, but Julius's tactical prowess and Vulcan's unmatched valor proved a formidable combination. The legions carved a path through the enemy lines, their discipline and technology leaving the barbarians in awe. The clang of swords and the roar of the legions' war cry echoed across the plains as they pushed towards Constantinople, the jewel of the East.

Each victory brought them closer to their ultimate goal, each step a testament to the might of Rome and the wisdom of the Illuminati. The Senate's faith in their leaders grew stronger, yet whispers of the society's influence grew louder. The people of Rome looked to the horizon, their hearts filled with hope and fear. For they knew that the fate of the empire rested not just in the hands of their elected o cials, but in the shadows of a secret order that had woven itself into the very fabric of their lives.

The city of Constantinople grew larger in the distance, its gleaming domes and spires a symbol of the East's wealth and power. The legions marched on, their eyes fixed on the prize that awaited them. Yet, unbeknownst to them, the true battle was not just ahead but also within their own ranks.

Julius, the stoic general, remained an enigma. His past shrouded in mystery, he had risen from the ranks of obscurity to become a legend on the battlefield. Some whispered of battles fought against the barbarians beyond the Danube, where his tactical brilliance had turned the tide of war. Others spoke of his time in the East, where he had honed his skills against the cunning Persians. His arrival in Rome had been swift and silent, his loyalty to the Illuminati unwavering. His stoic demeanor and unmatched experience in warfare had earned him the respect of the legions, yet his true intentions remained a puzzle.

Vulcan, ever the diplomat, had embraced his new comrade with open arms. Yet beneath the veneer of camaraderie, he couldn't help but feel a twinge of doubt. Was Julius truly committed to the Illuminati's vision of a unified and enlightened world, or did he harbor ambitions of his own? The bond between them grew stronger with each victory, yet Vulcan knew that in the shadowy world of politics, trust was as fragile as glass.

The march to Constantinople was not without its challenges. The barbarian hordes, though outmatched by Roman discipline and technology, were fierce and cunning. Yet under Julius's leadership, the legions faced each encounter with a tactical superiority that left the enemy in disarray. His strategies were a blend of the ancient Roman military doctrine and innovative tactics that had earned him fame across the empire.

The Illuminati's influence was evident in the meticulous planning and execution of each battle. Intelligence networks provided by the society allowed for swift strikes and strategic retreats, minimizing casualties and maximizing the impact of their forces. The legions moved with the precision of a well-oiled machine, each soldier aware of their role in the grand design. The barbarians, though brave, were no match for the combined might of Rome and the society's cunning.

With each victory, the legions grew more confident, their spirits bolstered by the knowledge that they were fighting for a cause greater than themselves. The society had painted a picture of an empire united under the banner of enlightenment, and the soldiers had bought into this vision. The promise of a new world order, one where knowledge and reason reigned supreme, fueled their valor and their will to conquer.

The city of Constantinople grew ever closer, its walls a testament to the might of the Eastern Roman Empire. Yet, as the legions approached, the Illuminati's spies reported growing unrest within the city. The Senate, eager for victory, pushed for a swift siege, but Julius cautioned patience. His tactical superiority had led to minimal losses thus far, and he was not one to squander lives unnecessarily.

Under the cover of darkness, Julius and Vulcan devised a daring plan to infiltrate the city. They would strike at the heart of the enemy's defenses, using the element of surprise to their advantage. The Illuminati's influence had reached the city's underbelly, and they had secured the loyalty of a contingent of the city's guards. The legions would march under the cover of a decoy force, their true destination known only to the trusted few.

The final approach was fraught with tension. The legions moved silently through the night, their footsteps mu led by the soft earth beneath their sandals.

Julius and Vulcan had identified a handful of senators who remained unaligned with the Illuminati's vision. These men, steadfast in their traditionalist beliefs, posed a potential threat to the society's growing power. One by one, these senators began to su er a series of unfortunate "accidents." Some fell ill with sudden, inexplicable ailments, others met with untimely ends in the labyrinthine streets of Rome. The whispers grew louder, the fear of the Illuminati's reach inescapable.

In their stead, the Illuminati appointed loyalists, men and women whose ideals aligned with the society's grand design. The Senate chamber, once a bastion of diverse thought and heated debate, slowly transformed into a hall of nodding heads and muted opposition. The Senate's policies and decisions began to subtly shift, reflecting the society's influence. The Senate's once proud independence was eroding, piece by piece, as the Illuminati's grip grew tighter.

The Senate's transformation was not lost on the people of Rome. They watched as their leaders fell in line, one by one, and wondered what lay behind the sudden unity.

In the heart of the city, whispers grew into murmurs, and murmurs into whispers. The Senate, once a beacon of Roman virtue, now echoed with the footsteps of shadows. The Illuminati's hand had reached into the very marble halls of power, and the air was thick with tension.

The Senate meetings grew shorter, the debates less fiery. The once-proud orators spoke in hushed tones, their eyes darting to the shadows where they knew the society's emissaries lurked. The topics of discussion shifted from the mundane to the strategic, the Senate's focus now aligned with the Illuminati's grand vision.

The Senate's decree to fund the construction of the bridge to Africa was met with astonishment and trepidation. It was a monumental project that would cement Rome's dominance over the continent, but it was also a stark reminder of the society's unyielding influence. The Senate had become an extension of the Illuminati's will, their once-noble intentions now a mere reflection of the society's grand design.

The few remaining independent senators were a dwindling minority. Their numbers had been steadily depleted by a string of mysterious "accidents." The death of Senator Livius, a vocal critic of the Illuminati, in a suspicious carriage accident had sent a chilling message throughout the Senate. His replacement, a young and ambitious tribune named Flavius, was a known ally of the society. His appointment had been swift and silent, leaving no room for doubt as to the Illuminati's power.

The Senate chambers had grown colder, the once vibrant debates now replaced by a tense silence. The air was thick with the scent of fear, and the shadows seemed to hold secrets that could topple empires. The Illuminati's emblem, the all-seeing eye, was etched into the very fabric of the marble walls, a silent sentinel watching over the proceedings.

The Senate's policies began to shift in favor of the society's vision. Debates on religious tolerance and the integration of foreign ideas grew increasingly one-sided. The conservative factions that had once held sway were now a fading memory, their voices drowned out by the Illuminati's insistent whispers. The Senate had become a tool in the society's quest for enlightenment, their decisions a mere formality in the grand design.

Augustus, ever the master of ceremonies, had planned a grand event to celebrate Rome's new era of enlightenment. The city was adorned with banners and lights, heralding the Enlightenment Festival. The cobblestone streets were lined with stalls displaying inventions from across the empire, the air buzzing with excitement and curiosity. The festival was a testament to the Illuminati's influence, a public declaration of their triumph over the old ways.

Prominent figures, all secretly aligned with the society, took to the podium, their words a symphony of progress and unity. They spoke of a Rome that was a beacon of knowledge, a city that would shine like a star in the darkness of ignorance. The crowd, intoxicated by the promise of a brighter future, listened with rapt attention. The festival culminated in a spectacular display of fireworks that painted the night sky with colors that mirrored the vibrant tapestries of the society's influence.

The new Illuminati church was the crown jewel of the festival. Its opulent design, with gleaming gold and marble, towered over the cit a tesamen to the society's power and the Senate's endorsement. Its construction had been swift, almost as if the very stones had been shaped by the society's will alone. The dome, a marvel of engineering, was said to have been inspired by the grandeur of the Pantheon but infused with a symbolism that spoke of the Illuminati's cosmic vision. Symbols were gently wove into the dome and the walls of the prestegious build.

The festival's climax was the grand procession to the church. Senators and society members walked side by side, their faces lit by the torches that lined the path. The air was filled with the scent of incense and the sound of hymns sung by a choir of a thousand voices. The procession was a visual feast, a testament to Rome's newfound enlightenment. The public was invited to bear witness to the dawn of a new era, where knowledge was king and ignorance was banished.

At the heart of the celebration, an elder council meeting was held in the church's vast sanctum. The air was thick with the scent of burning candles and the weight of their collective purpose. The council members, all clad in the society's crimson robes, sat in a circle, their eyes reflecting the flickering light. The map of Africa lay before them, a canvas for their ambitious plans. They discussed the continent's future with the same passion and vigor they had once reserved for philosophical debates in the clandestine chambers of the Illuminati's hidden lair.

The council spoke of agriculture, trade, and the spread of Roman culture and knowledge. They spoke of the promise of a continent united under the society's enlightened rule, a bastion of progress and civilization amidst the barbarian lands. The construction of the bridge was not just a feat of engineering but a symbolic gesture, a lifeline connecting the old world with the new. The Illuminati's influence would stretch from the Mediterranean to the edge of the known world, bringing the light of reason to the darkest corners of the earth.

As the echoes of the festival's final hymns faded into the night, the council members stood, their eyes gleaming with determination. They knew that the road ahead was fraught with danger, that their enemies were numerous and their resources stretched thin as it was, with two war fronts going on. Yet, the Illuminati had always thrived in the shadows, turning adversity into opportunity.

The celebration of the stars aligning with the pyramids was more than a mere astronomical event. It was a symbolic representation of the Illuminati's power, a celestial a rmation of their divine right to rule. In the grand public square, a colossal map of the known world was laid out, with each continent marked by a shimmering crystal. The crowd gathered around it, their eyes wide with wonder, as Aurelius took the podium. His words flowed like honey, sweet and convincing, speaking of a Rome that was not just a city but a beacon of light that would illuminate the world.

Prominent figures, all secretly aligned with the Illuminati, took to the podium during the Enlightenment Festival. Their speeches resonated through the grand amphitheater, echoing the society's vision of a Rome that was a beacon of light in the darkness of the world. They spoke of unity and knowledge, their words weaving a tapestry of hope and ambition that captivated the masses. The crowd was a sea of faces, each one reflecting the flaming torches that lined the arena's perimeter, creating an aura of divine revelation around the speakers. The air was electric with anticipation, as if the very gods themselves had descended to bless the society's grand design.

The Illuminati church stood tall and gleaming, a monument to the society's power. Its opulent design, with gold and marble that seemed to flow like liquid in the flickering torchlight, was a stark contrast to the austere temples of the old gods. The dome, a marvel of engineering and symbolism, drew the eye upward, inspiring awe and devotion. The structure was not just a place of worship; it was a beacon that cast its light over the city, a physical manifestation of the society's influence over Rome's destiny.

From the church's steps, a procession of prominent figures, their robes fluttering in the evening breeze, made their way to the grand festival stage. Each one of them had been carefully selected by the Illuminati to represent the society's vision of a new Rome. They spoke of unity and enlightenment, their words a siren's song that promised a brighter future under the society's guiding hand. The crowd, drawn by the allure of progress, listened with rapt attention, their hearts swelling with hope.

Senator Flavius, the Illuminati's newest ally, took the podium. His youthful face radiated with conviction as he recounted tales of

Rome's storied past, weaving in the society's ideals of knowledge and reason. He spoke of Rome as a "beacon of light," a city that would illuminate the barbarous lands with the flame of enlightenment. His voice grew stronger as he described a future where all peoples lived in harmony, guided by the society's wisdom. The crowd's murmurs grew into a thunderous applause, their faces a mirror to the torchlight that danced across the amphitheater's walls.

The procession moved through the city streets, passing the gleaming façade of the Illuminati church. Its opulent design reflected the society's newfound power and wealth, a stark contrast to the humble beginnings of their secretive meetings. The gold and marble gleamed in the torchlight, an unmistakable symbol of their influence. The structure's grandeur was not just for show; it was a bastion of the society's beliefs, a testament to their unyielding commitment to reshape the world.

Inside the church's sanctum, the elder council gathered. The room was a cocoon of crimson, the walls adorned with gold-leafed symbols of the Illuminati's power and reach. The air was thick with the scent of incense, a sacred veil that shrouded their clandestine proceedings. They had gathered to finalize their plans for Africa, the continent that would be the jewel in their enlightened empire's crown.

Tiberius, a man whose ambition was matched only by his tactical acumen, stepped forward to announce the Iron Horse project. This grand endeavor would not only unite the continent under Roman rule but also serve as a testament to the Illuminati's ingenuity. A network of steel railways would stretch from the shores of Carthage to the distant lands of Egypt, bringing the fruits of Roman civilization to the furthest corners of the continent. The council nodded in unison, their eyes gleaming with the prospect of unbridled power and influence.

The Iron Horse was not merely a means of transportation; it was a conduit for culture and enlightenment. Along its path, new cities would rise from the sands, each a bastion of Roman architecture and Illuminati wisdom. These urban centers would be the crucible for a new breed of citizenry, forged in the fires of innovation and knowledge. The society's emblem would be etched into the very stones of these cities, a silent declaration of their presence and intent .

The Illuminati's influence grew bolder with each turn of the spade. Their members operated openly now, their crimson robes a stark contrast against the dusty tunics of the laborers. They guided the construction with the precision of master architects, ensuring that each city was a reflection of their grand design. The railway was not just a path for trade and travel; it was the spine of a new Rome that stretched into the heart of Africa.

The cultural renaissance that swept through the continent was palpable. Schools and libraries sprang up alongside the railways, bringing the light of Roman knowledge to the masses. The local populace, once skeptical of the foreign invaders, embraced the society's ideals. They saw in the Illuminati a chance for a better life, a future where their children could rise above the cycle of poverty and ignorance that had plagued them for centuries.

The wealth of Africa flowed back to Rome on the Iron Horse's gleaming tracks, filling the city's co ers with gold and diamonds.

Cairo, once a mere gateway to the exotic lands of the Nile, had been transformed into a bustling port, a hub of trade that saw ships from the furthest reaches of the Mediterranean arrive daily, laden with the continent's riches. The Illuminati's symbol, the all-seeing eye, watched over the bustling docks, a constant reminder of the society's guiding hand in this new era of prosperity.

The cities that had sprung up along the railway grew into bastions of Roman culture and Illuminati philosophy. Their gleaming marble facades and grand temples stood as monuments to the society's power and the new Rome's grandeur.

In the heart of Cairo, the Iron Horse's terminus was a marvel to behold. Its gleaming steel tracks stretched into the horizon, a testament to the Illuminati's mastery over the continent. The city had been transformed from a dusty outpost to a bustling metropolis, its streets lined with markets and scholars eager to share their knowledge. The port, once a sleepy dock, now thrummed with the cacophony of trade. The scent of exotic spices mingled with the tang of metal and the sweat of laborers, as ships from across the Mediterranean unloaded their cargoes of gold and diamonds.

The Illuminati's crimson robes had become a common sight in the city's streets, their members openly guiding the development of the new world they had envisioned. The society's insignia, the all-seeing eye, was emblazoned on public buildings, bridges, and even the coins that changed hands in the bustling markets. The cultural renaissance that swept through Africa was not merely an Illuminati creation; it was a testament to their ability to harness the power of human aspiration and bend it to their will.

In every corner of the continent, schools and libraries bore the society's emblem, o ering a sanctuary of knowledge to those who sought it. The local populace, once wary of the Romans, now saw the Illuminati as benevolent guides, leading them out of darkness and into the light of progress. The society's philosophies were taught alongside the classics, and the youth of Africa grew up knowing that the society's wisdom was the key to their prosperity.

The wealth of Africa poured into Rome, funding the society's ambitious projects. The city's skyline grew taller, with new marvels of engineering rising alongside the ancient ruins. The Senate, now a mere shell of its former self, approved every proposal brought forth by the Illuminati-backed o cials. The Senate's treasury overflowed with gold and precious gems, fueling a building spree that had not been seen since the days of Julius Caesar.

Cairo's port grew into a colossal trade hub, a bustling nexus where ships from the furthest reaches of the empire docked, their holds brimming with exotic goods and precious metals. The Iron Horse's gleaming tracks stretched out like veins, carrying the lifeblood of wealth and culture to the heart of the new Rome. The city's skyline was a jagged silhouette of cranes and sca olding, a testament to the Illuminati's unbridled ambition. Yet, amidst the clamor of progress, whispers of dissent grew louder.

In the shadows of the gleaming temples and bustling markets, a rebellion took root. The Iron Hand, once thought vanquished, had regrouped and grown stronger in the wake of the Illuminati's expansion. Their numbers swelled with disa ected Romans who feared the society's growing power and the erosion of traditional values. They saw the society's influence as a cancer, corrupting the very soul of Rome.

Aurelius and Claudia, now seasoned leaders, were caught between the idealistic vision of a unified Rome and the harsh reality of dissent. The Iron Hand had infiltrated every level of society, from the Senate to the legions. Their tactics grew bolder, their saboteurs wreaking havoc on the Illuminati's projects and their agents spreading fear through the city's streets. The society's once unassailable power now faced a formidable challenge, and the cracks in their façade were beginning to show.

The Illuminati's response was swift and merciless. The leaders of the rebellion were rounded up in a series of midnight raids, their clandestine meetings shattered by the clatter of soldiers' boots and the gleam of drawn swords. They were brought before the Senate, now a mere echo chamber for the society's will, and charged with treason. The trials were a spectacle, a public reminder of the consequences of defying the new order. Some were sentenced to the mines, their backs bent under the weight of their treachery. Others were sent to the Colosseum, their fate to be decided by the roar of the crowd and the whims of fate.

Sextius, ever the devoted champion of the society, threw himself into his training with renewed vigor. The upcoming races were not just a show of strength and skill; they were a battleground where the Illuminati's dominance would be rea rmed. His eyes burned with a fierce determination, his muscles sculpted by the countless hours under the relentless sun of the training grounds. Each swing of his sword was a declaration of his loyalty to the society, each step a stride towards victory.

The Colosseum was once again the stage for the unfolding drama of power and retribution. The leaders of the rebellion were brought before the masses, their heads bowed in defeat. The Senate, now a puppet of the Illuminati, condemned them to various fates, from a life of toil in the mines to a swift and public end in the arena. The air was thick with the scent of fear and the acrid tang of bloodlust as the crowd awaited the spectacle that would be their punishment.

The next day, the Colosseum roared to life as the races commenced. The Illuminati had orchestrated a spectacle to both entertain the masses and reinforce their dominance. The leaders of the Iron Hand were led into the arena in chains, their heads held high despite their fate. The crowd watched with a mix of fear and morbid fascination as the first gladiator stepped into the sand.

The trials were swift and brutal. The rebels, once feared and revered, were now mere pawns in the Illuminati's public display of power. The clang of steel and the screams of the condemned echoed through the vast amphitheater, a grim reminder of the price of dissent. As the gladiators fell, one by one, the society's message was clear: Comitt treason and be hung.

In the midst of this spectacle, Sextius trained harder than ever before. The Illuminati had entrusted him with the critical task of maintaining their grip on Rome through the games. His every move was calculated, each swing of his sword a silent oath to secure victory for the society. His eyes reflected the flaming torches that illuminated the training ground, a mirror of the fiery determination that burned within his soul .

The day of the race arrived, the Colosseum alive with anticipation. The air was thick with the scent of sweat and fear, the very essence of the gladiatorial spirit. Sextius took his place, his muscles taut with tension. The chariots thundered forth, the crowd's roar a deafening crescendo. He raced with a ferocity that seemed almost superhuman, his eyes never leaving the prize ahead.

Yet, even as the Illuminati's grip on Rome tightened, the whispers of dissent grew louder. The Iron Hand had not disappeared; they had merely retreated into the shadows, waiting for their moment to strike. Sextius knew that his role in the upcoming games was not just to entertain the masses but to crush any semblance of hope that the Iron Hand might still harbor. He trained tirelessly, pushing his body to its limits, driven by the knowledge that victory was not merely a personal triumph but a declaration of the society's might.

The day of the chariot race dawned, the Colosseum buzzing with an electric anticipation that could be felt in the very air. Sextius mounted his chariot, his gaze steely and unwavering. The race was a blur of dust and thundering hooves, the screams of the crowd a cacophony that seemed to fuel his every move. He pushed his team to their limits, the wind whipping his hair back as he maneuvered through the treacherous circus, each turn a dance with death.

But fate had other plans. As the chariots rounded the final bend, a rogue gladiator emerged from the shadows, a contender not listed on the day's program. His chariot, sleek and unmarked, surged forward, and in a breathtaking display of skill, he overtook Sextius. The crowd erupted in shock and awe as the mysterious charioteer claimed victory, his identity as enigmatic as the circumstances of his appearance.

The Senate, caught o -guard by the unexpected turn of events, scrambled to regain control. A hush fell over the Colosseum as a herald announced a new competition. The four most formidable gladiators, each handpicked by the Illuminati, would engage in a brutal contest. The last man standing would not only claim victory but also symbolize the society's unyielding strength in the face of adversity.

The gladiators entered the arena, each one a picture of stoic determination. The crowd held their breath as the games began, their eyes flicking from the crimson-robed Illuminati o cials to the battle unfolding before them. The sand churned under the gladiators' feet, their weapons flashing in the sunlight. It was a spectacle of skill and strategy, a microcosm of the larger struggle for power that played out beyond the Colosseum's walls.

The contestants fought with the ferocity of cornered animals, each blow a silent testament to their desperation. The Illuminati's influence had reached into the very fabric of Roman society, and the bets placed on this race were more than just wagers on the outcome; they were investments in the society's power. As the dust began to settle and the gladiators fell, one by one, the weight of their failure hung heavy in the air.

Sextius watched from the shadows, his jaw clenched in anger and embarrassment. He had been the society's champion, the embodiment of their strength and resolve. Yet, the unforeseen victory of the mysterious charioteer had cast a pall over their triumph. The bets had been lost, and with them, the trust of many of Rome's elite. He knew that he had to regain their confidence, not just for the society's sake, but for his own reputation.

The four gladiators who had been chosen for the special exhibition were a motley crew, each with their own unique skills and weapons. There was the burly Barbarian with his massive sword, the nimble Egyptian with his whip-like flail, the swift Iberian with his twin short swords, and the enigmatic Roman, clad in gleaming bronze armor, his face obscured by a helmet adorned with the visage of a fierce wolf.

The crowd watched with bated breath as the gladiators were released into the arena. The Egyptian and the Iberian circled each other, their weapons flashing in the sunlight, while the Barbarian and the Roman approached more directly, their heavy steps echoing through the Colosseum. The Roman gladiator's eyes were cold and calculating, his movements precise and deliberate. His adversary, the Barbarian, was all brute strength and rage, his sword swinging in wild arcs that could cleave a man in two.

The battle was a dance of death, each combatant testing the others, seeking weaknesses to exploit. The Egyptian's flail sang through the air, a deadly pendulum that could dismember with a flick of his wrist. The Iberian darted and weaved, his twin swords a blur as he sought an opening in the Egyptian's defense. The Barbarian's heavy blade crashed against the Roman's shield, the impact resonating through the stands. The mysterious Roman gladiator remained a silent, unyielding force, his every move a study in discipline and control.

The clang of steel and the thud of sandaled feet grew deafening as the fight raged on. The crowd's cries of excitement melded into a single, undulating roar that seemed to pulse with the rhythm of the battle. Each gladiator fought with the ferocity of a cornered beast, their eyes reflecting the desperation of men who knew that defeat meant death. The arena floor grew slick with sweat and blood, the smell of fear mingling with the coppery tang of spilled life.

The Iberian's speed proved too much for the Egyptian, his swords slicing through the air with a deadly grace that left the latter no room to maneuver. With a swift and precise strike, the Egyptian crumpled to the ground, his crimson life's essence staining the sand. The Roman and the Barbarian continued their brutal exchange, each blow a testament to their unyielding strength and will to survive. The crowd held their breath as the gladiators clashed, their every movement a silent narrative of power and determination.

The Roman's shield was dented and scarred, the Barbarian's chest heaving with exhaustion, but neither man would yield. Their duel was a symphony of steel, a battle of wills that seemed to defy the very laws of endurance. The crowd watched, transfixed by the spectacle before them, their loyalties torn between the stoic resolve of the Roman and the primal fury of the Barbarian.

The Iberian and the Roman locked eyes across the arena, each sizing up the other. The Iberian's twin swords whispered menace as he approached, his every step a promise of swift death. The Roman, unfazed, raised his sword in a silent challenge. The air grew taut with tension as the gladiators circled each other, their eyes never leaving their opponent's.

The first clash was like the collision of thunder and lightning, the Roman's sword flashing out to meet the Iberian's swords in a storm of steel. Sparks flew as the blades met, the sound of metal on metal ringing through the Colosseum. The Roman's shield bore the brunt of the Iberian's frenzied assault, holding firm despite the relentless barrage. The crowd leaned forward, their collective breath held in suspense, as the two warriors danced in a deadly ballet.

The Barbarian watched the display with a predatory gaze, his chest still heaving from his own grueling battle. He knew that the Roman was his true challenge, a foe that would not fall easily. The Roman's blade was a silver streak, cutting through the air with surgical precision. The Iberian's speed was dazzling, but the Roman's defense was impenetrable, his shield a wall that no amount of fury could breach.

As the battle raged on, the Roman's shield arm grew heavy, his breaths coming in ragged gasps. Yet, he did not falter. His eyes never left the Iberian's, searching for the tiniest opening. With a sudden twist of his wrist, he sent his sword in a swift arc that found purchase in the Iberian's side. The smaller man's eyes widened in shock, his swords dropping from his hands as he crumpled to the ground. The crowd erupted in a roar of approval, the sound echoing through the ancient stones of the amphitheater.

The final contest was set. The Roman and the Barbarian faced each other in the center of the arena, the sun casting long shadows behind them. The air was thick with the scent of blood and sweat, a heady perfume that seemed to intoxicate the crowd. The two men circled, each sizing up the other, their eyes narrowed with the focus of predators. The Roman's sword was a gleaming arc in the sunlight, a silent promise of death. The Barbarian's massive blade was a blur as he tested the Roman's defenses, seeking a weakness.

The gladiators clashed, their swords ringing out a deadly symphony that echoed through the Colosseum. The Roman's shield was a bastion against the Barbarian's relentless assault, each blow a testament to their indomitable wills. The crowd leaned in, their eyes gleaming with the excitement of the brutal dance unfolding before them.

The Roman's blade darted and weaved, finding no purchase against the Barbarian's thick fur cloak and iron armor. Yet, the latter's heavy sword was slowed by the Roman's agility and the unyielding wall of his shield. The two men moved in a deadly waltz, their breaths labored, their muscles screaming with the e ort of holding back the inevitable.

Suddenly, the Roman feigned a stumble, his shield momentarily lowering. The Barbarian saw his opening and lunged, his sword aimed for the kill. But the Roman was not as unsteady as he seemed. He spun on his heel, the edge of his sword catching the Barbarian's weapon and sending it flying. With a snarl, the Roman pounced, driving his blade into the Barbarian's unprotected chest. The crowd erupted into a deafening cheer as the giant of a man collapsed, his life's blood staining the sand.

The Illuminati's influence had been rea rmed through brutal spectacle, their power a bloody tapestry woven in the arena's sands. Yet, the mysterious charioteer's victory earlier in the day lingered in the air, a question mark that none could ignore. Who was this new contender? What did he represent? These whispers grew into a murmur that rippled through the city's streets, reaching even the highest echelons of power.

Aurelius, watching from the Senate's private box, felt a twinge of doubt. The Iron Hand had struck a symbolic blow, and he knew that their true intentions were yet to be revealed. He glanced at Augustus, whose eyes gleamed with a mix of excitement and calculation. The emperor had always been a master of the game, and Aurelius wondered if he had anticipated this move, if he was playing a deeper game that none could see.

The four gladiators that once stood was down to one. The Roman, whose valor had not been seen in the games for years, basked in the deafening applause of the Colosseum. His crimson cape billowed in the breeze, stained with the grime of the sands, as he stepped over the bodies of his vanquished foes. The emperor Augustus, his gaze sharp and assessing, rose from his seat in the Senate's box, silencing the crowd with a raised hand.

"Who is this hero that fights in the name of Rome?" Augustus's voice boomed across the arena, resonating with the power of a man who had seen empires rise and fall. The gladiator, Adonis, looked up, his visor raising to reveal a stoic face, etched with the lines of battle and the pride of victory. The crowd held their breath, waiting for the man who had captured their hearts to speak.

"I am Adonis," he declared, his voice strong and clear, carrying over the tumult of the crowd. "I fight for the glory of Rome, for the light of knowledge, and for the will of the Illuminati!" The crowd erupted again, their cheers a testament to the power of his words. Augustus's eyes narrowed slightly, the name of the society not lost on him. This was not just a gladiator; this was a symbol, a living embodiment of the society's influence that had seeped into every aspect of Roman life.

The emperor's gaze remained fixed on Adonis, his expression unreadable. "Your valor is unmatched, Adonis," Augustus spoke, his words echoing through the Colosseum. "Your victory today serves as a beacon of hope to those who believe in the power of enlightenment and progress. Tell me, how did you come to embody the spirit of the Illuminati?"

Adonis took a deep breath, his eyes scanning the sea of faces before returning to Augustus. "I am a son of Rome, raised in the shadow of her greatness," he began, his voice steady and proud. "I have seen the darkness that ignorance breeds, the su ering that a lack of knowledge can inflict upon the masses. The Illuminati o ered me a path to bring the light of understanding to those shrouded in shadow. It is for them, and for Rome, that I fight."

The crowd's roar grew louder, a wave of approval that washed over Adonis as he stood tall, basking in his victory. The emperor's question hung in the air, a silent challenge that seemed to echo through the very fabric of the Colosseum.

Adonis had indeed come from nothing, the product of a Roman mother and a forgotten father from the conquered lands. His early years had been a battle for survival in the unforgiving streets of Rome, where the only law was the sharpness of your blade and the speed of your wit. He had learned to fight with whatever he could lay his hands on, from sharpened sticks to discarded swords, honing his skills in the shadow of the great city's grandeur.

When he was found, it was in the dank and desperate underbelly of the city, where the games were more than just entertainment—they were a means of escape. They had seen in him a spark of potential, he was now a flame that could be fanned into an inferno that would illuminate the path of their cause. They had plucked him from the squalor of the slave quarters and given him a room with a bed and a bath, a luxury beyond his wildest dreams. The weapons and armor that were now his to wield were once the stu of legends, and the women who now sought his favor were the very same who had once looked down upon him with disdain.

But Adonis knew that his newfound status was not just a gift; it was a tool. The Illuminati had recognized his potential, had molded him into a weapon of their own, a living symbol of their might and their cause. He had become their gladiator, their champion, fighting not just for his freedom but for the spread of their enlightenment. His victories in the arena were not just personal triumphs but a declaration of the society's power to shape the destiny of Rome.

Yet, amidst the adoration and the trappings of success, Adonis could not shake the feeling that he was still a pawn in a game much larger than himself. He knew that his life was not truly his own, that he was bound by invisible chains to the Illuminati's will.

One day, the Illuminati elders paid Theseus a surprise visit his chambers. Their faces were stern, their eyes unyielding as they presented him with an ultimatum. The society demanded a hefty tax from the goods that flowed through the new African trade routes, a tithe to fund their ever-expanding projects and cement their grip on power. The elders made it clear that refusal was not an option.

Theseus felt a cold knot form in his stomach. He knew that to oppose them would be to invite destruction upon his city, his people, and everything he had worked so hard to achieve. Yet, the very thought of bending the knee to these shadowy figures filled him with a searing anger. His mind raced, weighing the cost of defiance against the price of compliance.

He thought of the gleaming spires of Rome, the bustling markets of Cairo, and the quiet beauty of his own Crete. Each place represented a bastion of civilization under threat from the Illuminati's insatiable hunger for power. Theseus knew that if he gave in, he would be complicit in the erosion of the very freedoms he had sworn to protect. Yet, he also knew that the society's reach was long, their influence pervasive.

After a tense silence, Theseus made his decision. He would not betray his principles, but neither would he risk the lives of his people. He looked the Illuminati elders in the eye and spoke with a firm resolve. "Your cause is noble, and your vision for Rome is grand. But do not mistake our friendship for weakness. The prosperity of Crete is not yours to plunder."

The elders exchanged glances, their faces unreadable. One of them, a man named Virgil, spoke, his voice low and measured. "Our intentions are not to harm your people, Theseus. But the path to enlightenment is not a cheap one. The gold we seek is not for our own pockets but to fund the advancement of knowledge, to bring the light of civilization to the darkest corners of the earth."

Theseus's heart raced as he considered his words. He knew that the Illuminati's projects had indeed brought change to the world, but at what cost? The gold they sought was not just a symbol of wealth; it was the lifeblood of his city, the very essence of his people's freedom. Yet, the power they wielded was undeniable. The society had already transformed Rome, bringing innovation and culture to its people, but with it came a rigid control that chafed against his own belief in democracy.

With a heavy sigh, he reached for a cup filled with a rich, golden liquid that the elders had brought with them. "Gold juice," they had called it, a symbol of the wealth that flowed through the Illuminati's veins. He raised it to his lips, the liquid glinting in the candlelight. This act of unity was a public show of his acceptance of their demands, but in his heart, Theseus knew it was a temporary measure. He would find a way to balance the scales, to ensure that the prosperity of Crete remained in the hands of its people.

The Illuminati's influence grew stronger by the day, their innovations reshaping the face of Rome and her provinces. Yet, whispers of dissent grew louder, and the Iron Hand's shadowy presence was a constant reminder of the fragility of their power. The Senate was a hotbed of rumor and intrigue, with senators switching allegiances as quickly as the winds of the Mediterranean.

Amidst the chaos, Augustus remained a steadfast pillar of the Illuminati's cause. His reign had brought unprecedented peace and prosperity to the empire, but at what cost? The Senate's traditional power was waning, supplanted by the society's insidious grip. Yet, the emperor's popularity remained unshaken. His public appearances were met with adoration, his speeches of unity and enlightenment resonating with the masses who knew no other way.

The economic shifts brought by the Illuminati's projects were profound. Africa's integration into the empire had turned Cairo into a bustling hub of trade and culture, a gleaming jewel that drew the envy of neighboring lands. Yet, the disparity between the wealthy elite and the common folk grew wider, a chasm that threatened to swallow the very society the society claimed to uplift.

In the Senate, whispers grew into debates, the once-unified body now a battleground of conflicting ideologies. Some senators embraced the Illuminati's vision, their eyes alight with the promise of progress and power. Others, wary of the society's reach, called for caution, their voices a distant echo of the Republic's lost virtues. The Illuminati's grip on the political structures of Rome tightened, their members infiltrating the Senate and the military, ensuring that their will was done.

The Roman legions, once the bulwark of the Republic, now marched under the banner of the Illuminati. Their military might was now a tool of expansion and control, spreading Roman influence—and the society's ideals—far beyond the traditional borders of the empire. The Iron Horse, a marvel of engineering and power, snaked through the sands of Africa, a serpentine symbol of the Illuminati's reach.

In Rome, the Senate chambers buzzed with tension as the Illuminati's influence grew more overt. The once-great institution was now a stage for the society's grand designs, their puppets playing out a script of unity and enlightenment. Yet, the whispers grew louder, the shadows darker, as the Iron Hand's agents worked tirelessly to undermine the Illuminati's grip. The Senate was no longer a bastion of democracy but a chessboard for a secret war of ideologies.

Amidst the gleaming spires and bustling markets of the transformed Cairo, the Illuminati's cultural institutions grew like a forest of enlightenment, casting long shadows over the traditional ways of life. Schools taught the children of the city in the Roman fashion, filling their heads with the society's ideals of progress and unity. Yet, the whispers of the Iron Hand could not be silenced, their presence a stark reminder of the tension between the public face of enlightenment and the secretive control the society exerted.

One fateful evening, the Senate was ablaze with torches, the shadows flickering o the marble walls as the senators debated the future of Rome. In the midst of the cacophony, a sudden cry pierced the air, cutting through the din like a knife. Senators turned in their seats to see a figure stumble into the chamber, crimson staining his toga. It was Seneca, a man who had once been a beacon of wisdom and a pillar of the Republic, now clutching at a gaping wound in his chest.

Panic and chaos ensued as the Senate erupted into a cacophony of shouts and cries of disbelief. The Iron Hand had struck at the very heart of Roman power, their message clear: no one was safe from their wrath. As Seneca fell to the floor, the room grew still, the echoes of his last gasps a grim reminder of the price of dissent.

Augustus's face grew dark with anger and fear, his fists clenching the marble railing of the Senate box. He had underestimated the Iron Hand's reach, and now it had struck at the very heart of his alliance. The Illuminati had brought Rome into a new era, but it seemed the price was steeper than he had anticipated. The Senate's chaos mirrored the tumult in his own mind as he tried to piece together the implications of this brutal act.

The guards swarmed around Seneca's lifeless body, their shouts for order lost in the panic. The Illuminati elders exchanged furtive glances, their once-smooth faces etched with concern. They had underestimated the Iron Hand's resolve, their actions had provoked a creature of shadows into the open.

Aurelius, standing at the edge of the chaos, felt the weight of his own conflicted loyalties. He had dedicated his life to the Illuminati, but the sight of a friend lying in a pool of his own blood was a stark reminder of the cost of their ambition. He knew that this was only the beginning of a new chapter in their silent war, one that would demand sacrifices from all sides.

The Senate guards secured the chamber, the clatter of their armor a harsh counterpoint to the hushed whispers of the shocked senators. The crimson pool around Seneca's body grew larger, a grim reminder of the Iron Hand's ruthlessness. The once-proud man lay still, his eyes staring vacantly at the ceiling, the light of the torches playing over his lifeless features.

Augustus's voice cut through the silence, cold and commanding. "This is a declaration of war," he announced, his fists tightening around the marble railing. "The Iron Hand will pay for their treachery. They shall feel the full might of Rome!" The Senate murmured in agreement, their fear giving way to anger and a desire for retribution.

Aurelius, torn between his loyalty to Augustus and his burgeoning doubts about the Illuminati, watched the scene unfold with a heavy heart. He knew that the Iron Hand's violence was only a symptom of the deeper divide that now threatened to split Rome apart. As the guards rushed to arrest any suspected Iron Hand supporters, he couldn't help but wonder if their cause was truly just.

The Illuminati's response to the attack was swift and merciless. Across the empire, those suspected of loyalty to the Iron Hand were rounded up and made to serve as slaves, a stark reminder of the fate that awaited any who dared oppose them. Yet, amidst the fear and repression, the society continued to celebrate their power with grand festivals, their influence stretching to even the farthest reaches of Egypt .

In Cairo, the festivities were more elaborate than ever, with the Illuminati showcasing their mastery of the heavens themselves. The night of the aligned stars was a spectacle, with the pyramids serving as a backdrop to a celestial ballet of lights and sounds that seemed to defy the very fabric of reality. The air was electric with excitement and fear as the society demonstrated its power over the very cosmos.

The Illuminati had spared no expense for this event, with their engineers constructing intricate machines that mimicked the movements of celestial bodies, casting shadows that danced in harmony with the real stars above. The Sphinx, a symbol of ancient wisdom, had been adorned with a gleaming crown of gold, its eyes glowing with an inner light that seemed to pierce the very soul of all who gazed upon it.

The people of Egypt watched in awe as the grand procession of Illuminati-backed chariots paraded through the streets, the glittering spectacle a stark contrast to the shadows that had claimed Seneca's life. The air was thick with incense, the sweet scent mingling with the tang of fear that clung to the city like a second skin. Yet, amidst the grandeur, whispers of the Iron Hand grew louder, a reminder that not all of Rome's citizens were content to bask in the Illuminati's light.

In the chaos that followed Seneca's murder, a call went out for a full sweep of Iron Hand supporters. The society's agents fanned out across the city, rounding up anyone who dared to speak against their cause.

The crackdown was swift and decisive. The streets of Rome echoed with the clank of iron chains and the cries of the condemned. The Illuminati's power was on full display as they systematically dismantled the Iron Hand's network. Secret meetings were infiltrated, clandestine messages intercepted, and the society's hidden cells exposed to the harsh light of day.

The trials that followed were public spectacles, a deliberate show of force. The Iron Hand's leaders were paraded through the streets, their heads bowed in defeat. They were brought before the Senate, where Augustus himself presided, his face a mask of cold, calculated anger.

The charges were read, and the verdicts were swift and severe. The accused were sentenced to a fate worse than death: a lifetime of slavery, their bodies broken on the very projects they had once sought to destroy.

As the Iron Hand's influence waned, so too did the resistance to the Illuminati's grand designs. The Senate, now fully in Augustus's thrall, passed law after law, granting the society unprecedented power over Rome's military and economy. The society's projects grew more ambitious, their reach stretching across the Mediterranean and into the heart of Asia. The once-mighty Republic was becoming a tool of their will.

The public, still reeling from the recent unrest, found solace in the grandeur of the Illuminati's triumphs. The society's influence grew stronger with each new spectacle, their power seemingly unassailable. Yet, in the quiet corners of the city, whispers of dissent remained, a stubborn ember that refused to be extinguished.

The Illuminati's victory was not without cost. The once-noble Senate was now a stage for their power plays, a marble-clad theater of oppression where fear ruled alongside enlightenment. The trials of the Iron Hand's leaders were a gruesome spectacle, each sentencing meted out with a dramatic flourish, designed to crush the spirits of any who dared to oppose the society's will.

The public executions were held in the Colosseum, the very same arena where Adonis had become a hero to the masses. The air was thick with the scent of fear and sweat, the cries of the condemned echoing o the ancient stones. The Iron Hand leaders were brought forth, their heads held high despite their shackles, their eyes burning with the fire of conviction.

One by one, they were sentenced to the same fate that had once been reserved for the lowest of criminals: to fight for their lives in the arena. Yet, even in their final moments, they did not bend the knee to the Illuminati. Instead, they shouted defiant words that were drowned out by the roar of the crowd, their cries for freedom lost amidst the clamor of the games.

The chariot races had become more than mere entertainment; they were a tool of the Illuminati's social engineering. The society meticulously scheduled the tournaments to coincide with key political events, ensuring that the public's attention remained fixed on the Colosseum rather than the machinations of the Senate. The outcomes of these races were carefully orchestrated, the victors handpicked to bolster the society's narrative of strength and unity.

Aurelius watched from the sidelines, his heart heavy with the knowledge of the manipulation behind the scenes. He had once been a firm believer in the Illuminati's cause, but the events of the past few months had shaken his faith. The games had become a farce, a means to an end that was increasingly di cult to justify.

The Celestial Celebration in Cairo was a testament to the Illuminati's grandeur. The night sky was a canvas for their spectacle, with fireworks that painted the heavens in an array of colors, their brilliance reflected in the Nile's dark waters. Dancers from provinces across the empire graced the makeshift stages, their movements a tapestry of diverse cultures woven into the society's narrative of unity. The Sphinx looked on, a silent witness to the tumultuous dance of power and ambition that played out before it.

The African Circus was the crown jewel of the festivities. Exotic animals from the farthest reaches of the empire were brought into the arena, their eyes wide with fear and confusion as they were paraded before the rapturous crowd. Acrobats from the deserts of Numidia and the jungles of Aethiopia leapt and tumbled, their lithe forms a testament to the human spirit's boundless potential. The air was thick with the scent of their fear and the sweat of the performers, a heady mix that filled the vast space with a palpable energy.

Roman citizens packed the benches, their faces a mix of wonder and horror as the exotic animals of the African Circus snarled and roared, their fiery eyes reflecting the pyrotechnics that painted the night sky. The Celestial Celebration had transformed Cairo into a playground of the gods, a spectacle that drew people from all corners of the empire to bear witness to the Illuminati's power. The grandeur was intoxicating, a potent reminder of the society's influence over the very fabric of reality.

The acrobats from Numidia and Aethiopia danced in the air, their limbs a blur as they performed impossible feats of strength and agility. The crowd held its collective breath, transfixed by the beauty and danger that intertwined in their every move. Their bare feet barely touched the sand as they leaped from rope to rope, the flaming torches in their hands casting a frenetic pattern of light and shadow across the arena.

The jesters, with their painted smiles and tattered garb, danced among the spectators, their antics a stark contrast to the solemnity of the Illuminati's message. They were a reminder that even in the face of great power, there was room for laughter and levity. Yet, the tension in the air was palpable, the shadow of the Iron Hand's rebellion lurking just beneath the surface of the festivities.

The African Circus was a cacophony of sound and color, a symphony o beasts and humans, each vying for the audience's attention. The acrobats from Numidia and Aethiopia were the stars of the show, thei daring feats captivating the Roman citizens who had never seen such a display of skill. Their bare chests gleamed with sweat, their muscle: rippling in the torchlight as they tamed the fiercest creatures of the continent .

The exotic animals, brought from the depths of the African jungles and the vast savannas, roared and snarled in the enclosed space of the arena. The scent of their fear mingled with the aroma of roasting meats and spilled wine, a potent bouquet that spoke of the power of the empire to conquer even the wildest beasts.

The Illuminati had announced an international tournament, a spectacle to surpass all others. The news spread like wildfire across the empire and beyond, reaching the furthest corners of the known world Charioteers from the deserts of Africa, the gleaming streets of Rome the ancient palaces of Crete, the mystical lands of Asia, and the opulen courts of Persia were invited to showcase their skills in a race tha would determine the ultimate master of the Colosseum.

Rome buzzed with excitement as the day of the tournament approached. The once-crumbling racing facilities were now gleaming marble and steel, their grandeur restored to reflect the Illuminati's vision of a united empire. The city's best architects and engineers had been commissioned to expand and renovate the Colosseum, turning it into a gleaming bastion of Roman might.

The charioteers from across the empire had arrived, each bringing with them their own unique styles and traditions. The Africans, renowned for their speed and agility, had painted their chariots with vibrant images of the savannah, their horses snorting and pawing the ground with excitement. The Romans, with their disciplined precision, practiced in meticulous formations, their chariots adorned with the society's emblem. The Cretans, with their storied history of the labyrinth, brought with them a sense of strategy and cunning, their chariots intricately designed to reflect the twists and turns of their legendary maze. The Asians, mysterious and enigmatic, practiced in the shadows, their chariots whispering of ancient secrets and arcane power. And the Persians, with their opulent gold and jewels, brought a flair for the dramatic, their vehicles bedecked with the finest silks and fabrics, a stark contrast to the utilitarian designs of their rivals.

The Illuminati had not overlooked any detail in their preparations. The city swarmed with foreign dignitaries and envoys, each eager to witness the spectacle that would showcase Rome's dominance and the Illuminati's might. Palaces were emptied to accommodate the esteemed guests, their halls now echoing with the sound of foreign tongues and the clink of golden chalices. The air was filled with the scent of exotic spices and the cries of birds from distant lands, a testament to the empire's reach and diversity.

The racing facilities had been transformed into gleaming arenas of marble and steel. The Colosseum, once a symbol of Roman might, had been reborn as a monument to the Illuminati's power. Its arches now gleamed with gold, reflecting the setting sun and casting a warm glow across the city. The chariot tracks had been resurfaced, each stone meticulously laid to ensure a smooth and swift race. The stables hummed with the energy of the finest horses from across the empire, their eyes wild with anticipation of the battles to come.

Security was tight, with the Illuminati's best agents mingling among the crowds. They watched with hawk-like vigilance, their eyes searching for any sign of Iron Hand infiltration. The society had learned from the shadows that birthed it, and it had become a master of surveillance and subterfuge. The Gold Faction, ever eager to capitalize on the event, had orchestrated an elaborate scheme to manipulate the outcomes of the races. Their agents whispered in the ears of trainers and jockeys, o ering bribes and threats in equal measure to ensure the desired results.

The machinations of the Gold Faction were as intricate as the gears of the society's own machines. They had infiltrated the betting houses, rigging the odds and planting misinformation to lead the unsuspecting to wager on their predetermined champions. The Illuminati's gold flowed freely, greasing the palms of race o cials and whispering sweet promises to the charioteers. The games had become a battleground for power and wealth, the very essence of Rome's soul.

In the bustling stables, the air was thick with the musky scent of horses and the metallic tang of sweat and fear. The Illuminati's agents moved among the stalls, ensuring that their chosen champions were well-tended and that any potential threats were swiftly dealt with. The charioteers, oblivious to the shadowy deals being struck in their name, honed their skills and whispered prayers to the gods for victory.

The night before the tournament, a tense silence fell over the city. The usually raucous taverns were subdued, the conversations hushed as if in anticipation of a storm. The Illuminati's emblems, once proudly displayed, were now hidden, their owners fearful of the Iron Hand's retribution. The Gold Faction's agents scurried through the shadows, finalizing their plans and laying the groundwork for the grand deception that would unfold in the Colosseum's sands.

The next day dawned bright and clear, the sun casting its golden light on the gleaming chariots that lined the starting gates. The stands were a sea of togas and tunics, a kaleidoscope of colors that stretched as far as the eye could see. The air was electric with excitement and tension.

Vulcan and Julius had led their 15,000-strong army with strategic brilliance, conquering the city of Constantinople with swift and decisive blows. The siege had been a masterclass in military strategy, with the Illuminati's technological advancements giving them an edge that the defenders could not match. Key battles had raged across the city's storied hills and waterways, each victory a testament to the society's might. The turning point came when they breached the city's formidable walls with a new invention: a giant battering ram, powered by steam and imbued with the strength of Vulcan himself.

With the city secured, Flavius was appointed mayor of the newly-christened Istanbul. He faced a city torn by conflict and fearful of its new rulers. His first act was to convert an ancient mosque into the

Illuminati's headquarters, a move that was both symbolic and strategic. The grand dome and minarets, once a bastion of faith, now bore the society's emblem, a stark reminder of the power shift that had taken place.

Flavius implemented "enlightenment" programs, promising prosperity and progress to the conquered populace. The Illuminati's engineers set to work, constructing new infrastructure and introducing advanced technologies that had not yet graced the city's ancient streets. Schools were founded, teaching the society's progressive ideals alongside traditional Roman virtues. These institutions were a double-edged sword, o ering knowledge and opportunity to those who embraced the Illuminati's vision, while subtly indoctrinating the youth into their way of thinking.

The transformation of the mosque into the Illuminati's headquarters was a deliberate and powerful symbol of their dominance. The grand dome, once a beacon of faith, now gleamed with the golden light of the Illuminati's emblem. The muezzin's call to prayer was replaced by the steady tick of clockwork, marking the passage of time under the society's watchful eye. Yet, the society was not blind to the cultural significance of the site. They allowed the local clergy to maintain a small place of worship within the complex, a gesture that was as much about pragmatism as it was about respect.

The Illuminati's arrival in Istanbul was met with a mix of awe and apprehension. The people watched as the once-sacred ground was transformed into a bastion of power, its ancient stones bearing witness to the birth of a new order. Yet, amidst the uncertainty, there were whispers of hope. The society's promises of a better future were seductive, and many found themselves drawn to the allure of progress.

In the shadows of the bustling city, recruitment e orts began. Local intellectuals and ambitious young men were approached with whispers of secrets and power. The Illuminati's message of unity and enlightenment resonated with those seeking a new way forward, and their numbers grew. The society's influence stretched beyond the city walls, weaving through the fabric of the provinces and into the very heart of the empire. The Gold Faction's emblem, once a symbol of greed and corruption, was now a beacon of hope for many.

The Illuminati's presence grew stronger in the East, with the society's teachings infiltrating the very soul of Constantinople. The conquered city saw the rise of a new breed of Romans, those who embraced the society's vision for a modern empire. The recruitment process was meticulous, identifying those whose hearts burned with the desire for knowledge and power. They were drawn into the Illuminati's embrace with whispers of hidden truths and the promise of a place in the grand design of the world.

The society's agents moved with the grace of shadows, seeking out the brightest minds and most ambitious souls. They o ered them a chance to transcend the confines of their mundane lives, to become architects of a new era. The allure of the Illuminati was undeniable, a siren's call that resonated with those who yearned for more than the drudgery of the traditional Roman hierarchy. The support base grew, a network of hidden allies ready to serve the society's will.

When Vulcan's triumphant legions returned to Rome, the city erupted in a frenzy of celebration. The heroes of Constantinople were paraded through the streets, their chariots adorned with the spoils of war. The air was filled with the scent of incense and the sweet smell of victory. The people of Rome threw flowers and coins, their cheers echoing through the ancient streets as they hailed the conquerors.

The Illuminati had orchestrated the return to coincide with the arrival of the racers for the grand tournament. The Colosseum was a bustling hive of activity, with charioteers from Africa, Rome, Crete, and Persia setting up camp alongside the Illuminati's four factions. Each faction had its own distinct area, their emblems proudly displayed in a riot of color that matched their team's livery. The Gold Faction's area was the most opulent, with velvet tapestries and gleaming gold accents that spoke of their wealth and power.

The day before the races, the gladiatorial battles began. The Colosseum's sands were stained red with the blood of the brave and the desperate. Adonis, the society's chosen champion, emerged victorious from each fight, his sword flashing in the sunlight as he bested his opponents with graceful ease. The crowd roared with approval, their voices a thunderous crescendo that echoed through the ancient amphitheater.

In the final battle, Adonis faced the Iron Hand's most feared warrior, a brute of a man with arms as thick as tree trunks and a snarling visage that struck fear into the hearts of the weak. The clash of steel rang out, the sound of their struggle resonating with the very foundation of the city. Adonis's blade danced around the brute's clumsy swings, each strike a silent testament to the Illuminati's superior training and strategy. The crowd held its breath as the two titans locked eyes, the air crackling with the tension of a lightning strike.

And then, with a swiftness that seemed almost supernatural, Adonis struck. His sword pierced the warrior's heart, and the Iron Hand's champion fell to the ground, lifeless. The crowd erupted into a frenzy of cheers and applause, the sound washing over the Illuminati like a tidal wave of approval. Vulcan, watching from the sidelines, felt a surge of pride swell within him. This victory was not just for Adonis, but for all of them.

The gladiatorial battles were merely a prelude to the main event: the chariot races. The Colosseum had been divided into four quadrants, each representing one of the Illuminati factions. The Gold Faction's quadrant was a bastion of wealth and power, with its emblems of golden lightning bolts glinting in the sun. The Red Faction, with its focus on the Senate, was a sea of crimson and marble. The Blue Faction, representing the Merchants' Guild, was a display of opulent tapestries and luxurious fabrics. And the Green Faction, the society's engineers and architects, showcased their innovative spirit with mechanical wonders that whirred and clicked.

The racers from Africa, Rome, Crete, and Persia had arrived and were preparing for the tournament. Each had their own distinct style and strategy, honed on the sands of their homelands. The Africans, swift and agile, had painted their chariots with fierce beasts of the savannah. The Romans, disciplined and precise, had adorned theirs with the grandeur of the empire. The Cretans, crafty and strategic, had crafted their chariots with intricate maze patterns. And the Persians, with their flair for drama, had brought vehicles that shimmered with gold and jewels, reflecting their opulent culture.

Vulcan, the Illuminati's most feared and revered leader, was promoted to captain of the Roman army. The news sent a wave of excitement through the city, the air crackling with anticipation. The crowd in the Colosseum went wild, their cheers bouncing o the gleaming steel and marble. The charioteers felt the weight of their people's expectations on their shoulders, each eager to prove their worth in the grand spectacle of power and skill.

The races began, two chariots at a time, thundering onto the track. The crowd held its breath as the racers sped by, their hooves kicking up clouds of dust that hung in the air like a fog of war. Each faction's supporters roared their approval, their loyalties as clear as the emblems on the chariots. The first few heats were a showcase of speed and daring, as the lesser-known contenders jockeyed for position alongside the established champions.

In the first round, the Gold Faction's Sextius surged ahead of the Cretan charioteer, the wheels of his chariot biting into the sand as he urged his horses to greater speed. The Cretan's strategy was no match for the Illuminati's superior tactics and power. The crowd erupted in a frenzy of gold confetti as Sextius crossed the finish line, the first victory for the society in the tournament.

Next, the Red Faction's chariot, bedecked in the crimson of the Senate, clashed with the swift Africans. Despite their best e orts, the Romans were outmatched by the Africans' superior agility and tactics. The victory was decisive, and the crowd, though momentarily stunned, grew increasingly excited as the underdogs began to make their mark.

The Green Faction faced o against the Persians, whose chariots gleamed with gold and jewels, a stark contrast to the sleek, industrial design of the Illuminati's own. The race was tight, the chariots locked in a fierce battle as they rounded the Colosseum's curves. The Persian charioteer, an enigma wrapped in silk, handled his team with a mastery that seemed almost supernatural. Yet, the Green Faction's technological marvels could not match the Persian's ancient wisdom and cunning.

The final stretch saw the Persian chariot surge ahead, the whip cracking through the air like a snake's hiss. The Green Faction's chariot, once a bastion of hope, now lay in ruins, the wheels splintered and the horses whinnying in terror. The Persian victory was met with a mix of awe and fear from the crowd, the society's influence spreading like a shadow across the empire.

In the grand finale, Sextius of the Gold Faction and the mysterious charioteer from Africa took to the track along with the racer from Persia. The air was charged with electricity, the very essence of the Illuminati's power su using the Colosseum. The chariots, gleaming under the setting sun, were poised like predators waiting for the hunt to begin. The crowd was a sea of banners and shouted allegiances, each person eager to see their chosen faction rise to victory.

The starting gates crashed open, and the horses bolted forward. The chariots rumbled over the freshly packed sand, their wheels throwing up plumes of dust. Sextius, the Illuminati's poster boy, fought tooth and nail with the African charioteer, each vying for the lead. The

Persian, a silent and enigmatic figure, remained a constant threat, his gold-and-jewel-encrusted chariot a dazzling blur in the sun's glare.

As the race progressed, the Persian made his move. He swerved dangerously close to the African's chariot, the wheels screeching in protest. The crowd gasped as the two racers exchanged glares, their hatred palpable. It was a dance of steel and horseflesh, a ballet of power and destruction. The Persian's whip lashed out, and for a moment, it seemed as though he would overtake his rival. But fate had other plans.

In a heartbeat, the Persian's chariot careened out of control. A misstep a flaw in the design, perhaps divine intervention—whatever the cause the chariot flipped, sending the Persian tumbling into the dust. The crowd's collective breath caught in their throats as the chariot shattered into a hundred gleaming pieces. The Persian lay still, a tragic testament to the capricious nature of victory.

Now it was down to Sextius and the African. The Illuminati's golden hope and the unyielding spirit of a continent that had never fully bowed to Rome's rule. They raced around the Colosseum, their horses' hooves beating a rhythm of destiny. The Gold Faction's supporters roared for Sextius, their voices a symphony of power and entitlement. The Africans, a motley crew of traders and soldiers who had followed their hero to Rome, cheered with a desperate passion, their futures hanging in the balance.

The final lap approached, and Sextius pulled ahead, his face a mask of concentration. The African racer, a whirlwind of dust and determination, remained relentless. The crowd's roar grew deafening as the two chariots raced neck and neck, each desperate for the prize.

Sextius leaned into his chariot, his muscles straining as he urged his horses to one final burst of speed. The African, his eyes alight with the fire of competition, matched him stride for stride. The sun dipped low in the sky, casting long shadows across the Colosseum, painting the racers in stark relief.

In the final turn, the African's chariot slammed into a wall, the impact sending a shudder through the very air. The crowd gasped, the fate of the race hanging in the balance. Sextius, seeing his opportunity, dug his heels into his horses' flanks, and they responded with a snort of e ort. The gap between them grew smaller, a heartbeat, a breath, and then...

Sextius's chariot lunged forward, crossing the finish line a hair's breadth ahead of his rival. The Illuminati's supporters erupted in a delirium of gold, their cheers shaking the very foundations of the Colosseum. The Gold Faction had claimed victory, and the society's power grew a little more absolute.

The triumphant charioteer was showered with laurels and gold as the Colosseum reverberated with the roar of the ecstatic crowd. Sextius, the embodiment of the Illuminati's might, raised his hands in victory, the very essence of the society's spirit reflected in his gleaming eyes. The air was thick with the scent of victory, the sweet aroma of power and the acrid smell of burnt sand.

The celebration spilled out into the city streets, a tide of gold and euphoria. The citizens of Rome, caught in the fervor of the moment, danced and sang in the flickering torchlight. The Illuminati's emblems were everywhere, painted on walls and draped from windows, the city itself becoming a canvas for their glory. The clanging of metal and the pounding of drums accompanied the chariots as they paraded through the city, a testament to the society's dominance.

Statues of the Illuminati's leaders, once hidden in shadowy corners now stood proudly in the city's plazas, bathed in the warm glow of a thousand torches. The Colosseum, a gleaming bastion of power, threw its shadow over the city as the final notes of the victory song echoed through the streets.

Sextius, the golden hero of the day, led the procession through the city, his chariot adorned with the spoils of his triumph. The people of Rome, their spirits high on the thrill of the games, showered him with flowers and gold. The city's buildings, once stoic and proud, were now draped in a tapestry of the Illuminati's colors: gold and crimson, the hues of power and ambition. The cobblestone streets, usually baked to a dusty brown by the relentless sun, were now a canvas of color, painted with the joy of the citizens.

The celebration grew wilder as the night deepened. The air was thick with the scent of roasting meats and the heady aroma of spiced wine. Laughter and music filled the streets, the melodies of flutes and lyres mingling with the raucous cheers of the crowd. Bonfires blazed in the city's squares, their flames reaching for the stars as if to o er the gods a piece of the victory. The Illuminati's emblems were painted on every surface, a reminder to all that this new Rome was their creation.

The Illuminati leaders watched from the shadows, their faces a mix of triumph and contemplation. They knew that with every victory, with every conquest, the seeds of their power grew stronger. Yet, they also knew that with great power came great responsibility. The balance of the empire rested precariously on the edge of a knife, and one misstep could send it all tumbling into chaos.

The night grew long, the festivities stretching into the early hours of the morning. The streets of Rome were a maelstrom of revelry, with the citizens abandoning themselves to the euphoria of victory. In the heart of the city, the Colosseum stood tall, a gleaming beacon of the society's dominance. Its arches framed the night sky, a silent sentinel to the new order that had taken root.

As the celebrations reached their peak, a hush fell over the city. The music faded, the laughter grew softer, and the torches burned lower. The Illuminati's leaders, their faces a mask of satisfaction, gathered in a hidden chamber beneath the Colosseum, the very room where the society had been born. The air was heavy with the scent of incense and the weight of their ambitions.

Vulcan, now Captain of the Roman Army, stood at the head of the table, his eyes flitting over the maps and scrolls that littered its surface. The victory in the chariot races was a symbol of their might, but it was merely the opening act in the grand play for power. The real work, the strategic dance that would shape the future of the empire, was about to begin.

Augustus and Tiberius Falvius, the new leaders of Rome and Constantinople, were summoned to the chamber. Each was given a mission that would further entwine their cities with the Illuminati's vision. Augustus, the crafter of Rome's new order, was tasked with ensuring the Senate remained in line with their goals. Falvius, the keeper of the East, was to fortify Constantinople against any threats, both internal and external. The weight of their responsibilities was etched into their furrowed brows, but their eyes shone with the same fiery determination that had carried them to their current positions.

Aurelius, however, felt a twinge of unease. The Illuminati's tactics, once a tool of necessity, now felt like a tightening noose around the very essence of what he had fought to preserve. He knew that the time had come for the society to step out of the shadows, to make their presence known to the world. The chariot races had been a public display of their power, but it was time to bring their influence into the light of day.

As the celebrations wound down, Tiberius was called into the meeting with the key players in the Illuminati. The room was dimly lit, the flickering candles casting eerie shadows on the walls adorned with the society's insignia. The air was thick with the scent of victory, yet there was an undercurrent of tension that seemed to hum beneath the surface of the jovial atmosphere.

Vulcan addressed the group, his voice a commanding baritone that carried the weight of their collective ambition. "The time has come for us to emerge from the shadows," he announced, his eyes gleaming with a mix of excitement and calculation. "The people of Africa have shown us their mettle, their spirit unbroken by the harshness of the land and the cruelty of their past. They will be the face of our new Rome, the embodiment of our strength and progress."

The room grew quiet as the implications of Vulcan's words sank in. The Illuminati had always operated in the shadows, manipulating events from behind the scenes. To come out into the open was a bold move, one that could either cement their power or leave them vulnerable. Tiberius nodded, understanding the gravity of his new role.

"Africa will be the jewel in our crown," Vulcan continued, his hand sweeping over the map of the continent. "Their untapped resources and unbridled spirit will fuel our empire's growth. But we must be careful not to alienate them with our ambition. We must make them believe that this is their victory, their rise to greatness."

Tiberius was assigned the task of leading the Illuminati's integration into African society. His mission was to establish a new order, one that would bring the continent into the Illuminati's fold willingly. He was to be the face of this new era, the emissary of enlightenment and progress. The room was thick with anticipation as he absorbed the gravity of his assignment.

The Illuminati had long recognized the potential of Africa, its riches, and its people. They had quietly infiltrated the continent, laying the groundwork for a more significant presence. Now, with the victory in the chariot races, the time had come to step into the light and o er the Africans a future of prosperity under their rule. The challenge lay in convincing them that this was not a conquest but a partnership.

Tiberius knew that the key to their hearts was through their culture. He would need to embrace the continent's rich heritage and blend it with the Illuminati's ideals. He set out on a whirlwind tour, holding press conferences from the sands of Carthage to the jungles of Nubia. His words, once whispered in the shadowy corridors of power, now echoed across the vast savannas and bustling marketplaces.

"Do not hide your a liation with the Illuminati," he declared, his voice resonating through the ancient ruins. "Embrace it! Treat it like a religion, a faith that guides you to a better tomorrow. We are not your conquerors; we are your partners in progress. Together, we will forge a new Rome, one that knows no bounds and no darkness."

The people listened, their eyes wide with hope and suspicion. They had su ered under the yolk of Roman oppression for so long, yet here was a man, a leader, telling them that they were the architects of their own destiny. He spoke of schools and trade routes, of technology that would transform their lives, and of a world where their gods would be revered alongside the Roman pantheon.

Tiberius traveled from the sand-swept ruins of Carthage to the lush jungles of Nubia, his words carrying on the wind like the whispers of destiny. He stood before crowds that grew larger with each passing day, his voice a siren's call to a brighter future. The Illuminati's symbol was everywhere, etched into the very fabric of the land, a declaration of their intentions.

In the bustling markets of Alexandria, he promised knowledge and power, the wisdom of the ancients brought to life through the society's enlightenment programs. In the dusty streets of Carthage, he spoke of rebuilding, of restoring the city to its former glory and more. The Africans, so long downtrodden by the heavy hand of Rome, looked upon him with a mix of hope and skepticism. Yet, his words were a balm to their souls, a promise of a world where they were not merely subjects but equals in a grand empire.

Tiberius's journey through the continent was a pilgrimage of power, each step a declaration of the Illuminati's intent. He climbed the great pyramids of Giza and stood before the Sphinx, its enigmatic gaze seeming to nod in approval. He traversed the Nile, the lifeblood of Egypt, speaking of a new age of prosperity that would flow from its banks like the river itself. In the gold-rich lands of Nubia, he promised a world where their treasures would be theirs to share, not merely to plunder.

At every turn, the Illuminati's symbol grew stronger, weaving itself into the very fabric of African culture. The chariot races had been a mere prelude to this grand symphony of ambition. As Tiberius continued his tour, the society's influence grew more overt, their insignia emblazoned on temples and palaces alike. The people began to see the Illuminati not as an invading force but as a guiding light, a beacon of hope in a world of chaos.

In the heart of the continent, Tiberius encountered the most fierce resistance. The warrior tribes of the Sahara, whose traditions were as ancient as the desert sands, eyed him with suspicion. Yet, even here, the promise of progress was a siren's call that could not be ignored. He shared tales of the steam train that now connected Rome to Ciaro, of the wonders that awaited those who embraced the society's vision. He spoke of unity, of a world where the sun never set on their empire.

Slowly, the tides of doubt began to turn. The chieftains of the Sahara, once steadfast in their opposition, listened to his words with growing interest. They saw in Tiberius not a conqueror but a fellow dreamer, a man who o ered them a place at the table of power. The Illuminati's message of progress and unity began to resonate, and the seeds of a new alliance were sown in the fertile ground of African pride.

Tiberius's journey culminated in a grand assembly in the heart of the continent, where he was greeted by a sea of faces, each one a tapestry of hope and wariness. He stood before them, bathed in the golden light of the setting sun, and raised his arms. "Do not hide your a liation with the Illuminati," he called out, his voice carrying across the vast plain. "Wear it as a badge of honor! Let it be known that Africa stands united with us, for we are all children of the same star!"

The crowd murmured, then grew silent, their eyes locked on Tiberius. He knew that in this moment, the fate of the Illuminati's vision for Africa hung in the balance. With a deep breath, he called forth the essence of his own transformation, the blend of Roman stoicism and the fiery spirit of the society that had become his second skin.

"Look around you," Tiberius began, gesturing to the horizon where the sun painted the sky in fiery hues. "You see not just the end of the day, but the dawn of a new era. An era where the light of knowledge pierces the darkest corners of our world." He paused, allowing the words to sink in, watching as the chieftains exchanged glances, some nodding in quiet agreement.

The Illuminati's public presence grew more pronounced with each passing day. The society's symbol was no longer hidden, but etched into the very fabric of daily life. Public ceremonies were held in their honor, a fusion of Roman grandeur and African spirituality that captivated the masses. The Illuminati's leadership was acknowledged openly, their influence celebrated rather than feared.

In the bustling cities, schools sprang up, teaching the philosophy of the Illuminati alongside traditional African wisdom. The children's eyes shone with curiosity as they learned of a world beyond the desert, a world of science and reason that o ered them a future filled with possibility. Public lectures drew crowds eager to hear the enlightened thinking that had propelled Rome to such heights, and the society's teachings began to take root in the minds of the continent's leaders.

The Illuminati's economic policies bore fruit as well. New trade agreements were forged, favoring regions under their guidance. The once-dusty roads grew busy with caravans bearing goods from the far corners of the empire, and the markets buzzed with the energy of commerce. Agriculture boomed with the introduction of Roman innovations, and industry grew with the construction of new factories that hummed with the promise of progress. The continent's wealth grew, and with it, the society's influence.

Yet, amidst the blossoming prosperity, societal changes were not without their challenges. The old ways clashed with the new, and traditional social hierarchies shifted under the weight of Illuminati membership. Some embraced the change eagerly, seeing in it a chance to rise above their station. Others felt the sting of displacement, their power and status waning in the face of the society's relentless march forward.

The cultural fusion was most evident in the grand temples that now stood in the heart of every major African city. Their gleaming marble facades bore the likeness of African gods alongside the Roman deities, a visual representation of the Illuminati's promise of unity and shared destiny. Within their hallowed halls, priests and philosophers from both traditions debated and shared knowledge, weaving a new tapestry of belief that transcended borders.

The public ceremonies grew grander, a spectacle that drew the curious and the devoted alike. The Illuminati's insignia, once a secretive emblem, was now a proud declaration of allegiance. The chariot races had been reborn, a symbol of the society's power and the continent's newfound unity. The roar of the crowd as the chariots sped by, the clatter of hooves on stone, and the flutter of gold and crimson banners in the wind were a testament to the society's influence.

The schools were centers of enlightenment, buzzing with the excitement of discovery. Children, once confined to the oral traditions of their ancestors, now had access to the vast libraries of the Illuminati, where the secrets of the ancients were laid bare. The walls of the classrooms were adorned with the symbols of both Roman and African gods, a constant reminder of the shared destiny that bound the continent to the society's vision. The air was thick with the scent of parchment and ink, a scent that spoke of knowledge and power.

Public ceremonies grew in grandeur, with the Illuminati's leaders now openly participating in the rituals that once were reserved for the emperors. The society's insignia was etched into the very soul of African culture, a constant reminder of the new world order. In the bustling city of Carthage, a colossal statue of Tiberius, flanked by the

African lion and the Roman eagle, was unveiled amidst the cheers of the populace. It was a symbol of unity, a declaration that Africa had found a new guardian in the Illuminati.

In the schools, the children of Africa learned not only the wisdom of the ancients but also the strategic thinking that had made Rome invincible. They studied the teachings of Marcus Aurelius and Augustus, their words echoing through the hallowed halls alongside the wisdom of African sages. Public lectures drew massive crowds, eager to hear the enlightened thinking that promised a world without limits. The society's philosophers and scientists shared the stage, their dialogues weaving a tapestry of progress that captivated the minds of the continent.

Economic policies under the Illuminati's guidance brought unprecedented growth to Africa. New trade agreements favoring their allies saw wealth flow into the co ers of the society's supporters. The introduction of Roman agricultural techniques and advanced engineering transformed the landscape. Fields once barren now teemed with life, and the continent's cities grew tall with gleaming structures that seemed to reach for the heavens. The steam engines that powered the Illuminati's industrial revolution were a marvel to behold, a symbol of the power that knowledge could yield.

But the society's gaze was not solely fixed on Africa. Their sights were set on the East, where the mighty city of Constantinople beckoned. The strategic bastion straddling Europe and Asia was ripe for fortification. The Illuminati knew that to control the world, they must first secure their own. Behind the scenes, they orchestrated a massive military buildup. The city's ancient walls were reinforced with new materials and design, turning the once impenetrable fortress into an unassailable bastion of their power.

Intelligence networks were woven through the fabric of the Ottoman Empire, the Illuminati's greatest threat. Spies whispered of the sultans' intentions, their every move scrutinized by the society's sharp eyes. The Illuminati's strategists studied the Ottoman military tactics, anticipating their every move. They knew the value of foresight in the game of power, and they were determined to stay one step ahead.

Diplomatic envoys were sent to the courts of neighboring states, their tongues silvered with the allure of mutual protection and shared prosperity. They whispered of the Illuminati's vision for a world united under the banner of knowledge and progress. In the grand halls of Constantinople, the air was thick with the scent of incense and intrigue as the society's leaders met with moderate Ottoman factions. They o ered friendship and mutual benefit, seeking to sway them from the path of conflict and into the embrace of a new era.

Meanwhile, the city's defenses grew stronger. The ancient walls, once a bastion of Roman might, were reinforced with the Illuminati's advanced techniques. The Green Faction's engineers worked tirelessly, crafting unbreakable barriers that would stand against the most relentless sieges. The Red Faction's strategists, under the watchful eye of Julius, oversaw the training of a new local militia. These men and women were not just soldiers; they were the embodiment of the society's ideals, a living shield to protect the knowledge and enlightenment that flowed through the city's veins.

A network of spies, the society's silent sentinels, stretched across Ottoman lands. They moved like shadows, their eyes and ears reporting every murmur of dissent and whisper of war. The Illuminati's intelligence grew more precise, painting a picture of the empire's inner workings. The leaders studied the information, piecing together the puzzle of their enemy's intentions. They knew that knowledge was power, and in the game of thrones, it was the invisible hand that often dealt the most significant blow.

The society's envoys crisscrossed the city of Constantinople, overseeing the meticulous fortification of the city's ancient walls. The scent of stone and mortar filled the air as the Green Faction's engineers worked tirelessly to integrate their innovative techniques. Each block laid was a testament to their unyielding resolve to protect the bastion of enlightenment that the Illuminati had cultivated. The Gold Faction's architects designed ingenious trapdoors and hidden passageways that could be used for surprise attacks or hasty retreats, turning the city into a labyrinth that no enemy could hope to navigate.

Julius, the master strategist of the Red Faction, personally oversaw the training of the local Constantinople militia. In the city's sprawling training grounds, men and women from all walks of life gathered to learn the art of war from the society's finest instructors. They drilled relentlessly, their muscles hardening under the weight of the new steel the Illuminati had brought with them. The air was filled with the clang of swords and the grunts of e ort, each strike and parry a declaration of their commitment to the society's cause.

The Gold Faction's envoys, meanwhile, were as busy as bees in the honeyed courts of the East. They whispered sweet nothings in the ears of neighboring kings and emperors, extending the hand of friendship and proposing mutually beneficial alliances. They painted a picture of a world where knowledge and enlightenment flowed like rivers, bringing prosperity and peace to all who sought it. Some were swayed by the promise of power and protection, others by the allure of technology and wealth. Yet, in every negotiation, the Illuminati's true intentions remained shrouded, like the moon behind a veil of clouds.

Julius, the cunning strategist, knew that the true strength of Constantinople lay not just in its walls but in the hearts of its people. The local militia grew more than just in number; their spirits swelled with pride and purpose as they trained under the Red Faction's watchful eyes. The society's tacticians taught them not only to fight with the e ciency of Rome's legions but also to think like the Illuminati, to anticipate and adapt. The city's defenders grew into a formidable force, their discipline and innovation a stark contrast to the chaotic hordes that threatened the empire's borders.

In the shadowed alleys of the city, the Illuminati's spy network grew like ivy, entwining itself around the very pillars of Ottoman power. The whispers of their agents echoed through the grand bazaars and the hushed corridors of the Topkapi Palace. They gathered intel on the sultans' strategies, the movements of their armies, and the whispers of dissent within their own ranks. The information flowed back to the Illuminati's strategic center, where it was dissected with the precision of a surgeon's blade. Each scrap of knowledge was a piece of the puzzle that would determine the empire's fate.

Simultaneously, the society's diplomats danced the delicate dance of alliances, their gold-embroidered togas gliding through the courts of neighboring states. They o ered friendship and protection, a bulwark against the encroaching shadow of the Ottoman Empire. The Gold Faction's envoys painted a vision of a world illuminated by the society's wisdom, where knowledge and prosperity were the true currencies of power. The allure of this vision was not lost on the rulers.

In the grand strategy sessions, held in the dimly lit chambers of Constantinople's most secure palaces, the Illuminati leaders discussed the possibility of a siege. The air was thick with the scent of candle wax and parchment as they pored over maps, their fingers tracing the city's labyrinthine streets and the contours of the surrounding landscape. They knew that the city's walls could stand strong against any invading force, but they also knew that a prolonged siege would test their resolve and resources.

Contingency plans were drawn up with meticulous care. Evacuation procedures were established for the city's non-combatants, ensuring that the most vulnerable could find refuge beyond the city's walls. Secret escape routes were forged through the city's ancient catacombs, known only to the society's most trusted members. The Illuminati's blueprint for survival was a tapestry of ingenuity and foresight, a testament to their belief in the enduring nature of knowledge and enlightenment.

The Green Faction's engineers designed ingenious siege engines, their gears and levers a silent promise of destruction. These machines of war could rain fire and stone upon any would-be conquerors, turning the city into a fortress capable of withstanding the longest sieges. The Red Faction's tacticians studied the art of urban combat, preparing for a battle that would be as much psychological as physical. They knew that to keep the city's morale high, they must strike at the enemy's resolve, turning fear into a weapon.

Civilians were taught the basics of defense, from the youngest children to the eldest scholars. Every man, woman, and child became a part of the city's shield, ready to stand firm against the inevitable storm. Granaries were stocked, waterways secured, and hidden storerooms filled with supplies that could sustain the city's population for years. The Illuminati had learned from the lessons of the past, where Rome had faltered, and were determined not to repeat those mistakes.

The society's strategists anticipated the Ottoman's every move, preparing countermoves with the cold precision of a chess master. The air was electric with tension, each day bringing new reports of the enemy's advancing forces. Yet, within the city walls, the rhythm of life continued, albeit with a newfound sense of urgency. The clang of blacksmiths hammering out weapons and the murmur of strategic discussions became the city's heartbeat, a steady drum that grew louder with each passing moment.

The day of the counterattack dawned, a crimson sunrise that seemed to bleed onto the horizon. The Ottoman's war drums pounded a war march, and from the dusty plains, an army of 10,000 men emerged, a sea of scimitars and banners that stretched as far as the eye could see. The Illuminati's fortifications, a blend of ancient Roman might and Illuminati innovation, stood tall and unyielding before them. The society's leaders had anticipated this moment, their preparations meticulous and thorough.

The city's defenders, a mix of Roman legionaries and Illuminati-trained local militia, watched the approaching horde with steely resolve. Their eyes, once filled with awe at the grandeur of the chariot races, now gleamed with the fire of war. They had become the living embodiment of the society's ideals, a bastion of knowledge and progress against the relentless tide of ignorance.

The battle was fierce, the clash of steel and the screams of the dying a cacophony that drowned out the city's usual bustle. The Illuminati's siege engines roared to life, sending a barrage of flaming projectiles soaring over the city walls to rain down upon the Ottoman invaders. The enemy's war machines were met with a hailstorm of arrows and bolts, their fiery destruction lighting up the night sky like a grim celestial ballet.

For every Ottoman foot that trod upon the city's outskirts, the Illuminati had an ingenious countermeasure. Traps and pitfalls lay hidden beneath the earth, claiming the lives of countless soldiers as they advanced. The society's knowledge of engineering had transformed Constantinople into a fortress that no traditional siege could hope to breach. The city's defenders, bolstered by the society's training and innovations, fought with a unity and ferocity that astonished their attackers.

The siege engines roared again and again, sending their deadly payloads arcing over the city walls. The Ottoman's own machines, though once feared, were rendered obsolete by the Illuminati's advanced designs. The Gold Faction's envoys had been busy indeed, ensuring that the society's allies had provided the latest in military technology. The clang of steel and the thunder of explosions echoed through the streets, a symphony of power that drowned out the cries of the invaders.

In the face of such a formidable defense, the Ottoman forces grew desperate. Their commanders, unable to outthink the Illuminati's strategies, resorted to brute force. Yet, the city's defenders held firm, a bastion of light in the shadow of the advancing horde. The society's leaders had anticipated the enemy's every move, and their preparations had been meticulous. The walls of Constantinople, once thought impenetrable, had become an unbreakable bastion under the Illuminati's guidance.

The siege dragged on, with the Ottoman forces throwing wave after wave of soldiers at the city's defenses. Yet, for every man they lost, the Illuminati's resolve grew stronger. The clang of swords and the roar of the siege engines became the city's new rhythm, a grim melody that played out day and night. The air was thick with the acrid scent of smoke and the metallic tang of blood, yet the society's banners remained aloft, a beacon of defiance in the face of the relentless assault.

Amidst the chaos, Aurelius found himself torn between his loyalty to Augustus and his burgeoning doubts about the Illuminati's methods. He watched as the city's defenders, fueled by the society's teachings, fought with a ferocity that seemed almost inhuman. The society's influence had become the very fabric of Constantinople, woven into the lives of its inhabitants like an invisible shield. Yet, he could not shake the feeling that something was amiss, that the path they had chosen was leading them away from the very enlightenment they sought to protect.

The tide of the battle began to turn as the Illuminati's innovations took their toll. The Ottoman's once-mighty siege engines lay broken and burning, their operators cut down by the very machines they had sought to deploy. The society's own war machines, a terrifying fusion of Roman steel and Illuminati innovation, continued their relentless bombardment, tearing through the enemy's ranks with a precision that was almost surgical. The defenders of Constantinople, a mix of Roman legionaries and Illuminati-trained local militia, fought with a fierce determination that seemed to be drawn from the very stones of the city itself.

The Ottoman commanders grew desperate, their tactics crumbling under the weight of the Illuminati's unyielding defense. They threw wave after wave of soldiers at the city's walls, but each was met with a hailstorm of arrows, bolts, and Greek fire that sent them reeling back. The city's streets ran with blood, but the society's banners remained unblemished, fluttering in the wind like the wings of an eagle that had claimed its prey. The air was thick with the smell of gunpowder and scorched earth, a testament to the power of knowledge in the face of brute force.

Amidst the chaos, the Illuminati's leaders remained unflappable. From their vantage points atop the city's fortifications, they coordinated the defense with the ease of conductors guiding an orchestra. They had anticipated the Ottoman's every move, and their counterattacks were swift and decisive. The Red Faction's tacticians had studied the enemy's formations, exploiting their weaknesses with a precision that had been honed through countless battles and the wisdom of the ancients.

In Rome, the political structure had shifted subtly but significantly under the society's guidance. The Senate, once a bastion of power, had become a mere puppet theater, enacting the will of the Illuminati elders who pulled the strings from the shadows. Their directives were law, and the Senate's role was to ensure their implementation with the veneer of democratic process. The Senate had become a tool for the Illuminati's agenda, a facade that allowed them to wield power without the burden of public scrutiny.

The economic prosperity of the empire grew under their stewardship. Advanced farming techniques, brought forth by the Illuminati's agricultural geniuses, transformed the once-barren lands into fertile fields that bore bountiful harvests. The society's influence on trade routes was unmistakable, with ships adorned with their insignia plying the waters of the Mediterranean, bringing exotic goods and wealth to Rome's markets. The Senate, now a mere echo chamber for the Illuminati's grand design, passed laws that enriched the empire's co ers and ensured that the fruits of progress flowed to those who embraced the society's vision.

The streets of Rome were a testament to the Illuminati's ingenuity. New inventions, born from the secretive workshops of the society's brightest minds, were woven into the fabric of daily life. Aqueducts carried clean water to the city's inhabitants, and steam-powered engines turned the wheels of industry. Public works projects, like the gleaming Colosseum, stood as monuments to the Illuminati's vision of a Rome reborn in the image of enlightenment. The society's influence had seeped into every corner of the city, transforming it into a gleaming bastion of innovation and power.

Under the watchful gaze of the Illuminati elders, the Senate had become an instrument of their will. The Senate's debates and decrees were a meticulously choreographed dance, each step designed to advance the society's agenda. While the senators believed they held the reins of power, it was the Illuminati's whispers that truly guided the empire's policies. The Senate was a facade, a mask worn by the true rulers of Rome, whose faces remained hidden in the shadows of their opulent chambers.

Crime rates plummeted as the society's influence grew. The Illuminati had introduced a new order to the chaotic streets of Rome, one that prioritized education and enlightenment over brute force. Through their network of schools and public forums, the people were taught the virtues of reason and civic responsibility. The once-rampant thieves' guilds and gangs of the city found themselves out of work, their former members drawn into the society's fold by the promise of a better life. The cobblestone streets, once slick with the blood of the innocent, now gleamed with the light of a thousand torches, each one a symbol of the Illuminati's vigilance.

The public's satisfaction with their improved living conditions grew with each passing day. The society had invested heavily in infrastructure, ensuring that clean water flowed to every household and that the city's markets were stocked with the finest goods from across the empire. The air, once choked with the fumes of open fires and the stench of the streets, had been cleansed by the implementation of advanced sanitation systems. The citizens of Rome, once mired in the squalor of the Republic's decline, now walked with their heads held high, their lives touched by the Illuminati's guiding hand.

The cultural renaissance that accompanied the Illuminati's rise was as profound as it was deliberate. The society had long recognized the power of art to shape the narrative, and they became generous patrons of those who would sing their praises. The greatest artists and architects of the age found themselves drawn to the society's orbit, their works reflecting the Illuminati's ideals of knowledge and power. The Colosseum, once a mere amphitheater for brutal games, had been transformed into a symbol of enlightenment, its frescoes and sculptures telling the story of a Rome reborn under their guidance.

The Illuminati's influence in the arts was not limited to grand public works. They sponsored playwrights and poets whose verses echoed their ideals, their words whispered in the ears of the elite and recited in the streets by roving bards. The tales they spun were not just entertainment but subtle propaganda, woven into the very fabric of Roman culture. History was rewritten, the society's origins intertwined with the legends of the Republic's greatest heroes. The public lapped it up, hungry for the myth of a golden age restored.

The society's hand was also evident in the city's educational system. Schools were founded in every district, their curriculum carefully curated to instill the virtues of reason and order. The youth of Rome were taught to revere the Illuminati as the guardians of wisdom, the shepherds guiding the empire through the dark ages of ignorance. The society's symbol, the all-seeing eye, was emblazoned upon every scroll and stone, a constant reminder that their influence was ever- present.

The cultural rebirth extended to religion as well. The society had long understood the power of faith, and they sought to bend it to their will. Temples dedicated to the old gods were remodeled, their statues adorned with the Illuminati's emblems. Priests and vestals whispered the society's tenets alongside traditional prayers, subtly shaping the faithful's beliefs to align with the society's ideals. The Illuminati's influence was not a replacement of religion but a synthesis, a marriage of the divine and the intellectual that promised to elevate humanity to new heights.

In the grand amphitheaters, once the stage for gladiatorial contests, philosophers and orators now held court. Their debates and lectures drew crowds that once cheered for blood and spectacle, their words resonating with a newfound thirst for knowledge. The games had not disappeared entirely; rather, they had evolved. Chariot races still drew the masses, but now the factions' colors represented not mere entertainment but the society's ideological divisions. The roar of the crowd was a chorus of approval for the Illuminati's strategies, their favorites a symbol of the faction they supported.

The Illuminati's patronage of the arts grew more sophisticated as they sought to weave their narrative into the very soul of the empire. Sculptures and frescoes adorned the city's public spaces, depicting scenes of enlightenment and progress. Artists competed for the society's favor, their works becoming vehicles for the Illuminati's vision of a world governed by reason and order. The Colosseum, once a grim reminder of Rome's brutal past, now served as a canvas for their ambitions, its walls a testament to the society's power to reshape the very essence of the empire.

Historians were subtly coerced to rewrite the annals of Rome, casting the Illuminati as the unsung heroes of the Republic's rebirth. Their origins were entwined with the legends of Julius Caesar and Augustus, spinning a tale of an ancient order dedicated to guiding the empire through the ages. The public, hungry for a narrative of continuity and greatness, devoured these new histories. The society's emblems, once whispered in secret, now adorned the pages of textbooks and the walls of public buildings.

The city's artists, once patronized by the whims of the elite, now found themselves in the service of a higher ideal. Their works no longer celebrated the vanity of individuals but the collective achievements of the society. The Colosseum's once blood-soaked sands saw the rise of grand theatrical productions that recounted the Illuminati's triumphs in the guise of myth and allegory. The audience watched in awe as scenes of their own history unfolded before them, shaped by the society's hand into a story of progress and enlightenment .

Sculptures and frescoes that once honored the gods now depicted the Illuminati as deities of knowledge and wisdom. The Pantheon, once the sacred domain of the Olympians, was transformed into a hall of Illuminati heroes. Their faces, stern and enlightened, gazed down upon the worshipping masses, a silent testament to the society's power to reshape belief. The very air of Rome seemed to vibrate with the society's influence, their symbols and messages embedded in every corner of the city.

The society's influence extended to the games themselves. The chariot races had become a microcosm of political power, with each faction's success or failure reflecting the shifting tides of the Illuminati's internal power struggles. The public, once indi erent to the outcome, now watched with bated breath, their futures seemingly tied to the fate of their chosen color. Each victory was a declaration of loyalty, each defeat a whispered betrayal.

Amidst this transformation, Africa began to experience a rapid growth unseen in its history. The Illuminati's message of progress and enlightenment had spread like wildfire across the continent. Curious seekers from other lands flocked to the cities under their control, drawn by tales of prosperity and wisdom. The Illuminati welcomed them with open arms, eager to share their knowledge and expand their influence. The migration patterns shifted dramatically, with caravans of hopeful immigrants arriving daily at the gates of the Illuminati's gleaming metropolises.

These new cities grew at a dizzying pace, constructed on the very principles that had made Rome great. The society's architects and engineers applied their innovative techniques to the sands of Africa, raising gleaming towers that pierced the sky and sprawling marketplaces that hummed with the energy of a thousand voices. The urban landscape was reborn, a testament to humanity's potential when guided by the light of reason. The cities grew not only outward but upward, their spires a declaration of the Illuminati's dominion over the continent.

The cultural exchange that accompanied this growth was as vibrant as it was tumultuous. The society's teachings melded with the diverse traditions of the African people, giving rise to new art forms and philosophies that reflected the blending of worlds. The Illuminati embraced this fusion, seeing in it the potential for a truly global enlightenment. They encouraged the sharing of ideas and knowledge, believing that from this crucible of cultures, a new humanity would emerge, united under the banner of reason.

Yet, with this rapid expansion came challenges. Resources were stretched thin, and the once-bustling markets grew crowded. The Illuminati's leaders had anticipated this growth and had already set into motion plans to manage it. They knew that the key to maintaining power was not just in the construction of cities but in the careful allocation of resources and the management of the people within them.

Aurelius, stationed in Africa, found himself at the forefront of this monumental endeavor. He had been tasked with ensuring the smooth integration of the continent into the Illuminati's growing empire. His days were spent mediating disputes between the society's newcomers and the established African elite, who were both eager to claim their place in the burgeoning cities. The society's principles of unity and knowledge were tested against the realities of cultural clashes and the scramble for power.

The Illuminati's approach to resource management was unprecedented. They introduced new agricultural techniques, drawn from the collective wisdom of their members, which allowed the desert lands to bloom. The Nile, once the lifeblood of ancient Egypt, now flowed with innovation as well as water. The society's engineers had constructed intricate systems of canals and aqueducts, bringing life to the parched earth and turning the desert into fertile farmland. The breadbaskets of Rome grew more abundant, and the empire's wealth swelled.

But the challenges of integration were not confined to the physical realm. The blending of cultures was a delicate dance, one fraught with misunderstandings and tension. The Illuminati's message of enlightenment was met with both eager embrace and suspicious skepticism. The society's emissaries worked tirelessly to bridge the gap, sharing their knowledge of science, medicine, and governance with the local leaders. They o ered a vision of a unified continent, where the light of reason would banish the shadows of ignorance and superstition.

In the bustling markets of the Illuminati's new African cities, the air was thick with the aromas of spices and the clang of metal on metal. Merchants from across the empire peddled their wares, while scholars and philosophers debated the merits of the society's teachings. The chariot races had become a unifying force, a spectacle that drew the diverse populace together under the auspices of sport and entertainment. Yet, beneath the veneer of unity, whispers of dissent grew louder.

The economic boom that accompanied the Illuminati's expansion had given rise to new industries that catered to the ever-growing influx of immigrants. Weavers, blacksmiths, and craftsmen found their skills in high demand, and the society's co ers swelled with the profits from trade. The volume of goods passing through the continent grew exponentially, with caravans stretching for miles across the desert sands, their camels laden with precious metals, silks, and exotic spices. The society's influence was not just felt in the grand halls of power but in the very fabric of daily life.

But with growth came strain. The resources that had once seemed inexhaustible now grew scarce, and the once-pristine streets of the Illuminati's cities began to show signs of wear. The infrastructure, built to accommodate a smaller population, groaned under the weight of the masses. Water was rationed, and food prices soared. The society's leaders knew that if they were to maintain their grip on power, they would have to address these issues swiftly and decisively.

Tensions simmered between the newcomers and the established residents. The society's message of unity and enlightenment was met with suspicion by those who had built their lives in the shadow of the desert. They saw the Illuminati's gleaming towers and bustling markets as a threat to their ancient ways, a harbinger of change that would sweep away their traditions like sand before the wind. The society's emissaries, armed with knowledge and goodwill, faced the daunting task of convincing these skeptics of the benefits of progress.

The strain on resources grew more pronounced with each passing day. Water, once plentiful thanks to the society's ingenious engineering, became a precious commodity as the cities grew. The aqueducts, once a marvel of human ingenuity, now struggled to meet the demands of the burgeoning populace. Fights broke out in the marketplaces as desperate citizens vied for the last drops, and the Illuminati's engineers worked around the clock to devise new solutions to the crisis. The gleaming façade of the Illuminati's utopia began to crack, revealing the stark realities of unbridled growth.

The Illuminati's leaders, gathered in their secret chambers, discussed the situation with furrowed brows and urgent whispers. They knew that to maintain their grip on power, they had to act swiftly. One of the elders, a man whose eyes gleamed with the light of a thousand calculations, spoke up. "We must build a new city," he declared, his voice echoing through the dimly lit room. "A city that will serve as a beacon of our enlightenment, a shining example of what can be achieved when humanity embraces reason and progress."

The room grew still as the implications of such an endeavor sank in. To construct such a city would require not just resources but a mastery of engineering and planning that surpassed anything the world had ever seen. Yet, the Illuminati had never shied away from a challenge. The very fabric of their existence was woven from the threads of innovation and ambition. They had transformed Rome from a crumbling Republic into a gleaming bastion of knowledge and power; surely, they could do the same for Africa.

The city, which they named Aurelia in honor of Aurelius's triumphs, would be a marvel of modernity. It would boast a sewer system that would put even Rome's to shame, carrying away waste and disease, leaving the streets clean and the air fresh. Running water, drawn from the Nile's mighty embrace, would flow through aqueducts to the very fingertips of the city's inhabitants. It would be a bastion of enlightenment, a gleaming jewel in the desert sands that would draw the eyes of the world to the Illuminati's power.

The Illuminati's architects set to work with a fervor that bordered on obsession. They studied the ancient texts of the Egyptians, whose mastery of hydraulic engineering had once allowed them to defy the very will of the Nile itself. Drawing on this ancient knowledge, they began to design a city that would not just survive in the desert but thrive. The society's engineers laid out grand plans for an intricate network of sewers and aqueducts that would bring clean water to every corner of Aurelia.

The construction of Aurelia was a monumental task, one that drew upon the collective might of the Illuminati's resources and ingenuity. Stone by stone, the city grew, its gleaming spires and gleaming streets a testament to the society's power. Yet, as the city took shape, so too did the challenges of integrating such disparate cultures into a unified vision. The society's leaders had to balance the demands of the Roman newcomers with the traditions of the native Africans, ensuring that each group felt a stake in the city's future.

Meanwhile, in Rome, the Senate, now firmly under the Illuminati's control, voted to pour vast sums of money into the African endeavor. The city's co ers were emptied, and legions of engineers, architects, and laborers were dispatched to the continent. The Iron Horse, a marvel of steam-powered transportation, stretched its iron fingers across the desert, bringing the bounties of Africa back to the heart of the empire. Its construction was a testament to the society's technological prowess, a symbol of their dominion over the very land itself.

The arrival of the Iron Horse marked the end of an era and the beginning of another. The ancient caravans that had once crisscrossed the desert gave way to the rhythmic chug of the locomotive's engine, belching smoke into the clear blue sky. The Iron Horse brought not just goods but knowledge, culture, and the Illuminati's unyielding spirit of progress. It was an umbilical cord that bound Africa to Rome, a lifeline that pumped the lifeblood of innovation into the veins of the empire.

Yet, even as the Iron Horse's tracks reached further into the heart of the continent, the Illuminati's leaders were not blind to the challenges ahead. The construction of Aurelia had revealed the depth of the cultural chasm that separated the Romans from the Africans. The society's envoys, tasked with spreading the message of unity and enlightenment, faced a tougher audience than they had anticipated. The Roman way of life, with its strict social hierarchies and rigid adherence to tradition, clashed with the egalitarian spirit of the African tribes.

In the bustling markets of the new city, whispers of discontent grew louder. The local leaders, once eager to embrace the Illuminati's vision, now watched with wary eyes as their ancient traditions were swept aside in favor of Roman innovation. The society's emissaries, accustomed to the hallowed halls of power, found themselves navigating a minefield of cultural sensitivities. They knew that to maintain their influence, they had to find a way to reconcile the old with the new, to weave the threads of Roman knowledge into the rich tapestry of African tradition.

The construction of Aurelia's sewer system was a Herculean task. The engineers faced not only the harsh desert conditions but also the skepticism of the local population. Yet, as the first waters flowed through the gleaming pipes, the city's streets transformed. The stench of waste lifted, and a new sense of pride swelled in the hearts of the inhabitants. They had seen their city rise from the sands, and now it gleamed with the promise of progress. The Illuminati had brought more than just cleanliness; they had brought a vision of a future where technology and tradition could coexist.

The Iron Horse's expansion into Africa was met with a mix of awe and fear. The great beast of steel and fire that devoured the desert sands brought with it not just goods but the very essence of Rome itself. The continent's traditional ways of life were irrevocably altered as the tracks laid down by the Illuminati's engineers stretched further into the heart of the land. Yet, amidst the chaos of change, the society's leaders remained steadfast in their vision. They knew that to truly integrate Africa into their empire, they had to o er more than just the trappings of power; they had to give the people the tools to build a better future.

In Rome, the Senate, now a mere puppet to the Illuminati's will, approved vast sums for the continent's development. The city's treasury, once brimming with gold and silver, was now a river of coins that flowed into Africa. The society's architects and engineers were tasked with reconstructing cities to include the marvels of Roman infrastructure. The construction of sewer systems and aqueducts became a priority, aimed at improving the quality of life for the populace and ensuring their unwavering loyalty to the empire.

The Illuminati's influence grew stronger with each city they touched. The clatter of hammers and the scent of freshly hewn stone echoed through the air as the ancient lands were reshaped in the image of Rome. The aqueducts, arching gracefully over the savannah, brought water to the parched lips of the people, turning barren lands into fertile grounds for growth. The sewer systems, a feat of Roman engineering, banished the stench of waste, allowing the cities to breathe anew.

As the Iron Horse's tracks reached further into the continent, the society's influence grew more pervasive. The chugging locomotive brought not just goods and people but also the very essence of Roman innovation. The society's architects and engineers were in high demand, as they worked tirelessly to reconstruct African cities in the image of Rome. The Illuminati's vision was clear: a continent unified under the banner of enlightenment, where knowledge and progress flowed as freely as the water in their gleaming aqueducts.

The construction of Aurelia continued with fervent dedication. The city grew not just in size but in significance, a shining beacon of the Illuminati's power and a testament to their commitment to progress. Its gleaming spires and clean streets stood in stark contrast to the surrounding desert, a monument to humanity's ability to conquer the most inhospitable of lands. The society's leaders watched with pride as their vision took shape, a city where the finest Roman minds could coalesce and flourish.

The Iron Horse's expansion was not without its challenges. The vast distances and unpredictable terrain tested the limits of the society's technology. Yet, the engineers, driven by the Illuminati's unyielding spirit of innovation, overcame each hurdle with ingenious solutions. The completion of the final stretch of track was met with a cacophony of cheers and the clanging of metal as the first train pulled into Aurelia's gleaming station. The city's newfound connectivity to the rest of the empire brought with it a sense of excitement and urgency.

As Aurelia grew, so too did the society's influence. The Illuminati's architects worked alongside local artisans, blending Roman grandeur with African elegance. The city's layout was meticulously planned, with wide boulevards and public spaces designed to encourage the exchange of ideas. At the heart of the city stood the Great Library, a bastion of knowledge that drew scholars from across the continent. The society's leaders knew that true power lay not in the strength of their legions but in the wisdom of their people.

The sewer system and aqueducts were marveled at by the Africans. Water, once a scarce and precious commodity, now flowed freely through the streets, turning the once-parched land into a verdant oasis. The Illuminati had not just built a city but had tamed the desert itself, bending nature to their will.

The city of Aurelia grew in grandeur, with each stone laid and each beam raised in the name of progress. The Illuminati's leaders had meticulously selected the first 5,000 inhabitants, all of them society members who embodied the ideals of unity and knowledge. These chosen ones were tasked with setting the foundation for a society that would be a shining example to the world. They were architects, engineers, scholars, and artists, each bringing their unique talents to the table to create a utopia in the desert.

The selection process was rigorous, with candidates from across the empire vying for the honor. They were chosen not just for their skills but for their unwavering loyalty to the cause. Each new citizen was a testament to the society's belief in a better future, a future where the light of enlightenment would shine upon all corners of the world. These individuals were the vanguard of a new era, the foundation upon which Aurelia would stand tall.

The chosen 5,000 were a diverse tapestry of the Illuminati's membership. There were philosophers and warriors, scholars and administrators, all bound by a shared vision of progress. They arrived in Aurelia with a sense of purpose that could not be quenched by the desert heat. Their eyes gleamed with the light of discovery as they surveyed the city rising from the sands, each one eager to contribute their part to the grand design.

The first days in Aurelia were a flurry of activity. The chosen ones were assigned to various roles, from the meticulous planning of the city's layout to the intricate construction of the Great Library. Their days were long, but their spirits remained high, fueled by the promise of the city they were crafting. They worked tirelessly, driven by a shared vision of a society that would be the envy of the world.

The Illuminati's leaders had foreseen the need for a harmonious blend of Roman innovation and African tradition. They had carefully selected individuals who could navigate this cultural crossroads with diplomacy and finesse. Each new resident was a master of their craft, eager to share their knowledge and learn from others. The air was electric with the excitement of possibility as they collaborated on designs that would soon become a reality.

The society's architects had drawn inspiration from the grandeur of Rome and the elegance of African palaces to create a city that was both a bastion of innovation and a testament to the harmony of cultures. The Great Library of Aurelia grew from the sands, a monumental edifice that mirrored the society's aspirations. Within its gleaming marble halls, the catacombs were constructed with meticulous attention to detail, a maze of hidden chambers and tunnels that served as both a sanctuary and a symbol of the Illuminati's clandestine nature.

The catacombs beneath the Great Library were a labyrinth of knowledge and power. They housed the society's most precious artifacts and records, a treasure trove that contained the secrets of the ancients and the strategies of the modern world. The air was thick with the scent of parchment and the whispers of history as the Illuminati's scholars moved through the dimly lit corridors, their eyes scanning the shelves for the next revelation. The catacombs were not just a bastion of security but a living archive of human achievement, a testament to the society's commitment to enlightenment.

As the city of Aurelia took shape above, the Illuminati's influence grew stronger. The society's leaders had ensured that the city's layout was not only functional but also aesthetically pleasing, a symphony of Roman architecture and African elegance. The colossal aqueducts stood tall, bringing life-giving water to the thirsty sands, while the sewer system operated flawlessly, banishing the stench of waste to the shadows of the underground. The Great Library grew into a bastion of knowledge, its gleaming marble façade reflecting the desert sun and drawing the eye of every traveler who approached the city.

Within the library's grand halls, the Illuminati's scholars worked tirelessly, translating ancient texts and sharing their findings with the eager minds that flocked to the city. The catacombs beneath, once a mere concept, now sprawled in a complex network of hidden chambers and tunnels. Their walls were lined with the finest marble, veined with gold and jewels, each stone whispering secrets of the society's power and history. The air was cool and dry, a stark contrast to the scorching heat outside, and the catacombs were a sanctuary not just for knowledge but for the society's most vital operations.

The catacombs had become the city's beating heart, where the Illuminati's strategies were born and nurtured. It was here that the society's leaders met in shadow, their faces illuminated by the flickering light of torches, as they plotted the future of the empire. The air was thick with the scent of incense and the weight of secrets, as they discussed the challenges of maintaining their power in a world that was ever-changing.

The Illuminati's integration of African cultures into Aurelia was a delicate dance. They had to ensure that the city remained a bastion of Roman innovation while also respecting the traditions of the land they now called home. The Great Library was a shining example of this unity, its hallowed halls a testament to the power of knowledge. Within its gleaming marble walls, the wisdom of the ancients melded with the vibrant spirit of Africa, creating a symphony of thought that resonated throughout the empire.

The city's completion was celebrated with a grand festival, the likes of which had never been seen in the desert lands. The Illuminati had brought with them the finest artisans, musicians, and performers from across the empire to entertain the masses. The air was filled with the scent of exotic spices and the laughter of children as the citizens of Aurelia reveled in the fruits of their labor. The festival was not just a celebration of the city's birth but a declaration of intent: the society's influence would not just survive in Africa; it would flourish.

The Illuminati's leaders watched from the shadows, their eyes gleaming with the satisfaction of a job well done. The city of Aurelia had risen from the desert sands, a gleaming bastion of progress and enlightenment. Yet, even as the final stones were laid and the last aqueduct filled with life-giving water, whispers of a new land reached their ears. A place called America, a collection of only 13 colonies, but brimming with potential.

The society had long had its sights set on the distant shores of the New World, and the time had come to act. America was a canvas upon which they could paint their vision of an enlightened society. Its youth and burgeoning spirit of freedom made it ripe for their influence. The Illuminati's strategic council met in the heart of the Great Library, the echoes of their footsteps resonating through the hallowed halls. The air was thick with the scent of ambition as they discussed the potential of this new land.

Aurelia, gleaming in the desert sun, had been a testament to their power and knowledge. Now, they looked westward, their eyes alight with the promise of a new frontier. The leaders knew that the key to America's heart lay in its burgeoning Enlightenment movement, a perfect breeding ground for their ideals. They had watched the 13 colonies from afar, observing the seeds of rebellion against British tyranny, and they knew that the time was ripe for them to extend their hand.

The council members debated the best course of action. Some advocated for a soft approach, spreading their ideas through trade and culture, while others pushed for more direct political intervention. Yet all agreed that the continent's vast resources and burgeoning population presented an opportunity too great to ignore. They had transformed the desert into an oasis; surely they could mold the untamed wilderness of America into a bastion of their enlightened ideals.

Aurelius spoke with conviction, his eyes gleaming with the light of discovery. "We must send our brightest minds, our most eloquent speakers, and our most capable leaders to the shores of America. They are ripe for our influence, hungry for the wisdom we can provide." The other council members nodded in agreement, the flickering torches casting shadows on their stoic faces.

The Illuminati had always been adept at reading the currents of history, and the whispers of rebellion in the 13 colonies were a siren call they could not ignore. The society had been born in the shadows of power, and they knew that the seeds of change were sown in the hearts of the discontented. They would o er America not just a new way of life but a new way of thinking, a path to progress that would lead them out of the dark ages of colonial rule.